JOURNAL OF CLINICAL CHILD PSYCHOLOGY

**Official Journal of the
Section on Clinical Child Psychology
Section 1, Division 12, American Psychological Association**

Volume 23, Number 4   **December, 1994**

ARTICLES

Journal of Clinical Child Psychology
1994, Vol. 23, 346–348

Impact of Poverty on Children, Youth, and Families: Introduction to the Special Issue

Donald K. Routh

University of Miami

Provides background for this special issue of the Journal of Clinical Child Psychology on the "Impact of Poverty on Children, Youth, and Families," cosponsored by the Committee on Children, Youth, and Families of the American Psychological Association. As anticipated, the majority of the articles present original research, including controlled interventions, along with two comprehensive and critical reviews of issues relevant to policy. In addition to considering the impact of poverty itself (in the short and long term), the authors examine numerous correlated factors, including prenatal methadone exposure, low birthweight, other biological risks, racial and ethnic minority status, neighborhood disadvantage, need for integrated medical and psychosocial services, supportive home environments, parental anger, and divorce.

The call for papers for this special issue of the *Journal of Clinical Child Psychology* was issued in 1992 under the cosponsorship of Division 12's Section on Clinical Child Psychology and the American Psychological Association (APA) Committee on Children, Youth, and Families (CYF). The CYF committee operates under the APA Board for the Advancement of Psychology in the Public Interest. Its ultimate goal, in the words of the APA bylaws, is to advance psychology "as a means of promoting human welfare" (Lazo, 1993, p. xxii), in part by influencing the U.S. Congress and other policy-making bodies. Committees such as the CYF attempt to formulate policy statements for APA that can then serve as the basis for the entire organization's lobbying activities. They can also, as in the case of this special issue, simply encourage their colleagues to do research on relevant issues, and publish their findings, thereby making them available to policy makers. Such activities seems particulary important today, when new health care and welfare legislation is being considered nationally.

The need for CYF's focus on the effects of poverty came from the realization that, although the field of child psychology may be doing relatively well as a science and profession, many of the children and families it aims to serve are actually worse off than they had been in some preceding decades. Newspaper readers are constantly made aware of the fact that 20% to 25% of children in the United States are now living in poverty; in many other countries around the world, of course, the situation for children is much worse. Thus, even though they are not professional economists, psychologists should try to understand all they can about why such poverty persists, what its effects are, and what, if anything, can be done about the problem.

Of course, poverty is not a simple problem nor one that exists in isolation. As the original call for articles acknowledged, poverty is associated with an extremely diverse set of factors, including educational disadvantage, unemployment, racism, urban violence, fetal exposure to alcohol, childhood lead poisoning, and many others. A colleague, Robert Felner (personal communication, February 1992), described the impact of poverty using the metaphor of a gigantic tree with many roots (causes and correlates) and many branches (adverse outcomes). Thus, a proper understanding of poverty cannot emerge from a few simple experiments but must be obtained through a longitudinal ecological or epidemiological approach taking account of the many relevant variables simultaneously. Indeed, this is the approach taken by the authors contributing to this special issue.

Some Personal Background

Using my prerogative as the guest editor of this special issue, I begin by explaining why the impact of poverty on children, youth, and families seems so important to me. It would not surprise me if most (if not all) readers have had similar personal and family encounters with the effects of poverty, because it is truly one of the scourges of humanity.

My maternal grandmother, whom I never knew, died of pellagra, a disease marked by dermatitis, gastroin-

Requests for reprints should be sent to Donald K. Routh, Department of Psychology, University of Miami, P.O. Box 248185, Coral Gables, FL 33124.

testinal disorder, and symptoms involving the central nervous system. Pellagra is caused by a diet deficient in niacin and protein and is entirely preventable, but the disease was not uncommon, especially among poor people in the rural South, two generations ago. Because of my grandmother's death, my mother and her sister were parceled out to be raised by various aunts and uncles. In this way, poverty cast its shadow over my own childhood and caused my mother a lifelong preoccupation with the importance of holding the family together (and, incidentally, with the importance of proper nutrition).

When I was an undergraduate, I worked for a time as a caseworker in a county office of the Oklahoma Department of Public Welfare. Thus, I was brought into frequent contact with poor people, in the form of applicants and recipients of general assistance, old-age assistance, aid to the disabled, and Aid to Families With Dependent Children (AFDC). Even more distressing were those applicants who were equally poor but who, on investigation did *not* qualify for any of these categorical forms of assistance. From these experiences, I realized that not only "those people" were poor but so also were many other individuals (friends or even relatives) well known to me personally in what were better times for them.

So far, my personal experiences with being poor have been confined to times when I was struggling to stay in college and graduate school. Thus, in a sense they were voluntary. These experiences were no doubt much less severe than, for example, forced unemployment or disability. Nevertheless, in my graduate school days, my wife can vividly remember the stigma of having to go to the Mellon Bank office in Pittsburgh and stand in the food stamp line. She felt as if the tellers were looking at her as if she were a member of some lower species of animal.

Ever since those years, I have pondered the problem of poverty, its correlates, its causes, and the various outcomes associated with it. At first, I naturally thought that the facts and principles I was learning as an aspiring clinical psychologist would reveal some of the answers. Perhaps, I thought, it might even become evident to me how to "fix" the "welfare mess,"—for example, an AFDC system that provides an income below subsistence, stigmatizes the recipients, and apparently discourages their initiative. But this did not happen, and I found myself as a middle-aged professor no nearer to the answers than I had been in my days as a young caseworker. It seems that if we are ever going to have answers to such policy questions, we will have to study them directly, intensively, and for a long time. It was for this reason that a special issue of a journal such as this made sense as a way of encouraging colleagues to grapple with the problem now, not just wait for time to provide the answers (it probably will not).

Articles in This Issue

Fortunately, many high-quality manuscripts were submitted in response to the call for articles, and even after the pruning resulting from a rigorous review process, there remained a full journal issue of 10 substantive articles. These articles are printed in the order of their submission. In the remainder of this introduction, I highlight some unique aspect of each article, not only to suggest its content but also to encourage the reader to examine it in detail.

The first article, by Bernstein and Hans, is unique in the present issue in its focus on young children exposed to methadone. A researcher working in the animal laboratory would randomly assign subjects to receive exposure to methadone or placebo, systematically varying the timing and dosage level of the exposure. In the real world of methadone-exposed children, there is serious confounding of the drug effects with all manner of other factors, and Bernstein and Hans carefully take account of these in their design. No significant differences in outcome (e.g., Bayley scores) were found that could be attributed to methadone alone, yet cumulative environmental risk factors were more predictive in the methadone group, perhaps in part because of the wider range of risk factors in that group.

Liaw and Brooks-Gunn report a sophisticated secondary analysis of data from the Infant Health and Development Program, a major intervention study with low-birthweight infants. The principal findings of this analysis showed systematically lower 36-month IQ scores for children from poverty backgrounds than for those not living in poverty, as well as a complex interaction of poverty, other risk factors, and the effects of the intervention.

Adams, Hillman, and Gaydos were the only ones in this set to examine other biological risks in addition to low birthweight, including spina bifida, cerebral palsy, neurosyphilis, Trisomy 13, cleft lip, and sickle-cell anemia. They compared a low-risk control group to one with social risk only (poverty or one-parent families) and to a group with both biological and social risk. Social risk was found to be associated with significant behavioral difficulties among these preschoolers, whether or not it was also accompanied by biological risk factors.

The Wall and Holden study was unusual in its focus on inner-city children, 94% of whom were African American, who were seen in a primary health care setting. Among these children, the boys' behavior was found to be more vulnerable than that of the girls to maternal depression and anger. For example, depressed mothers had boys who were less assertive, and angry mothers had more submissive boys.

The study by Attar, Guerra, and Tolan had a unique focus on neighborhood disadvantage and stressful life events. As expected, elementary-school-age children living in more disadvantaged neighborhoods experienced more stressful life events. In turn, such stressful life events were related to higher levels of peer-rated aggression and predicted increased aggression a year later in these children. As might be expected, exposure to violence was also an important variable in this study.

Dubow and Ippolito's study, like that of Liaw and Brooks-Gunn mentioned earlier, was a secondary analysis of an existing data set, in this case a subset of the National Longitudinal Survey of Youth. This study was unusual in treating poverty as a dynamic rather than a static variable, in other words, recognizing that families' incomes vary over time. Thus, it was found that long-term poverty was a robust predictor of both children's academic performance and their antisocial behavior problems. Once prior poverty levels were controlled, however, measures of recent poverty did not add significantly to the predictions. Thus, poverty seems to have some effects that are not at all quickly reversible just by providing more funds to a family.

Mention of Illback's article requires a change of pace, because it is not a report of empirical research but a discussion of a current policy option, *services integration*. The family living in poverty may be technically eligible for services from several different government agencies, which offer health care, nutrition, education, mental health services, and so on, each with its own bureaucracy, red tape, and so on, not to mention the time it takes a parent to obtain services by going back and forth day after day from one office or clinic to another. Why not eliminate the duplication and offer "one stop shopping," or many services all at one place, by a single set of service providers? This idea is being discussed by many different professional associations around the country at present, including the APA's own Task Force on Comprehensive and Coordinated Services. Illback presents the work of this task force and his own experience in running an integrated services program. He discusses several recent demonstration projects showing the workability of the service integration concept, for example, in programs centered in the public schools. Within psychology, such a services integration project might have to begin with the radical step of requiring clinical psychologists to talk to school psychologists again!

As in Liaw and Brooks-Gunn, the article by Bradley, Whiteside, Mundfrom, Casey, Kelleher, and Pope was based on a secondary analysis of the Infant Health and Development Program data set. The subjects were low-birthweight infants living in poverty. The main findings reported by these investigators concerned the joint effects of the intervention and the number of protective factors in the infant's home on *resilience*, defined by cognitive competence, behavioral competence, health status, and growth status. Children in the intervention group were more likely to be resilient than those in the control group, especially if they had high numbers of home protective factors. These relations held up at both the 12-month and 36-month assessments.

Peterson, Ewigman, and Vandiver were interested in contributing to our understanding of the problem of physical abuse. They asked low-income mothers to respond to a set of standard vignettes describing child misbehavior (being messy, having a tantrum, pulling things from a grocery-store shelf, and refusing to follow directions). Maternal anger and the tendency to use physical discipline in such situations were directly related to the frequency of behavior problems reported by the mothers for their own children. Peterson and her colleagues acknowledged one limitation of the study (there was no middle-income control group), but nevertheless discussed its implications for abuse prevention.

The final article, by Duncan, reviewed the economic impact of divorce on children's development. One of the most obvious correlates of low income for a child in the United States at present is having parents who are divorced. Some of this kind of poverty seems to be an unanticipated result of such social trends as the women's movement and no-fault divorce. In addition, poverty seems to be one of the factors putting a marriage at risk for divorce, so the causal arrow points both ways. Duncan goes well beyond a review of relevant census data and other research to draw up specific recommendations for social policy, for example, the need for better enforcement of child support laws and children's need for help in coping with their parents' divorce.

As the guest editor of this special issue, I would like to be able to take credit for the high quality of the articles submitted and for their high social relevance. However, I am afraid that would be like the rooster taking credit for the dawn. Most of these articles came in without any direct solicitation. In any case, this is an excellent, timely set of articles, well worth the attention of psychologists and policy makers alike.

Reference

Lazo, J. A. (1993). Bylaws. (1993). In *Directory of the American Psychological Association* (pp. xxii–xxvii). Washington, DC: Author.

Received June 18, 1994

Journal of Clinical Child Psychology
1994, Vol. 23, 349–359

Predicting the Developmental Outcome of Two-Year-Old Children Born Exposed to Methadone: Impact of Social–Environmental Risk Factors

Victor J. Bernstein and Sydney L. Hans
Department of Psychiatry, The University of Chicago

Suggests that conclusions drawn concerning the development of drug-exposed children have been too extreme in either condemning the children as damaged or proclaiming them unaffected. Results from a longitudinal study of the development of methadone-exposed and comparison-group children are presented. Social–environmental risk factors, sex of child, and maternal communication are used to predict the children's developmental outcome at age 2 years. No significant differences in outcomes between the groups were found. For the methadone group only, cumulative environmental risk factors predicted poorer developmental outcome. We note that the problematic neurobehavioral profile of some drug-exposed children can result from either biological insult associated with drug exposure or environmental risk factors including maternal communication. The importance of early intervention for drug-exposed and comparison children and their families is emphasized.

Children born drug-exposed have received a great deal of attention from the media (e.g., "Cocaine Babies," 1986; "Crack Comes to the Nursery," 1988). The identification of fetal alcohol syndrome first demonstrated the long-term damaging effects of a drug on the growth and development of the child (Abel, 1984; Streissguth, Landesman-Dwyer, Martin, & Smith, 1980) and led the scientific community to investigate the effects of other substances. Early reports on newborns exposed to heroin, cocaine, and phencyclidine presented a disturbing picture of growth retardation and congenital and neurobehavioral abnormalities (e.g., Chasnoff, Burns, Hatcher, & Burns, 1983; Chasnoff, Burns, Schnoll, & Burns, 1985; Harbison, 1974). Stud-

ies of the postneonatal effects of *in utero* exposure to drugs other than alcohol have been less conclusive. Several studies have found no differences in development between exposed and nonexposed children (Chasnoff, Griffith, Freier, & Murray, 1992; Kaltenbach & Finnegan, 1987; Zuckerman & Frank, 1992). Where differences in development between exposed and nonexposed children have been found, the size of effects generally has been small (Fried & Watkinson, 1990; Hans, 1992).

Part of the difficulty in understanding the effects of drug exposure on children is that only rarely, if ever, is drug exposure the sole factor posing risk to development. In most studies of children born to substance abusers, *in utero* exposure to drugs is strongly associated with poor prenatal care, poor nutrition, limited parental education, family instability, family violence, inferior housing, extreme poverty, parental mental health problems (Hans, 1992), and a host of other social–environmental factors that threaten children's health and well-being. Almost always, multiple environmental risks co-occur with parental substance abuse (Myers, Olson, & Kaltenbach, 1992).

Independent of drug use, the effects of multiple environmental risks can have a profoundly negative impact on development (Greenspan, 1982). Sameroff, Seifer, Barocas, Zax, and Greenspan (1987) argued for the nonspecific and cumulative nature of multiple risks. Using data from the Rochester Longitudinal study, they reported that it was not any particular risk but rather the presence of 7 or more risk factors at birth and in infancy

We gratefully acknowledge the vision of Joseph Marcus, MD, who conceived this study in the mid-1970s and who recognized the importance of the parent–child relationship to development. We express our sincere appreciation to Rita Jeremy, PhD, who helped develop the first version of the Parent–Child Observation Guides and directed data collection; and to Linda Henson, who assisted in data analysis and in editing this article. Ora Aviezer, Steve Benner, Jeff Green, Maria Vasquez, and Lisa Fisher were wonderfully conscientious videotape raters. Karen Freel was the principal Bayley scales examiner and made most of the videotapes. Carrie Patterson's relationship with the participants allowed us to retain 75% of the families over the 2½ years of their involvement with our project. Last, we thank the families whose interest in their children's development provided us with the data contained herein.

This research was supported by grants from the Harris Foundation and by National Institute on Drug Abuse Grants PHS 5 R01 8 DA–01884 and R01 DA–05396–01A1

Requests for reprints should be sent to Victor J. Bernstein, Department of Psychiatry, The University of Chicago, MC 3077, 5841 South Maryland Avenue, Chicago, IL 60637.

that characterized children who were developmentally delayed at age 4 years. In a reanalysis of these data (Sameroff, Seifer, Baldwin, & Baldwin, 1993), the authors reported that this finding did not hold for the subgroup of African-American children in that sample. Being born African-American was one of the 10 original environmental risk factors. On the average, this subgroup of children was performing in the range of developmental delay, but the number of risk factors present, other than race, was unrelated to their level of performance.

Others have argued, however, that individual risk factors can combine with one another in a manner that is not simply additive. A particular combination of *environmental and constitutional* risk can be particularly potent. Crockenberg (1981) reported such a finding. In a study of middle-class families, she found that a low level of social support for the mother combined with a high level of neonatal irritability was the best predictor of infants' anxious attachments to mothers at age 1 year. In a study of children exposed prenatally to methadone, Hans (1989) reported that neither methadone exposure nor socioeconomic status (SES) alone predicted problematic cognitive performance of children at age 2 years, but children who were both exposed to methadone *and* living in extreme poverty were developmentally delayed. Thus, the effects of risk factors appear to be cumulative, but combinations of specific environmental and biological-constitutional risk factors may be especially damaging. One would expect children born drug-exposed to be at compound risk for developmental problems, and they may also be differentially vulnerable to particular risk factors (Parker, Greer, & Zuckerman, 1988).

The parent–infant relationship may play an extremely important role in determining developmental outcome in drug-exposed children. Parental substance abuse poses some unique challenges to the parent–child relationship. In addition to the multiple problems associated with poverty, mind-altering substances can affect the way behavior is organized in both the parent and the child; drugs can affect the ways in which the parent and child communicate with one another. Drug intoxication and preoccupation with procurement of illegal substances can restrict the parent's emotional availability, sensitivity, and skill in responding to the infant (Bernstein, Jeremy, & Marcus, 1986; Householder, 1980; Jeremy & Bernstein, 1984). Parental involvement in drug rehabilitation or recovery can lead to constricted, insensitive responding to the child's needs either because of the effects of drug withdrawal, the stresses associated with continuing abstinence, or the preoccupation with self that is required by the treatment process (Pawl, 1992). Drug-exposed neonates can be unclear in signaling their needs, unresponsive, or shut down at normal levels of stimulation (Griffith, 1991; Weston, Ivins, Zuckerman, Jones, & Lopez, 1989); or they can be disorganized, or persistently upset (Chasnoff & Griffith, 1989). Therefore, difficult parent–infant interactions may mediate the effects of parental drug use, transforming the probability of risk into actual experiences of success or failure for the child (Bernstein, Hans, & Percansky, 1991).

The goal of this article is to explore how some young children develop adequately and some do not in high risk environments—in particular, environments in which the mother is a user of narcotics. We attempt to replicate Sameroff et al.'s (1987, 1993) approach to how multiple social-environmental risks, including sex of child and maternal communication with her child, are related to cognitive and social outcomes in two groups of urban African-American children: (a) those born to women being maintained on methadone (a legal heroin substitute used in treatment for opioid addiction and the grouping variable) and (b) those born to drug-free women recruited from the same prenatal clinic. We explore three hypotheses deriving from the preceding discussion of risk:

1. Prenatal drug exposure is in itself a risk factor and drug-exposed children will be doing more poorly at 24 months, possibly because of the teratogenic, neurophysiological effects of having been exposed to drugs *in utero*.

2. Cumulative social–environmental risks, other than drug exposure, will have a more powerful and consistent adverse affect on development.

3. Poor maternal communication is a specific risk factor for poor development and will have its greatest impact on children made biologically vulnerable due to *in utero* drug exposure.

Method

Participants

Participating families were enrolled in a longitudinal study on the effects of prenatal exposure to methadone on child development. We report data from prenatal interviews with the mothers and observations of the mothers and infants at infant ages 4, 12, and 24 months. Between the years of 1978 and 1982 all methadone-using women attending prenatal clinics at Chicago Lying-In Hospital were identified and participated in a screening interview with research staff. Those who had no chronic medical problems such as diabetes, who had no obvious mental illness, and who were between the ages of 18 and 35 were asked to participate in the research project. Twenty-eight percent of the eligible women either refused participation or withdrew their consent prenatally or during the postpartum period. Altogether, a sample of 36 methadone-using women became participants in the longitudinal study. These women delivered a total of 42 infants, including one set of twins. These opioid-using women were all involved in low-dose methadone-maintenance programs for the treatment of chronic heroin addiction; their methadone dosages during pregnancy ranged from 3 to 40 mg per 24-hr period ($M < 20$ mg). Most had been involved in methadone maintenance throughout pregnancy; some had sought treatment during pregnancy. Most of the women occasionally used other drugs in addition to methadone, most commonly marijuana, heroin, cocaine, Valium, or Talwin. The extent of polydrug use in the sample was minimal compared to what would be expected today.

Potential comparison-group women were identified by conducting screening interviews in the waiting room of the obstetric clinics at Chicago Lying-In Hospital. Women were asked to participate in the study if their demographic characteristics (race, age, SES, education, parity) were comparable to women already enrolled in the methadone group, if they had no chronic physical illnesses or obvious mental illness, if they had no history of opioid use or abuse, and if they consumed less than 1 to 2 drinks of alcohol 2 to 3 times per month. Forty-five percent of the women who met these criteria either refused participation or withdrew their consent during the postpartum period. Altogether, a sample of 43 comparison women became participants in the longitudinal study. These women delivered a total of 47 infants, including one set of twins.

All mothers from the methadone and comparison groups were African-American women from low-income inner-city neighborhoods. All women received regular, scheduled prenatal care in the second and third trimesters of their pregnancies. The methadone-maintained women received specialized prenatal monitoring through a clinic for high-risk pregnancies. Attendance at prenatal appointments was required as part of their drug treatment. The methadone clinic provided transportation to the high-risk prenatal clinic. All infants remained with their mothers after birth.

The infants and mothers were followed longitudinally to the age of 2 years. The primary assessment instruments administered at 4, 12, and 24 months were the Bayley Scales of Infant Development (Bayley, 1969) and videotapes of mother–infant interaction. At the time of the 2-year-olds' assessments, the sample included 71 toddlers each within 2 weeks of their second birthday: 28 from the methadone group, 43 from the comparison group. Attrition over the 2 years was greater for the methadone group (15 children, 30%) than for the comparison group (4 children, 8.5%). Most of the attrition occurred early in the study. Participant loss in the methadone groups was related to infant death ($n = 4$) and a massive stroke occurring in a neonate ($n = 1$), family withdrawal of consent ($n = 3$), inability to locate family at 24 months ($n = 4$), child no longer in custody of mother at 24 months ($n = 1$), child hospital-ized in burn unit ($n = 1$), and technical problems with the videotape ($n = 1$). Attrition among comparison children was related to family withdrawal of consent ($n = 1$), inability to locate family ($n = 1$), child with cerebral palsy ($n = 1$), and technical problems with the videotape ($n = 1$). The sample described herein consists of 25 methadone-maintained women and their 28 infants and of 38 comparison women and their 41 children examined at age 2 years.

The typical mother in the sample at the time she gave birth was in her mid-to-late 20s (methadone $M = 27.1$, $SD = 3.7$ years; comparison $M = 25.3$, $SD = 4.1$ years), had two other children (methadone $M = 3.1$, $SD = 1.2$ years; comparison $M = 2.9$, $SD = 1.1$ years), was unmarried (methadone, 21%; comparison, 33%), but was living with the baby's father (methadone, 43%; comparison, 53%). These statistics characterize women represented in this article (those remaining 2 years after the birth of their children); women giving birth to more than one child are counted separately for each child. Women who dropped out of the sample did not differ on any variable from those remaining (Marcus, Hans, Patterson & Morris, 1984).

The methadone infants in the sample reported in this article are typical of those described in the literature on opioid-exposed children (see Hans, 1989). The methadone children were born at lower birthweight than comparison children (methadone $M = 2,880$ g, $SD = 616$ g; comparison $M = 3,238$ g, $SD = 397$ g) and had more pregnancy and birth complications as measured by the Rochester Research Obstetrics Scale (Zax, Sameroff, & Babigian, 1977; methadone $M = 5.33$, $SD = 3.0$; comparison $M = 3.58$, $SD = 2.4$). The infants went through a period of narcotics abstinence which generally had resolved by 1 month of age (Jeremy & Hans, 1985). Drug-withdrawing children were hypertonic, jerky, tremulous, very active, and irritable. None of the children had withdrawal signs so severe as to require pharmacological management. After the neonatal period, few differences were noted between the methadone and comparison infants in their behavior assessed on developmental scales (Hans, 1989, 1992).

Measures

The analyses in this article are are based on 10 risk factors (*in utero* exposure to methadone, five maternal social–environmental variables measured prenatally, child sex, and the mother's communication with the infant at three age periods) predicting to four child outcomes at 24 months (the child's communication with the mother and three outcomes derived from the Bayley Scales of Infant Development; Bayley, 1969).

Maternal social–environmental risk factors. Measures of social–environmental risk reported here were selected from the variables available in the data set to parallel those used by Sameroff et al. (1987). Because our sample was homogeneous for race we substituted sex of the child. In a manner similar to ethnicity, in recent years the child's sex has emerged as a psychosocial risk factor. Males have been found to have more difficulty dealing with stress (Rutter, 1970) and coping with the effects of divorce (Hetherington, 1989), to be less resilient growing up in an alcoholic family (Werner, 1986), and, within drug-using families, to be particularly susceptible to developing behavioral and learning problems (Hans, 1993).

During the last trimester of pregnancy, the women were interviewed in depth and assessed on a variety of psychological and psychiatric instruments, including the Wechsler Adult Intelligence Scale (WAIS; Wechsler, 1955) and a psychiatric interview, either the Current and Past Psychopathology Scales (CAPPS; Endicott & Spitzer, 1972) or the Schedule for Affective Disorders and Schizophrenia–Life version (SADS-L; Endicott & Spitzer, 1978) with supplemental items from the CAPPS. Using the third edition of the *Diagnostic and Statistical Manual of Mental Disorders* (*DSM–III*; American Psychiatric Association, 1980) diagnoses on all five axes were made based on these structured clinical interviews.

Five social–environmental risk factors were identified from the interviews irrespective of drug use. The risk variables included:

1. WAIS Full Scale IQ.
2. Years of education.
3. SES, measured using the two-factor Index of Social Position (Hollingshead & Redlich, 1958). All women represented the three lowest strata—semiskilled or unskilled working poor or persons receiving public assistance.
4. Severity of psychosocial stressors, derived from *DSM–III* Axis 4. Scores in the sample ranged from 4 (moderate, including pregnancy) to 6 (severe, including death of a close relative).
5. Level of adaptive functioning, derived from *DSM–III* Axis 5. Scores in the sample ranged from 1 (excellent functioning in both social relationships and work setting) to 5 (very poor functioning in both social relationships and work).

Parent interviewers were not blind to participants' group status because the psychiatric interviews included questions about substance abuse. Assessments of parental IQ were conducted by "blind" examiners.

Parent–child communication. Mothers and children were videotaped in the laboratory for approximately 15 min performing four everyday activities with their 4-month-old infants: diapering, feeding, playing with a rattle, and playing a game. At 12 months, the session lasted approximately 30 min, and seven situations were observed. Mothers were instructed to: "see if your baby is interested in the doll," "play a game you both enjoy at home," "let your baby play with toys," "help your baby play with toys you both enjoy," and "change your baby's diaper." Separation/reunion (a less-stressful variation of the Strange Situation paradigm) and free time were the two remaining situations observed at 12 months. At 2 years of age, "teach your child to use the shape sorter" was substituted for the doll situation, cleanup was substituted for separation/reunion, pottying was substituted for diapering, and a snack time was introduced. This video session lasted 40 min on average.

The Parent Child Observation Guides for Program Planning (PCOGs; Bernstein, Percansky, & Hans, 1987) are used to assess mother–infant interaction by observing aspects of mutual competence (Goldberg, 1977). The PCOGs are set of tools developed to make objective clinical judgments from the observation of the parent–child relationship. There are three forms: Feeding and Daily Routines (0 to 3 months), Infant (4 to 15 months); and Toddler (16 to 36 months). In our study, the Infant form was used at ages 4 and 12 months, and the Toddler form was used at age 2 years.

Parent categories of five items each include:

I. Actions to Meet Child's Needs (Dealing With Self-Assertion—Toddler form).
II. Responding to Child's Activity and Interests (Sensitivity/Pacing).
III. Positive Feelings Shown to Child.
IV. Helping Child Learn—Infant form (Learn Language—Toddler form).

The first three categories (15 parent items) are on the Feeding/Daily Routine forms; the the fourth category is added to the Infant and Toddler forms (20 parent items).

Child categories of four items each include:

I. Expression of Needs and Wants (Expression of Self—Toddler form).
II. Using Parent's Help.
III. Involvement With Parent.
IV. Positive Feelings Shown to Parent—Infant and Toddler form.
V. Language with Parent—Toddler form.

The first three categories are on the Feeding form (12 child items); the fourth category is added to the Infant form (16 child items); the fifth category is added in the Toddler form (20 child items).

Two PCOG raters blind to drug-group status evaluated videotapes from each session. Different raters were used at each age. Their disagreements were resolved by consensus and consensus scores were used for analyses. For the current study, data on the reliability, internal consistency, and stability of the PCOGs are as follows. Interrater reliability coefficients were .76 for the mothers' scores and .52 for the infants' at age 4 months, .75 for the mothers' and .82 for the infants' at age 12 months, and .79 for the mothers' and .60 for the toddlers' at age 2 years. Alpha coefficients were .82 for the mothers' scores and .60 for the infants' at age 4 months, .71 for the mothers' and .79 for the infants' at age 12 months, and .78 for the mothers' and .58 for the toddlers' at age 2. The stability of the mothers' scores was $r = .23$ ($p < .05$) from 4 to 12 months, $r = .08$ from 4 to 24 months, and $r = .28$ ($p < .05$) from 12 to 24 months. The stability of the children's scores were $r = .09$ from 4 to 24 months, $r = -.19$ from 4 to 24 months, and $r = .25$ ($p < .05$) from 12 to 24 months. Construct validity of the child scores was derived from relating the child's PCOG scores to the Bayley Infant Behavior Record (IBR) Social Resiliency subscale (see later section) at the same age. These coefficients were $r = .29$ ($p < .01$) at 4 months, $r = .16$ ($p < .10$) at age 12 months, and $r = .43$ ($p < .01$) at 24 months. Additional reliability and validity data from other studies have been reported elsewhere (Bernstein et al., 1991).

For the present report, because of the focus on the impact of social–environmental factors on development and out of concern for minimizing the numbers of statistical tests, maternal PCOG scores were summed across categories and that sum standardized to produce a global *parent communication score* for each of the three ages. These three maternal PCOG sum scores were used as predictor variables. Four child Toddler PCOG communication category scores from 24 months only were similarly summed and standardized. The Expression of Self category was excluded from the child interaction sum because it was negatively correlated with the other child categories. This child PCOG score was used as a child outcome measure. Standardized scores were used to simplify comparability of the scores from different ages for which different numbers of items were used to compute the sums.

Child's level of cumulative social–environmental risk. Following Sameroff et al.'s (1987) nonspecific, additive approach and rationale for high–low splits, the 9 predictors other than drug use were dichotomized, identifying the poorer portion as being an element of risk. High-risk status was defined as having an IQ score less than 85, having less than an 11th-grade education, having Hollingshead Level 5 SES, having more than moderate psychosocial stressors, having a "poor" level of adaptive functioning, and having been born male. For parent communication at the three ages, the poorest 25% were assigned at-risk status. We then computed a cumulative risk score by adding the (unweighted) variables together. The range of risk was from 0 to 7 of the 9 elements present. In computing the cumulative risk

scores for siblings, the parent data collected prenatally before the birth of the first child were used in computing cumulative risk for both children. Three of the 8 pairs of siblings used in data analysis had identical cumulative risk scores. Because of the variability of the remaining risk factors, only one pair, the twins, had an identical pattern of cumulative risks.

Bayley scales child outcomes. At 24 months, following interaction videotaping, infants were examined on the Bayley Scales of Infant Development, including the Infant Behavior Record (IBR), a series of items requiring clinical judgments. Three examiners, trained to reliability via clinical supervision, tested the infants and conducted the videotape sessions. All were blind to the child's drug status. Matheny (1980, 1983) identified factors for consolidating the 27 IBR items; the item composition of these factors differed slightly at different ages. Following Matheny's analyses, two subsets of IBR items showing strong patterns of intercorrelations at different ages were used in the present study. These subsets were labeled Attention and Social Resiliency. Attention included three IBR items: object orientation (Item 8), goal orientation (Item 11), and attention span (Item 12). Social Resiliency included five items: responsiveness to persons (Item 1), responsiveness to examiner (Item 2), cooperativeness (Item 4), general emotional tone (Item 7), and endurance (Item 13). All items within each subset were both positively and significantly correlated with one another; the magnitudes of the within-subset Pearson correlation coefficients ranged from .34 to .72. The unit-weighted sum of the three items from the Attention IBR subscale and five items from the Social Resiliency, along with the Bayley Mental Development Index (MDI), were used as the three Bayley scale child outcome measures in this study.

Results

The top portion of Table 1 presents descriptive statistics by drug group for the predictor variables. The groups did not differ significantly on WAIS Full Scale IQ, years of education, SES, or parent communication at 4 and 12 months. Differences were found between the groups on the following: The methadone-maintained women experienced more severe stressors, had a poorer level of adaptive functioning, and had poorer communication with their children by 24 months. The methadone group also had more cumulative risk factors.

To test the first hypothesis—that is, to determine whether drug-exposed infants performed more poorly than comparison infants—the two groups were compared on the four measures of child outcome. The bottom portion of Table 1 presents the descriptive statistics by group for the child outcome variables. For every child outcome, the methadone group functioned slightly more poorly than the comparison group. Although consistent, in no instance did these differences in outcome reach a level of statistical significance. Our first hypothesis was not supported.

To test the second hypothesis—that cumulative social–environmental risk factors other than parental substance abuse would be predictive of child outcome—correlations between the measures of 24-month developmental competence and cumulative risk were examined for the entire sample and for the two groups

separately. For the methadone group, cumulative risk was a significant predictor of all four developmental outcomes; for the comparison group, it predicted only the child's PCOG score at 24 months. Table 2 presents these Pearson correlations.

Figure 1 presents the scatterplots between cumulative risk and each of the outcome variables with LOWESS smoothing curves marking the shape of the distribution for methadone and comparison children (Cleveland, 1979, 1981; Wilkinson, 1990). For all of the Bayley scales outcome measures, the results replicated those of Sameroff et al. (1987). There is a steep drop between 0 and 2 elements of risk present; then, the

Table 1. *Descriptive Statistics for the Predictor and Child Outcome Variables*

		Group	
		Methadone[a]	Comparison[b]
Variables			
Predictors			
Maternal Risk Factors			
WAIS Full Scale IQ	M	89.5	89.7
	SD	9.1	12.4
	Range	71 to 102	68 to 120
Years of Education	M	11.1	11.4
	SD	1.5	1.3
	Range	9 to 14	8 to 14
SES	M	4.5	4.3
	SD	0.7	0.8
	Range	3 to 5	3 to 5
Severity of Stressors (*DSM–III*)	M	4.7	4.2*
	SD	0.7	0.4
	Range	4 to 6	4 to 5
Adaptive Functioning (*DSM–III*)	M	4.7	3.2*
	SD	0.8	0.8
	Range	4 to 6	1 to 5
Sex of Child			
Males		14	25
Females		14	18
Maternal Communication			
4 months[c]	M	−0.13	0.57
	SD	2.73	3.01
12 months[c]	M	−0.09	−0.03
	SD	3.00	2.70
24 months[c]	M	−1.37	0.88*
	SD	2.87	2.23
Cumulative Risk	M	3.89	2.47*
	SD	1.91	1.03
	Range	0 to 7	1 to 5
Child Outcomes (24 months)			
Bayley MDI	M	92.5	95.8
	SD	13.4	12.6
	Range	66 to 123	76 to 119
Bayley IBR Attention	M	16.4	17.5
	SD	2.9	2.6
	Range	11 to 23	11 to 22
Bayley IBR Social Resiliency	M	25.8	27.1
	SD	4.9	5.3
	Range	17 to 34	15 to 37
Child Communication[c]	M	−0.34	0.21
	SD	2.52	2.15

[a]Parents, *n* = 25; children, *n* = 28. [b]Parents, *n* = 39; children, *n* = 41. [c]Standardized.
*p < .01, one-tailed.

Table 2. *Pearson Correlations Between Cumulative Risk and 24-Month Child Outcome Variables*

| | Child Outcomes at Age 24 Months | | | |
Cumulative Risk	Bayley MDI	Bayley IBR Attention	Bayley IBR Social Resiliency	PCOG Child Communication
Entire Sample	.27*	.26*	.29*	.38**
Comparison Group	.00	−.04	.17	.33*
Methadone Group	.45**	.39*	.37*	.42*

Note: Signs of correlations have been adjusted so that positive signs reflect relations in the predicted direction.
*p < .05, one-tailed. **p < .01, one-tailed.

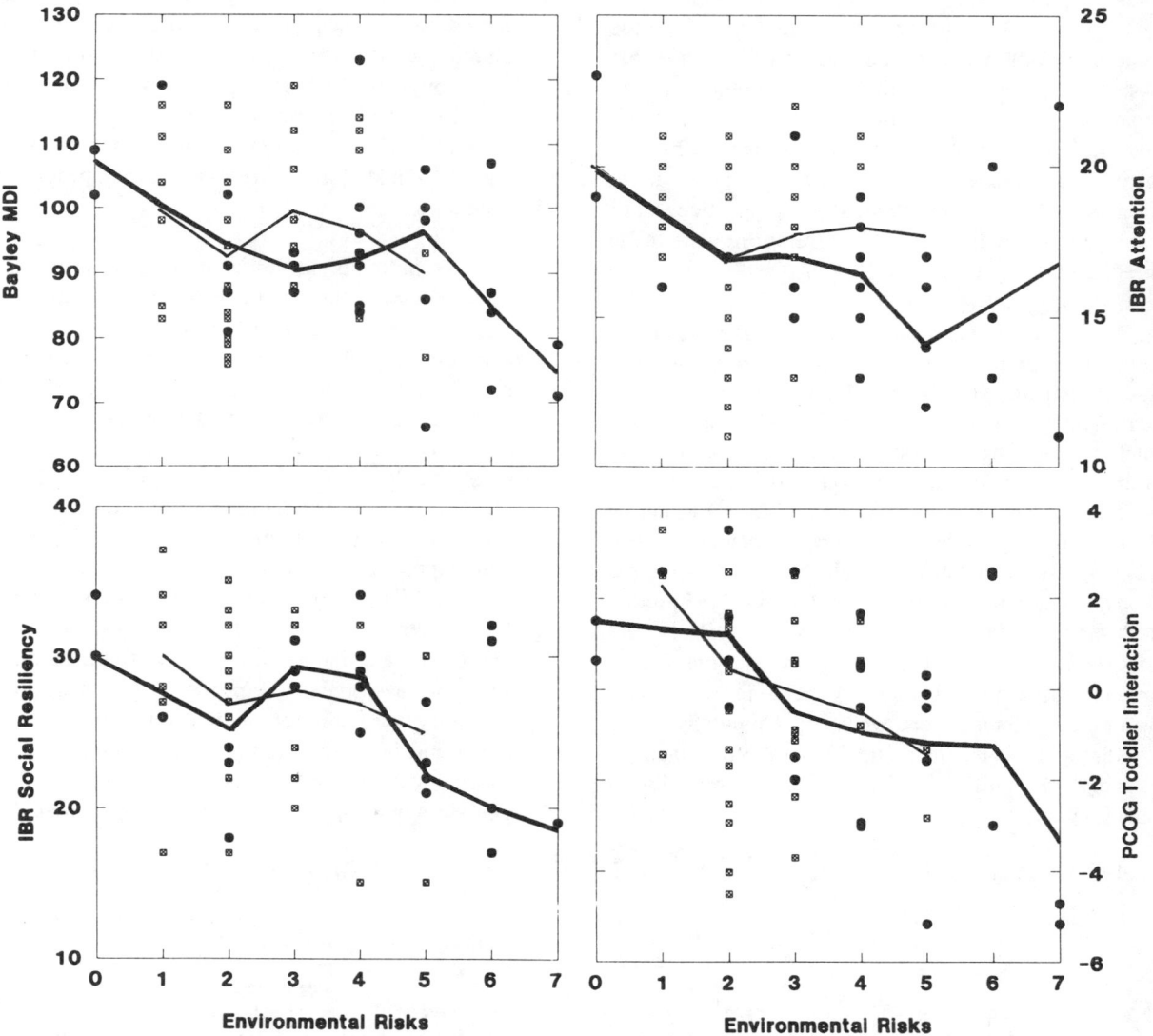

Figure 1. Scatterplots of cumulative social–environmental risks by 24-month-old child outcomes. Methadone group indicated by dark solid circles and a thick LOWESS smoothing line; comparison group indicated by light squares and a thin LOWESS smoothing line.

line levels off between 2 and 4 elements present; finally, the line declines steeply with 5 or more elements of risk present. The curve of best fit is considerably more linear for predicting child PCOG communication score at 24 months—the more risk elements, the poorer the child's communication.

Figure 1 indicates that the difference in magnitude of the correlations between the groups is somewhat misleading. The higher correlations for the methadone group are clearly related to the group's greater range of risk factors: The 2 methadone-exposed children with fewer risk factors than any comparison children were doing well, and of the 5 methadone children with more risk factors than any comparison children, most were doing quite poorly at age 2. Thus, the higher correlations for the methadone group are the result of greater predictability from the extreme ends of the methadone group—extremes not present in the comparison group. Excluding these outliers, our results would be similar to Sameroff et al.'s (1993) for African-American children. Except for 24-month child communication, the power of prediction of cumulative risk applied only to the extreme ends of the range of risks—extremes present only within the methadone group.

Our third hypothesis concerned whether a specific factor—poor maternal communication—is indeed a risk factor and whether it had greater impact on the outcomes for the methadone-exposed children. Table 3 shows the Pearson correlation coefficients between maternal communication at each of the three ages and the four 24-month outcomes. For the methadone group, all 12 correlations were in the predicted direction and 8 of the 12 were statistically significant. For the comparison group, only 7 correlations were in the predicted direction and only 1 of these was statistically significant.

We decided to test whether these differences in correlation magnitudes between the two groups were in fact statistically significant. This was done by using a series of general-linear-model prediction equations that included the drug group status categorical variable and a single maternal communication predictor as main-effect parameters followed by Group Status × Maternal Communication as the interaction parameter (Cohen & Cohen, 1975). Of the 12 models tested (the combinations of drug group status × 3 maternal PCOG predictors on the 4 child outcomes), 5 interaction effects were statistically significant. These significant interactions are indicated by a dagger (†) in Table 3. We also examined whether there were any Cumulative Risk Predictor × Group interactions by the same method. None were significant. The differential prediction of maternal communication occurred despite the fact that

the methadone and comparison mothers showed a similar range of poor to good communicating. The third hypothesis is partially supported.

Discussion

Three main findings from this study warrant further discussion:

1. Methadone exposure alone was not found to have a negative impact on the developmental outcomes studied.

2. Individual and cumulative risk factors other than methadone status generally predicted developmental outcomes only for the methadone group and then only for children at the extremes of the continuum of risk.

3. Although methadone exposure per se did not produce more problematic outcomes, the methadone-using women who had difficulty communicating with their children had children with particularly problematic outcomes.

The first finding of no simple drug effects is consistent with emerging longitudinal research on children exposed to substances other than alcohol. This research indicates, in general, that substance exposure does not affect older infants and preschool-age children's level of functioning as measured on standardized tests, or that the effects are so small as to be undetectable with relatively small samples (Chasnoff et al., 1992; Hans, 1992). This failure to reject the null hypothesis, however, does not necessarily mean that the development of drug-exposed children is no different from that of unexposed children. It may simply be that standardized tests of development and intelligence as measured in the laboratory are not sensitive to the effects of drug exposure on development. Some recent reports indicate that drug-exposed children demonstrate increased attentional and behavioral problems in school settings (Howard, Beckwith, Rodning, & Kropenske, 1989). The children in the current study were too young to be

Table 3. *Pearson Correlations Between Maternal Communication and 24-Month Child Outcome Variables*

Maternal Communication (By Group and Child Age in Months)	Child Outcomes at Age 24 Months			
	Bayley MDI	Bayley IBR Attention	Bayley IBR Social Resiliency	PCOG Child Communication
Methadone Group				
4	.34*†	.33*†	.43*†	.07
12	.32*†	.05	.58**†	.32*
24	.25	.26	.40*	.37*
Comparison Group				
4	−.25	−.14	−.06	.04
12	−.09	−.17	.10	.07
24	.17	.17	.08	.45**

*p < .05, one-tailed. **p < .01, one-tailed. †Significant statistical interaction effects (Maternal Communication × Group).

evaluated in these contexts. Traditional outcome measures for infants and toddlers may be inadequate for assessing the subtleties of behavior that act as precursors to the emergence of attentional and behavioral problems of children when they enter school (Meisels & Provence, 1989). In the sample, the consistent, although slight, pattern of the exposed children performing more poorly on all outcome measures, combined with the higher level of risk within some of these families, may portend a greater vulnerability to school adjustment problems. Most of these children enter overcrowded public schools with limited resources and classrooms containing at least several children with behavior problems. This combination of risks may well put them at risk of school failure and behavior problems.

The second hypothesis—that both individual and cumulative risk factors are predictive of children's outcome—yielded differential correlational findings for the two groups, but a similar pattern of poor prediction where the range of risk between the two groups overlapped. These results replicate both the 1987 and 1993 Sameroff et al. results from the Rochester Longitudinal Study. They replicate the 1987 results for all racial groups by identifying "thresholds" at the extremes for good and poor outcomes. They replicate the lack of predictability for African-American children among children in the midrange of risk—all of the comparison and most of the methadone group, those comparable to the participants in the Rochester study.

One could argue that this finding of a higher level of predictability within the methadone group is simply an artifact resulting from children in the methadone group having been exposed to a broader range of risk than the comparison children, but some of our findings suggest that this is not the case. It seems unlikely that all risk factors are nonspecific and equally potent. Parent communication predicts developmental outcome for the methadone group, but not for the comparison. The two groups had similar means and standard deviations on these differential predictors. The differential results for the two groups indicate the need to go beyond the sheer number of nonspecific risk factors and to examine risk factors in the context of social relationships. This should lead to a more complete understanding of how risk may operate to affect a child's development, perhaps in ways suggested by the third hypothesis.

The third hypothesis—that drug exposure would combine with poor maternal communication to have a particularly damaging impact on the development of drug-exposed children—was partially supported. The data are consistent with a transactional model of development—that the combination of biological risk (in this case methadone exposure) and nonoptimal parenting combine to limit development (Sameroff & Chandler, 1975).

Altogether, these data show that aspects of the social environment are related to methadone-exposed children's developmental outcomes—even with the rather limited set of social–environmental variables and laboratory measures of problematic maternal communication used herein. We did not begin to tap more subtle aspects of the social environment such as the structure of daily routines, communication in home settings, or relationships with nonmaternal figures.

Two other limitations should be noted. First, although our data show that the development of methadone-exposed children is linked to social–environmental factors, the data do not rule out the possibility that *some* of the children may be dealing with biological limitations placed on them by prenatal drug exposure and the perinatal experience of narcotics abstinence. Four of the original 42 methadone-exposed infnats died neonatally. Some preliminary studies of older drug-exposed children indicate continuing drug-related effects such as reduced head circumference and increased attentional and behavioral problems in school (Chasnoff et al., 1992; Fried & Watkinson, 1990; Griffith, 1991; Hans, 1992). Both children with known biological deficits (Greenspan, 1988; Williamson, 1988) and children from high stress environments (Garbarino, Kostelny, & Dubrow, 1991) are known to display similar types of behavior. Although our data indicate the importance of social–environmental factors for development, we did not address the interaction between social–environmental factors and biological markers other than simple prenatal exposure history.

The second limitation becomes apparent through examining the relative strength of early and concurrent predictors of outcome. Despite the cross-age predictability of maternal communication within the methadone group, contemporaneous factors were the strongest predictors of outcome in both children born exposed to methadone and unexposed children. Other than collection of data concerning parent–child communication and the Bayley scales, the bulk of the information gathered about the parents concerned factors occurring prenatally. Even better prediction might have been achieved had we had data on concurrent experiences beyond parent–child communication, factors such as support from social networks, maternal childrearing attitudes, and concurrent stressful life events known to contribute to the organization of children's behavior (Belsky & Isabella, 1988; Lewis, 1990).

Importantly, some of the methadone-maintained women in the study were communicating well with their children and their children were developing adequately. Perhaps they and the members of their extended families can act as resources for their children. This interpretation is consistent with other reports on the development of children born into substance-abusing families. Resilient adolescents born into an alcoholic family were the ones who received a great deal of positive attention from their primary caretaker (Werner, 1986). In a study of methadone-exposed children, the "surprise was not that some of the children did quite poorly but that, despite apparently overwhelming odds, some of the children managed to do quite well." (H. L. Johnson & Rosen, 1990, p. 282).

Especially because of how the media oversimplifies research results, researchers and clinicians need to remain cautious in explaining the developmental outcomes of drug-exposed children. At first, the pendulum of knowledge swung in the direction of asserting that all drug-exposed children would be born damaged by *in utero* exposure to drugs. It now appears to be swinging in the direction of claiming that drug-exposed children are no different from their unexposed counterparts ("New Research," 1992; Zuckerman & Frank, 1992). Our data indicate that both of these positions are too extreme. The developmental course of methadone-exposed children seems to differ from that for unexposed children in a manner related to social–environmental factors. The developmental implications of these differences await more refined, longitudinal study. Finally, for the children in both groups, given the relative power of concurrent predictors, the importance of early intervention around strengthening family relationships in low-income families should not be underestimated. Indeed, recent reports of successful intervention efforts with children born brain-injured (Vaucher, 1988), at environmental risk (D. L. Johnson & Walker, 1987; Lally, Mangione, & Honig, 1988), or drug-exposed (Griffith, 1991) support this contention.

References

Abel, E. L. (1984). *Fetal alcohol syndrome and fetal alcohol effects.* New York: Plenum.

American Psychiatric Association. (1980). *Diagnostic and statistical manual of mental disorders* (3rd ed.). Washington, DC: Author.

Bayley, N. (1969). *Bayley Scales of Infant Development.* New York: Psychological Corporation.

Belsky, J., & Isabella, R. (1988). Maternal, infant, and social–contextual determinants of attachment security. In J. Belsky & T. M. Nezworski (Eds.), *Clinical implications of attachment* (pp. 41–94). Hillsdale, NJ: Lawrence Erlbaum Associates, Inc.

Bernstein, V. J., Hans, S. L., & Percansky, C. (1991). Advocating for the young child in need through strengthening the parent–child relationship. *Journal of Clinical Child Psychology, 20,* 28–41.

Bernstein, V. J., Jeremy, R. J., & Marcus, J. (1986). Mother–infant interaction in multi-problem families: Finding those at risk. *Journal of the American Academy of Child Psychiatry, 25,* 631–640.

Bernstein, V. J., Percansky, C., & Hans, S. L. (1987, April). *Screening for social-emotional impairment in infants born to teenage mothers.* Paper presented at the biannual meeting of the Society for Research in Child Development, Baltimore.

Chasnoff, I. J., Burns, W. J., Hatcher, R. P., & Burns, K.A. (1983). Phencyclidine: Effects on the fetus and neonate. *Developmental Pharmacology and Therapeutics, 6,* 404–408.

Chasnoff, I. J., Burns, W. J., Schnoll, S. H., & Burns, K. A. (1985). Cocaine use in pregnancy. *New England Journal of Medicine, 313,* 666–669.

Chasnoff, I. J., & Griffith, D. R. (1989). Cocaine: Clinical studies of pregnancy and the newborn. *Annals of the New York Academy of Sciences, 562,* 260–266.

Chasnoff, I. J., Griffith, D. R., Freier, C., & Murray, J. (1992). Cocaine/polydrug use in pregnancy: Two-year follow-up. *Pediatrics, 89,* 284–289.

Cleveland, W. S. (1979). Robust locally weighted regression and smoothing scatterplots. *Journal of the American Statistical Association, 74,* 829–836.

Cleveland, W. S. (1981). LOWESS: A program for smoothing scatterplots by robust locally weighted regression. *American Statistician, 38,* 54.

Cocaine babies hooked at birth. (1986, July 26). *Newsweek,* pp. 56–57.

Cohen, J., & Cohen, P. (1975). *Applied multiple regression/correlation analysis for the behavioral sciences.* Hillsdale, NJ: Lawrence Erlbaum Associates, Inc.

Crack comes to the nursery. (1988, September 19). *Time,* pp. 85.

Crockenberg, S. B. (1981). Infant irritability, mother responsiveness, and social support influences on infant–mother attachment. *Child Development, 52,* 857–865.

Endicott, J., & Spitzer, R. L. (1972). The Current and Past Psycho-Pathology Scales (CAPPS). *Archives of General Psychiatry, 27,* 678–687.

Endicott, J., & Spitzer, R. L. (1978). A diagnostic interview: The Schedule for Affective Disorders and Schizophrenia (SADS–L). *Archives of General Psychiatry, 35,* 837–844.

Fried, P. A., & Watkinson, B. (1990). 36- and 48-month neurobehavioral follow-up of children prenatally exposed to marijuana, cigarettes, and alcohol. *Journal of Developmental and Behavioral Pediatrics, 11,* 48–58.

Garbarino, J., Kostelny, K., & Dubrow, N. (1991). *No place to be a child: Growing up in a war zone.* Lexington, MA: Lexington.

Goldberg, S. (1977). Social competence in infancy: A model of parent–infant interaction. *Merrill–Palmer Quarterly, 23,* 163–178.

Greenspan, S. (1982). Developmental morbidity in infants in multi-risk factor families. *Public Health Reports, 97,* 16–23.

Greenspan, S. (1988). Fostering emotional and social development in infants with disabilities. *Zero to Three, 9*(1), 8–18.

Griffith, D. L. (1991, April). Prenatal exposure to cocaine and other drugs: Developmental and educational prognoses. *Phi Delta Kappan,* pp. 30–34.

Hans, S. L. (1989). Developmental consequences of prenatal exposure to methadone. *Annals of the New York Academy of Sciences, 562,* 457–478.

Hans, S. L. (1992). Maternal opioid drug use and child development. In I. S. Zagon & T. A. Slotkin (Eds.), *Maternal substance abuse and the developing nervous system* (pp. 177–213). New York: Academic.

Hans, S. L. (1993). Sex differences in children of substance-abusing parents. In R. R. Watson (Ed.), *Addictive behaviors in women* (pp. 1–16). New York: Humana.

Harbison, R. D. (1974). *Perinatal addiction.* New York: Spectrum.

Hetherington, E. M. (1989). Coping with family transitions: Winners and losers. *Child Development, 60,* 1–14.

Hollingshead, A. B., & Redlich, F. C. (1958). *Social class and mental illness: A community study.* New York: Wiley.

Householder, J. (1980). *An investigation of mother–infant interaction in a narcotic-addicted population.* Unpublished doctoral dissertation, Northwestern University.

Howard, J., Beckwith, L., Rodning, C., & Kropenske, V. (1989). The development of young children of substance-abusing parents: Insights from seven years of intervention and research. *Zero to Three, 9,* 8–12.

Jeremy, R. J. & Bernstein, V. J. (1984). Dyads at risk: Methadone-maintained women and their 4-month-old infants. *Child Development, 55,* 1141–1154.

Jeremy, R. J. & Hans, S. L. (1985). Behavior of neonates exposed *in utero* to methadone as assessed on the Brazelton scale. *Infant Behavior and Development, 8,* 323–336.

Johnson, D. L., & Walker, T. (1987). Primary prevention of behavior problems in Mexican-American children. *American Journal of Community Psychology, 15,* 375-385.

Johnson, H. L., & Rosen, T. S. (1990). Difficult mothers of difficult babies: Mother–infant interaction in a multi-risk population. *American Journal of Orthopsychiatry, 60,* 281–288.

Kaltenbach, K., & Finnegan, L. P. (1987). Perinatal and developmental outcome of infants exposed to methadone in-utero. *Neurotoxicology & Teratology, 9,* 311–313.

Lally, J. R., Mangione, P. L., & Honig, A. S. (1988). The Syracuse University family development research program: Long-range impact of an early intervention with low-income children and their families. In D. Powell (Ed.), *Parent education as early childhood intervention: Emerging directions in theory, research and practice* (pp. 79–104). Norwood, NJ: Ablex.

Lewis, M., (1990). Models of developmental psychopathology. In M. Lewis & S. M. Miller (Eds.), *Handbook of developmental psychopathology* (pp. 15–28). New York: Plenum.

Marcus, J., Hans, S. L., Patterson, C. B., & Morris, A. J. (1984). A longitudinal study of offspring born to methadone-maintained women: I. Design, methodology and description of women's resources for functioning. *American Journal of Drug and Alcohol Abuse, 10,* 135–160.

Matheny, A. P., Jr. (1980). Bayley's Infant Behavior Record: Behavioral components and twin analyses. *Child Development, 51,* 1157–1167.

Matheny, A. P., Jr. (1983). A longitudinal study of stability of components from Bayley's Infant Behavior Record. *Child Development, 54,* 356–360.

Meisels, S. J., & Provence, S. (1989). *Identifying and assessing young disabled and developmentally vulnerable children and their families: Recommended guidelines.* Washington, DC: National Center for Clinical Infant Programs.

Myers, B. J., Olson, H. C., & Kaltenbach, K. (1992). Cocaine-exposed infants: Myths and misunderstandings. *Zero to Three, 13,* 1–5.

New research finds little lasting harm for "crack" children. (1992, January 29). *Education Week,* pp. 1, 10.

Parker, S., Greer, S., & Zuckerman, B. (1988). Double jeopardy: The impact of poverty on early child development. In B. Zuckerman, M. Weitzman, & J. Alpert (Eds.), Children at risk. *Pediatric Clinics of North America, 35,* pp. 1227–1240.

Pawl, J. H. (1992). Interventions to strengthen relationships between infants and drug-abusing or recovering parents. *Zero to Three,* 13, 6–10.

Rutter, M. (1970). Sex differences in children's response to family stress. In E. J. Anthony & C. Koupernik (Eds.), *The child in his family* (pp. 195–196). New York: Wiley.

Sameroff, A. J., & Chandler, M. J. (1975). Reproductive risk and the continuum of caretaking casualty. In F. D. Horowitz, E. M. Hetherington, S. Scarr-Salapatek, & G. M. Sigel (Eds.), *Review of child development research* (Vol. 4, pp. 187–244). Chicago: University of Chicago Press.

Sameroff, A. J., Seifer, R., Baldwin, A., & Baldwin, C. (1993). Stability of intelligence from preschool to adolescence: The influence of social and family risk factors. *Child Development, 64,* 80–97.

Sameroff, A. J., Seifer, R., Barocas, R., Zax, M., & Greenspan, S. (1987). Intelligence quotient scores of 4-year-old children: Social–environmental risk factors. *Pediatrics, 79,* 343–350.

Streissguth, A. P., Landesman-Dwyer, S., Martin, J. C., & Smith, D. W. (1980). Teratogenic effects of alcohol in humans and animals. *Science, 209,* 353–361.

Vaucher, Y. E. (1988). Understanding intraventricular hemorrhage and white matter injury in premature infants. *Infants and Young Children, 1,* 31–45.

Wechsler, D. (1955). *Wechsler Adult Intelligence Scale.* New York: Psychological Corporation.

Werner, E. E. (1986). Resilient offspring of alcoholics: A longitudinal study from birth to age 18. *Journal of Studies on Alcohol, 47,* 34–40.

Weston, D. R., Ivins, B., Zuckerman, B., Jones, C., & Lopez, R. (1989). Drug exposed babies: Research and clinical issues. *Zero to Three, 9,* 1–7.

Wilkinson, L. (1990). *SYGRAPH: The system for graphics.* Evanston, IL: SYSTAT, Inc.

Williamson, G. G. (1988). Motor control as a resource for adaptive coping. *Zero to Three, 9,* 1–7.

Zax, M., Sameroff, A. J., & Babigian, H. M. (1977). Birth outcomes of mentally disordered women. *American Journal of Orthopsychiatry, 47,* 218–230.

Zuckerman, B., & Frank, D. (1992) "Crack kids": Not broken. *Pediatrics, 89,* 337–339.

Received February 16, 1993
Final revision received August 16, 1993

Journal of Clinical Child Psychology
1994, Vol. 23, No. 4, 360–372

Cumulative Familial Risks and Low-Birthweight Children's Cognitive and Behavioral Development

Fong-ruey Liaw and Jeanne Brooks-Gunn

Columbia University

Examines the prevalence, contributions, and cumulative effects of 13 biological, economic, maternal, family-structural, and parenting-belief risk factors in poor and nonpoor families separately on low-birthweight premature children's 36-month IQ scores and behavior problems (N = 704). Children were part of the Infant Health and Development Program (IHDP), a multisite, randomized clinical trial providing early pediatric follow-up and educational and family support services. Risk factors occurred more frequently in poor families than in nonpoor families. Different sets of risk factors were associated with children's IQ scores and behavior problem scores. As the number of risk factors increased, child IQ decreased. Behavior problems did not change as a function of risk factors. Early intervention had a beneficial effect on IQ scores regardless of the number of risks experienced.

Risk has often been broadly defined as biological and environmental conditions that increase the likelihood of negative developmental outcomes (e.g., Brooks-Gunn, 1990a; Garmezy & Rutter, 1983; Werner & Smith, 1982). Factors that have been considered risks include biological (e.g., low birthweight, LBW), economic (e.g., poverty, unemployment), parental (e.g., maternal ability and education, parental mental health), family structural (e.g., large family size, father absence), and extrafamilial (e.g., adverse neighborhoods, economic recession, inadequate health care systems) variables. Poverty has been considered a major risk for physical health problems (Butler, Starfield, &

Stenmark, 1984; Klerman, 1991; McCormick & Brooks-Gunn, 1989), mental health problems (McLoyd, 1990; McLoyd & Wilson, 1991), and deficits in cognitive development and school achievement (Duncan, Klebanov, & Brooks-Gunn, 1994; Levin, 1991). Poverty is also linked to other risks, such as unemployment, father absence, maternal depression, inadequate parenting, low social support, and stressful life events (Chase-Lansdale & Brooks-Gunn, in press; Huston, 1991; McLoyd, 1990; Parker, Greer, & Zuckerman, 1988; Wilson, 1987). These risks are sometimes termed *poverty cofactors* (McCormick & Brooks-Gunn, 1989). Some researchers suggest that poor families are exposed to more risk factors than nonpoor families, and that the consequences of risk factors are more severe for children who reside in poor families than for children who reside in more affluent families (e.g., McLoyd, 1990; Parker et al., 1988).

LBW is a biological risk factor; it is likely to place the infant at risk for neurodevelopmental problems, which subsequently place the infant at risk for developmental delays and behavior disorders (Hunt, 1983; Institute of Medicine, 1985; McCormick, 1989; Sameroff, 1986). This is particularly true for very-low-birthweight (VLBW) children (birthweight < 1,500 g; Hack, Fanaroff, & Merkatz, 1975; McCormick, 1989; McCormick, Brooks-Gunn, Workman-Daniels, Turner, & Peckham, 1992). Several studies have examined the interaction between biological risks and family socioeconomic status (SES) on child development (Beckwith & Cohen, 1984; Escalona, 1982; Sameroff & Chandler, 1975). For example, in Werner's classic two-decade study of the children of Kauai, an interaction between perinatal problems and SES was found,

This article is based on data from the Infant Health and Development Program and was presented at the meeting of the Society for Research in Child Development, New Orleans, March 25, 1993. The Infant Health and Development Program was funded by the Robert Wood Johnson Foundation. Additional support was provided by the Pew Charitable Trusts and by the Bureau of Maternal and Child and Resources Development, Health Resources and Services Administration, Public Health Services, Department of Health and Human Services; and by the National Institute of Child Health and Human Development (NICH). The writing of this article was partially supported by a fellowship to Fong-ruey Liaw from the Educational Testing Service and by grants from the March of Dimes Foundation, NICHD, and the Pew Charitable Trusts. Additionally, the continuation of the Infant Health and Development Program was supported by grants from the sources listed earlier to the Longitudinal Study Office, Albert Einstein College of Medicine and Columbia University; and the Data Coordinating Center, Johns Hopkins University.

We thank Ruth Gross, Donna Spiker, Cecelia McCarton, Jim Tonascia, and Pat Belt for assistance in data preparation and coordination. We also thank Pamela Klebanov for her comments on an early draft.

Requests for reprints should be sent to Jeanne Brooks-Gunn, Center for Young Children and Families, Teachers College, Columbia University, New York, NY 10027.

such that perinatal problems were associated with much lower IQ scores at age 2 years in low-SES than high-SES families (Werner, Bierman, & French, 1971).

LBW births are often associated with poverty and its cofactors (e.g., low maternal education, high unemployment, and teenage motherhood), which are themselves associated with decreases in child well-being (Hunt, 1983; Institute of Medicine, 1985; McCormick & Brooks-Gunn, 1989). However, most previous studies of LBW infants' development focused either on a specific risk factor—such as severity of illness (Field, Dempsey, & Shuman, 1979; Klein, Hack, Gallagher, & Fanaroff, 1985; Meisels, Plunkett, Pasick, Stiefel, & Roloff, 1987), poverty (Drillien, 1964; Escalona, 1982; Sameroff & Chandler, 1975), parent–child interactions (Cohen & Parmelee, 1983), maternal depression (Field, 1981), or social support (Hall, Williams, & Greenberg, 1985)—or on a small set of risk factors, such as neonatal illness and low maternal education (Hunt & Cooper, 1989). Few studies examined the potential cumulative effects of multiple risks likely to be experienced by LBW children.

A cumulative risk model of development posits that adverse developmental outcomes can better be predicted by combinations of risk factors than by single risk factors (Sameroff, Seifer, Baldwin, & Baldwin, 1993; Sameroff, Seifer, Barocas, Zax, & Greenspan, 1987; Schorr, 1988; Werner & Smith, 1982). The premise is that the number of risks, rather than individual risk factors, accounts for developmental delays. This model would also account for: (a) some children in poor families doing well, because not all poor families may experience multiple negative events in addition to poverty; and (b) some children in more advantaged families not doing well, perhaps because of the presence of multiple negative events. Little research directly tests this model, however.

The best example of the cumulative risk model may be the study conducted by Sameroff et al. (1987, 1993) which looked at the cumulative effects of socio-environmental risk factors in predicting normal-birthweight children's IQ scores at ages 4 and 13. The 10 risk factors accounted for 16% of the variance in children's IQ scores at age 4, above and beyond family SES. In addition, multiple risk factors had a greater effect than would be expected from looking at each singly: As the number of risks increased, IQ scores decreased at both ages. The effect of cumulative risks seemed more pronounced in low-SES families than in high-SES families at age 4, but this differential effect was not tested.

Services that poor families receive, such as early intervention and home-visiting programs, often improve poor children's cognitive development and reduce the likelihood of grade failure, special education placement, and probably delinquent behavior and conduct disorder later on (Bronfenbrenner, 1975; Brooks-Gunn, 1990b; Bryant & Ramey, 1987; Clarke-Stewart

& Fein, 1983; Haskins, 1989; Lazar, Darlington, Murray, Royce, & Snipper, 1982; Woodhead, 1988; Zigler, 1992). Intervention programs developed for biologically at-risk children often report similar benefits in cognitive development and, to a lesser extent, in social and emotional development (for reviews, see Brooks-Gunn, 1990b; Field, 1981; Meisels, Dichtelmiller, & Liaw, 1993). Most studies have not examined whether early intervention programs are helpful for subgroups of children who are exposed to different numbers of risk factors, probably due to lack of risk data or insufficient sample size. Thus, little is known about whether the intervention can help buffer the adverse effects of risks, especially for children who experience multiple risks. Given that both LBW infants and children from poor families are likely to be exposed to multiple risks, this line of investigation is an important addition to the intervention literature.

Based on Sameroff et al.'s (1987, 1993) studies of the effects of cumulative risks on child IQ, the impact of risk factors on cognitive development of the child at 3 years of age was examined in this study. Our investigation included 13 risk factors other than family poverty status; factors were similar to those examined by Sameroff et al. (1987, 1993). Associations between risk factors and outcomes were examined for children from both poor and nonpoor families. Four major questions are addressed:

1. How prevalent are risk factors experienced by LBW children from poor and nonpoor families? We expect risk factors to be more prevalent in poor than in nonpoor families.

2. What are the effects of risk factors, and are the effects different for poor and nonpoor families?

3. Are the effects of risk factors cumulative? We expect that risk factors will have negative effects on child IQ scores and that, as the number of risks increases, cognitive well-being will suffer. We also expect the effects of risk factors (individually or cumulatively) to be more severe for poor children, given the "double jeopardy" proposition.

4. Does the provision of early intervention service reduce the adverse effects of risk factors? We expect that the adverse outcomes will be ameliorated by participation in early intervention irrespective of number of risk factors. Because the Infant Health and Development Program, on which the study was based, was not designed to test the intervention effect on reducing risk factors or their effects, these analyses are exploratory.

Emotional well-being was also assessed when the children were 3 years of age, using a behavior problem scale. Consequently, we were able to examine links between behavior problems and risk factors. Because less is known about how family factors influence behavior problems as opposed to cognitive development,

361

our predictions are more speculative. Typically, family factors account for less variance in behavior problems than in cognitive outcome, so that overall models should be less predictive. Factors such as maternal depression and parenting beliefs may play a more significant role in behavior problems than in cognitive scores. The accumulation of risk factors is expected to contribute to behavior problems, though (Benasich, Brooks-Gunn, & McCormick, in press).

Method

Program

The data are drawn from the Infant Health and Development Program (IHDP). The IHDP was a multisite randomized clinical trial that included 985 low birthweight, premature infants (birthweight ≤ 2,500 g, gestational age ≤ 37 weeks) at eight sites.[1] Of those eligible, 21% refused consent. Infants were stratified by sites and by two birthweight groups: *heavier* (birthweight between 2,001 and 2,500 g) and *lighter* (birthweight < 2,001 grams). Two thirds of the sample came from the lighter group and one third from the heavier group. One third of the sample from each birthweight group was randomly assigned to the intervention group ($n = 377$) and two thirds to the follow-up-only group ($n = 608$) immediately after nursery discharge (IHDP, 1990). The intervention and follow-up-only groups of children did not differ in terms of measures collected prior to randomization, specifically, birthweight, sex, race/ethnicity, neonatal health, maternal age and education (see Gross, Brooks-Gunn, & Spiker, 1992; Infant Health and Development Program, 1990).

The intervention was provided for 3 years, from the infants' hospital discharge to their third birthday, and included three modalities: (a) home visits, (b) children's attendance at a full-day Child Development Center, and (c) parent-group meetings. Home visits were made weekly in the first year and bimonthly in the second and third years. The home visitor provided information and support to the parents and implemented two specific curricula: *Partners for Learning* (Sparling & Lewis, 1985), a program of learning

activities for the parent to use with the child; and *Problem Solving for Parents* (Wasik, 1984), a systematic approach to help parents to deal with childrearing and personal problems. The Child Development Center provided an enriched educational curriculum beginning at 12 months (corrected for gestational age) and continuing until the last child at the site reached 36 months (corrected age). The teacher–child ratio was 1:3 in a class of six children from 12 to 24 months and 1:4 in a class of eight from 24 to 36 months. The intervention children attended the Child Development Center 5 days a week. The curriculum emphasized cognitive, linguistic, and social development (Sparling, Lewis, & Neuwirth, 1988). Parent-group meetings were held every 2 months in the second and third years to provide the parents with childrearing information and social support. (For detailed information regarding recruitment and the intervention services, see IHDP, 1990; Ramey et al.,1990; and Sparling et al., 1991.)

The children and mothers in the IHDP were followed up at 40 weeks and at 4, 8, 12, 18, 24, 30, and 36 months postterm (corrected for gestational age), during which time sociodemographic and developmental information of the family was collected. Children's cognitive and behavioral functioning was assessed annually at 12, 24, and 36 months, and observations were made in home at 30 months. Attrition was low at 3 years (only 7%). Attrition did not differ by treatment groups (IHDP, 1990).

Sample

The sample for this study included 704 children who had family income data and complete data on all risk factors that were under investigation. About 28.5% (281) of the original sample were excluded due to missing data across the 3-year period. Descriptive analyses comparing the selected and the excluded samples indicated significant differences in maternal race/ethnicity, age, and education, but not in child's birthweight, neonatal health, or sex. No differences as a function of treatment group were found. The current sample compared with the excluded sample, was more likely to have been Caucasian (39.3% vs. 30.6%), $\chi^2(1, N = 984) = 10.3$, $p < .01$; to have had an older mother (8.5% vs. 15.3% teenage mothers), $\chi^2(1, N=984) = 9.9$, $p < .01$; and to have had a mother with more education (64.9% vs. 47.7% having completed high school or more), $\chi^2(1, N = 984) = 24.84$, $p < .001$. Thus, our sample is somewhat more advantaged than the entire sample, and limitations in generalization to other families should be observed.

The sample of children was 50% male, 52% African American, 9% Hispanic American, and 39% Caucasian. Sixty percent were in the follow-up-only (FOL) group, and 40% were in the intervention (INT) group. Families were classified into *poor* and *nonpoor* catego-

---

[1]The IHDP was a joint collaboration of eight participating medical institutions at eight sites. The participating universities and site directors were Patrick H. Casey, University of Arkansas for Medical Sciences (Little Rock); Cecelia M. McCarton, Albert Einstein College of Medicine (New York); Michael W. Yogman, Harvard Medical School (Boston); Charles R. Bauer and Keith G. Scott, University of Miami School of Medicine (Miami); Judith Bernbaum, University of Pennsylvania School of Medicine (Philadelphia); Jon E. Tyson and Mark Swanson, University of Texas Health Science Center (Dallas); Clifford J. Sells and Forrest C. Bennett, University of Washington School of Medicine (Seattle); and David T. Scott, Yale University School of Medicine (New Haven, CT).

ries based on the family's income at 12 months (using 1986 poverty thresholds). A family was classified as poor if the annual income (adjusted for family size) fell below the poverty threshold by an income–needs ratio of 1.5 (56.4% of the sample; $n = 230$ in the FOL group and $n = 167$ in the INT group), whereas a family was considered nonpoor if its annual income exceeded this 1.5 income–needs ratio (43.6% of the sample; $n = 193$ in the FOL group and $n = 114$ in the INT group).[2]

When examining the first three questions (i.e., prevalence, contributions, and cumulative effects of risk factors), children in the FOL group were included in the analyses. When testing the effect of early intervention, both the FOL and the INT groups were used.

Measures

Risk factors. The risk factors examined here include 13 biological, socioeconomic, maternal characteristic, and family structural factors that have been associated with adverse child parent outcomes in the literature. Whenever possible, risk factors were constructed from measures taken when the child was born (i.e., birthweight, neonatal health status, race/ethnicity, and maternal age and education). Otherwise, risk factors were constructed based on the earliest time the measures were taken (i.e., unemployment, maternal mental health, stressful life events, social support, father absence, and family density at 12 months; mother's score on a verbal ability test at 18 months). The risk factors, the criterion for high risk, and the sample composition of the high-risk groups are next described by type of risk:

1. *Biological* risks included birthweight and neonatal health. VLBW children (defined as birthweight < 1,500 g; 23.9% of the sample) were considered at high risk because VLBW is associated with higher incidence of cognitive problems and neurological defects than is heavier birthweight (Klein, Hack, & Breslau, 1989; McCormick, 1989; McCormick et al., 1992). LBW

children who are severely ill at birth may be at higher risk for adverse outcomes than LBW children who are not sick at birth (McCormick, 1989; Meisels & Plunkett, 1988). Children whose Neonatal Health Index (NHI, an index calculated based on length of stay in the newborn nursery, adjusted for birthweight and standardized to a mean of 100 and a standard deviation of 16, with high scores indicating better health; Scott, Bauer, Kraemer, & Tyson, 1989) was less than the 25th percentile (NHI < 92) were considered at high risk (24.3% of the sample).

2. *Socioeconomic* risks included race/ethnicity and unemployment of the head of the household. African-American or Hispanic-American children are more likely to live in poverty and to experience persistent poverty than Caucasian children (Duncan et al., 1994; Duncan, Hill, & Hoffman, 1988; Duncan, & Rodgers, 1988). In addition, minority children are at substantially higher risk than Caucasian children for experiencing developmental and social-emotional problems (Gibbs, 1989; McLoyd, 1990; Myers & King, 1983; Neisser, 1986; Spencer & McLoyd, 1990). Following Sameroff et al.'s (1987, 1993) study, being African American or Hispanic American was considered a risk factor (60.7% of the sample).[3] Unemployment of the head of the household was also considered a risk (34.8% of the sample).

3. *Maternal characteristic* risks included maternal education, verbal ability, mental health, stressful life events, and low social support. Mothers who had not completed high school were considered at risk (35.1% of the sample). Mothers' scores on the Peabody Picture Vocabulary Test–Revised (PPVT–R; Dunn & Dunn, 1981) lower than the 25th percentile (PPVT–R score < 66) were another risk (23.0% of the sample). Mothers' mental health (e.g., depression, high stressful life events, and low social support) is associated with children's cognitive and social-emotional development (Billings & Moos, 1981; McLoyd, 1990; Orvaschel, Weissman, & Kidd, 1980). Maternal depression was evaluated by the General Health Questionnaire (GHQ; Goldberg, 1978) when the child was 12 months of age. The GHQ is a 12-item scale, tapping depression, somatization, and anxiety. A total GHQ score was computed, with higher values indicating more psychological distress (range = 0 to 32).[4] High risk was defined as having a total score higher than the highest 25% (i.e., GHQ > 13), indicating higher depression (21.9% of the sample). Mother-reported stressful life events were

---

[2]The economic status of the family was designated at 12 months by dividing each family's income by its corresponding poverty threshold. Because family income is a categorical variable that indicates a range, this variable was recoded with the mean of the income range. Income was then divided by the poverty threshold, a level of income determined by the U.S. Department of Commerce (1986), Bureau of the Census, based on the size of the family. For example, in 1986, which coincides with the 12-month IHDP assessments, U.S. poverty threshold for a family of three, was roughly $8,737. Families with annual incomes, before taxes, that exceed these thresholds by an income–needs ratio of 1.5 are considered nonpoor, whereas families with incomes falling below them are considered poor. Thus, a family of three with an income of $20,000 would have an income–needs ratio of about 2.3 and be considered nonpoor in that year. On the other hand, a family of six on the same income, would have a poverty threshold of $14,986, an income–needs ratio of about 1.3, and would be considered poor (Brooks-Gunn et al., 1993; Duncan et al., 1994).

[3]Separate analyses were not conducted for African-American and Hispanic children, because Hispanic children were present in only three of the eight sites and thus constituted a small sample. However, the findings with African-American and Hispanic children's data combined are essentially the same as when analyses were performed with African-American children alone.

[4]All ranges given are sample ranges.

measured at 12 months. A stressful life event score was computed by summing the occurrences of 18 stressful life events (including maternal illness; friend/relative illness or death; change in schooling, work, or residence; and need for services; range = 0 to 9). High risk was defined as the highest 25% on the scale (number of stressful events > 3; 15.3% of the sample). Mothers' social support network was measured by six vignettes asking mothers to report sources of monetary, emotional, and child-care support (Cohen & Lazarus, 1977; McCormick & Brooks-Gunn, 1989; McCormick et al., 1987). An overall score was obtained by summing support across the vignettes (range = 0 to 12), with higher values indicating more social support. High risk was defined as the lowest 25% of scores on the scale (total score < 7; 23.6% of the sample).

4. *Family structural* risks included teenage motherhood, father absence, and high family density. Teenage mothers have been found, in some but not all studies, to be less verbal, less responsive, and more punitive in interacting with their children than older mothers (e.g., Brooks-Gunn & Furstenberg, 1986; Chase-Lansdale, Brooks-Gunn, & Zamsky, 1994; Garcia-Coll, 1988; Garcia-Coll, Hoffman, & Vohr, 1987; Oppel & Roystom, 1971; Roosa, Fitzgerald, & Carlson, 1982). Mothers who were younger than 18 years when the child was born were considered high risk (8.5% of the sample). Father presence was determined by whether the husband or father of the child lived in the household when the child was 12 months old. Approximately 48% of the sample had no father in the home. Family density was represented by a child–adult ratio in the household at 12 months, reflecting not only family size but the availability of human resources in the home. High-risk was defined as having a child–adult ratio greater than 2 (19.3% of the sample).

5. *Parenting-belief* risk was reflected by the extent to which parents held a categorical view of child development. Parental beliefs were measured by the Concepts of Development Questionnaire (CODQ; Sameroff & Feil, 1985) at 12 months. The CODQ is a 20-item scale reflecting two levels of parental beliefs about development: At the *categorical* level, a parent holds a rigid simplistic view of child behavior; at the *perspective* level, parents have a more sophisticated view of child behavior, seeing development as subject to multiple influences. A total score was obtained (range = 1.05 to 2.65); higher scores indicated a more perspectivistic view, and lower scores a more categorical view. The high-risk group consisted of mothers whose scores were lower than the 25th percentile (CODQ < 1.65; 19.5% of the sample).

Outcome measures. The Stanford–Binet Intelligence Scale (3rd revision, Form L–M; Terman & Merrill, 1973) was administered to all children at 36 months corrected age across sites. Testers were trained and monitored centrally and were blind to the child's assignment to treatment group. An overall IQ score was calculated ($M = 90$, $SD = 19$, range = 43 to 144).

Children's behavior problems were measured by the Child Behavior Checklist for Ages 2–3 (CBCL/2–3; Achenbach, Edelbrock, & Howell, 1987; McConaughy & Achenbach, 1989) at 36 months. The CBCL/2–3 is a 99-item questionnaire in which parents rate their children's behavior problems within the past 2 months on a 3-point scale ranging from *not true* (0) to *very/often true* (2). A total raw score was computed ($M = 45$, $SD = 20$, range = 3 to 121), with higher scores indicating greater behavior problems (Brooks-Gunn, Klebanov, Liaw, & Spiker, 1993). Approximately 19% ($n = 76$) of the children had a score above 63, an index for severe behavioral problems (Achenbach et al., 1987). A dichotomized behavior problem measure was used in this study to signify *severe* behavior problems (total score > 63; coded as one) versus *less severe* problems (total score ≤ 63; coded as zero). The correlative between IQ and behavior problems was .27.

Covariates. We included clinical sites and the child's sex as covariates in all our analyses. Child's sex was dummycoded (female = 1, male = 0), and the eight clinical sites were coded into seven dummy variables, with the eighth site (Yale) as the control group.

Results

Frequency of Risk Factors

Chi-square analyses were performed to compare the percentages of risk factors in poor versus nonpoor groups in the FOL group. Poor families were more likely to be at high risk on 11 of the 13 risk factors under investigation (see Table 1). Looking at the number of risk factors experienced, 2% of the poor families had no risk factors, 6% had 1 risk, 19% had 2 risks, 17% had 3 risks, 14% had 4 risks, 17% had 5 risks, and 35% had 6 or more risks ($n = 230$). In contrast, for families who were not poor, 19% had no risk factors, 31% had 1 risk, 21% had 2 risks, 12% had 3 risks, 7% had 4 risks, 6% had 5 risks, and 5% had 6 or more risks ($n = 193$). Poor families, on average, experienced more risks than nonpoor families (the average number of risks experienced was 5 for poor families and 2 for nonpoor families), $t(422) = 12.97$, $p < .001$.

Contributions of Risk Factors

Hierarchical regressions were conducted to examine: (a) the associations between individual risk factors and outcomes, independent of the effects of family poverty status, clinical site, child's sex, and other risk factors; and (b) the Risk Factor × Poverty interaction

Table 1. *Percentages of High Risk in Poor and Nonpoor Families, Follow-Up-Only Group*

Risk Factor	Total[a]	Poor[b]	Nonpoor[c]	χ^2	*F* Value
Biological					
Very Low Birthweight[d]	25.1	28.3 (27.4)	21.2 (22.1)	2.75	1.28
Poor Neonatal Health[e]	25.3	22.2 (26.8)	29.0 (24.4)	2.60	0.26
Socioeconomic					
Minority[f]	60.0	80.0	36.3	83.65***	
Unemployment[g]	30.5	46.1 (41.6)	11.9 (16.4)	57.81***	30.18***
Maternal Characteristic					
Low Maternal Education[h]	32.6	47.8 (45.2)	14.5 (17.2)	53.00***	34.67***
Low Maternal PPVT-R[i]	22.5	33.9 (28.4)	8.8 (14.3)	37.98***	11.40**
High Maternal Depression[j]	22.7	27.8 (29.4)	16.6 (15.0)	7.56**	10.07**
High Stressful Life Events[k]	16.5	30.0 (27.4)	13.0 (15.6)	17.64***	10.50**
Low Social Support[l]	22.2	38.3 (36.0)	23.3 (25.5)	10.87***	7.17**
Family Structural					
Teenage Motherhood[m]	8.0	11.3 (10.4)	4.1 (5.0)	7.27**	3.35
Father Absence[n]	43.7	64.8 (57.3)	18.7 (26.1)	90.75***	47.69***
High Family Density[o]	17.3	25.7 (24.1)	7.3 (8.8)	24.87***	14.71***
Parenting					
Categorical Childrearing View[p]	20.1	29.1 (24.6)	9.3 (13.9)	25.63***	6.76*

Note: Values in parentheses indicate the adjusted percentages of high risk, adjusted for minority status, derived from SPSS–X (SPSS, Inc., 1990) MANOVA procedures.
[a]$n = 423$. [b]$n = 230$. [c]$n = 193$. [d]Birth weight < 1500 g. [e]Child's NHI at birth lower than the 25th percentile (NHI < 92). [f]African American or Hispanic. [g]Head of the household unemployed when the child was 12 months of age. [h]Mother's education less than high-school completion when the child was born. [i]Mother's score on the PPVT–R less than the 25th percentile (PPVT–R < 66). [j]Mother's GHQ score higher than the 75th percentile (GHQ > 13). [k]Reported stressful life events when the child was 12 months of age were higher than the 75th percentile (total stressful events > 3). [l]Reported social support score when the child was 12 months was lower than the 25th percentile (total score < 7). [m]Mother's age < 18 years when the child was born. [n]Husband or father of the child not present in the household when the child was 12 months old. [o]The child–adult ratio in the household when the child was 12 months old was greater than 2. [p]Mother's CODQ score lower than the 25th percentile (CODQ < 1.65).
*$p < .05$. **$p < .01$. ***$p < .001$.

effects on outcomes (see Cohen & Cohen, 1983).[5] Family poverty status (equal to or below 150% of the poverty line = 1, above 150% of the poverty line = 0), site, and child's sex were entered in the first step. In the second step, the 13 variables that were used to construct the risk factors were entered, including birthweight (in grams), NHI, race/ethnicity (African American/Hispanic American = 1, Caucasian = 0), unemployment (unemployed = 1, employed = 0), maternal education (< 12th grade = 1, high school graduate = 2, some college = 3), maternal PPVT–R score, maternal depression (GHQ score), stressful life events, social support, maternal age (< 18 years = 1, ≥ 18 years = 0), father absence (absent = 1, present = 0), family density, and maternal view of childrearing. In the third step of regressions, a particular Risk Factor × Poverty interaction term was entered (hence, requiring 13 regressions; p at .01 to adjust for multiple analyses). The results of regressions are summarized in Table 2.

Children's IQ scores. The results show that the 13 risk factors as a whole explained a substantial proportion (13%) of the variance in children's IQ score, above and beyond family poverty status, site, and sex

of child (total R^2 for the entire model = .47, $p < .001$). Significant associations were seen with poverty status, NHI, race/ethnicity, maternal education, PPVT–R score, and maternal depression. Poor African-American and Hispanic-American children, and children of depressed mothers, were likely to show lower IQ scores. In contrast, children who were born with better neonatal health, or who were born to mothers of higher education and higher verbal ability, had higher IQ scores. Additionally, the results of the Risk × Poverty interactions show that family poverty status interacted with race/ethnicity and maternal verbal ability in relation to children's IQ scores at age 3. An examination of the mean IQ scores of high- versus low-risk children within poor and nonpoor groups shows that the effects on child IQ of being African American or Hispanic American and of having mothers with low verbal ability on child IQ were greater for children who were not poor than for those who were poor. Specifically, within the nonpoor group, the IQ scores for minority African-American and Hispanic-American children were, on average, 14.8 points lower than those for Caucasian children, and children of low-PPVT–R mothers scored 6.5 points lower than did those of high-PPVT–R mothers. In contrast, for the poor group, the IQ scores of minority children were, on average, 5.3 points lower than those for Caucasian children, and children of low-

---

[5]Associations among the risk factors were not high enough to cause problems of collinearity.

PPVT–R mothers scored 0.5 points higher than did children of high-PPVT–R mothers.

Children's behavior problems. Regressions on children's behavior problems indicated that the risk factors accounted for 12% of the variance, after controlling for family poverty, site, and child's sex (total R^2 for the entire model = .16, $p < .001$). Major contributors were mother's PPVT–R, maternal depression, stressful life events, and maternal age. Mothers with low verbal ability, high depression, frequent stressful life events, and being younger than 18 years at the child's birth were more likely to report more severe behavior problems in their children. No significant Risk × Poverty interaction effects were found.

Cumulative Effects of Risk Factors

A multiple-risk score was created as the total number of high risks experienced by each family (range = 0 to 12). Because the number of families falling in the high end of multiple risks tended to be small, families were collapsed into six groups for analyses—0 or 1 risk, 2 risks, 3 risks, 4 to 5 risks, and 6 or more risk factors. The cumulative effect of risk factors on child and parent outcomes was tested with the FOL group via hierarchical multiple regressions. The covariates (site and child's sex), the multiple-risk score, and poverty status were entered in the regression model first. The potential

differential effect of multiple risks for poor and non-poor families was tested by entering the interaction term of Multiple-Risk Score × Poverty in the second step.

Children's IQ scores. Results of the hierarchical regressions on children's IQ scores show significant main effects of the multiple-risk score, $t = -5.88$, $p < .001$, and poverty, $t = -4.63$, $p < .001$ (Ns for regression = 423). That is, as the number of risks increased, children's IQ scores decreased; the IQ scores of children from poor families were always lower than those of children from nonpoor families across risk status (see Figure 1 for the adjusted means of IQ scores, adjusted for site and child's sex, by the number of risks for poor and nonpoor groups, respectively).

The Multiple-Risk Score × Poverty interaction was significant, $t = 2.69$, $p < .05$ (N for regression = 423). The cumulative effect of risk factors on IQ scores was similar for children who were poor and not poor when they experienced few risks, but when children were exposed to a large number of risk factors (5 or more), the IQ scores of children from families who were not poor dropped dramatically and converged with the IQ scores of children from poor families.

Children's behavior problem scores. Regression results for children's behavior problems show a similar cumulative effect of multiple risks, $t = 3.19$, $p < .001$:

Table 2. *Standardized Regression Coefficients of Risk Factors Predicting Outcomes (Follow-Up-Only Children)*

Predictor	Stanford–Binet IQ	Severe Behavior Problems
Covariates		
Site	–	–
Female	.05	−.05
Poverty	−.17***	.00
Risk Factors		
Birthweight	.06	−.00
NHI	.09*	−.00
Minority	−.26***	−.09
Unemployment	.00	−.01
Maternal Education	.15**	.09
Maternal PPVT–R	.15*	−.33***
Maternal Depression	−.09*	.18***
Stressful Life Events	.06	.10*
Social Support	−.01	−.01
Maternal Age < 18 Years	.02	.11*
Father Absence	.00	.03
Family Density	−.07	−.04
Perspectivistic View of Child-Rearing	.01	−.06
R^2 Change Due to Risk Factors	.13***	.12***
Total R^2 Due to Covariates and Risk Factors	.47***	.16***
Significant Poverty × Individual Risk Interaction[a]		
Poverty × Minority	.23***	ns
Poverty × Maternal PPVT–R	−.42**	ns

[a]Each of the 13 Risk × Poverty interactions was entered individually in the third step of regressions; only the significant interactions are presented.

*$p < .05$. **$p < .01$. ***$p < .001$.

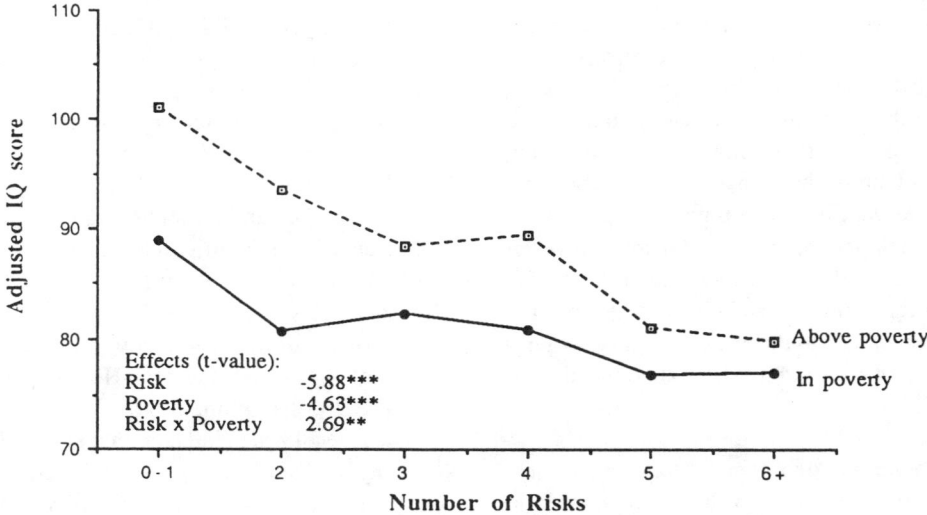

Figure 1. Adjusted IQ scores by risk groups and poverty status follow-up-only groups ($N = 423$).

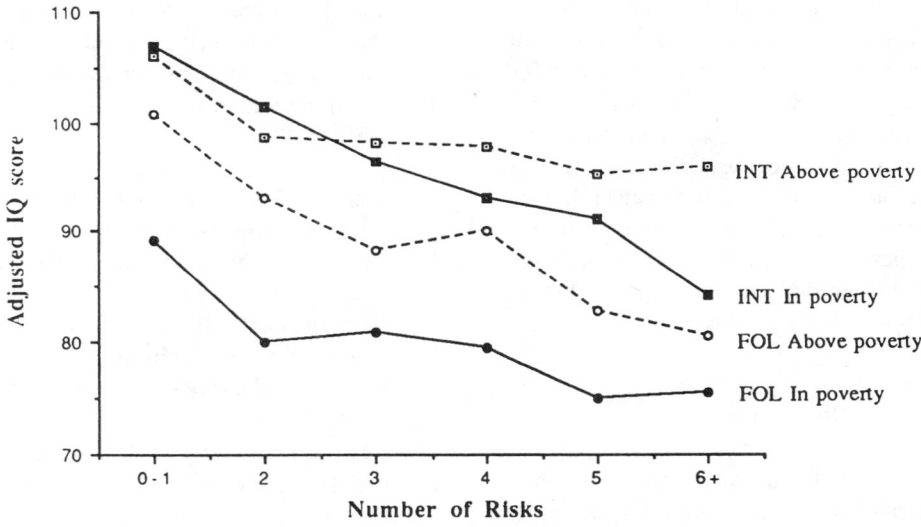

Figure 2. Adjusted IQ scores by treatment and risk groups ($N = 704$).

As the number of risk factors increased, incidence of mother-reported severe behavior problems increased. However, neither a main effect of poverty, $t = 0.17$, $p > .05$, nor a Multiple-Risk Score × Poverty interaction effect, $t = -0.38$, $p > .05$, was found for behavior problems.

Treatment Effect

The effect of the IHDP intervention was tested by hierarchical regressions with predictors being entered in the following order: (a) the covariates (site and child's sex), (b) the multiple-risk score and the treatment status (INT group = 1, FOL group = 0), and (c) the Treatment × Multiple-Risk Score interaction. Anal-

yses were conducted for children from poor and non-poor families separately.

Children's IQ scores. Regression results indicate significant main effects on IQ scores of the treatment for poor, $t = 9.00$, $p < .001$, and nonpoor, $t = 3.60$, $p < .001$, children and of the number of risk factors for poor, $t = -6.45$, $p < .001$, and nonpoor, $t = -5.26$, $p < .001$ children. That is, regardless of family poverty status, children in the intervention group, on average, had higher IQ scores than children who did not receive the intervention; IQ scores generally decreased with the increase in risks (see Figure 2 for the adjusted mean scores of IQ, adjusted for site and child's sex). The Treatment × Multiple-Risk Score interaction was significant for children who were poor, $t = -2.34$, $p < .05$, but not for children who were not poor, $t = 1.43$, $p >$ .05). An examination of the adjusted means of IQ by the number of risks for children from poor families suggest that the intervention had a greater effect for children who had experienced fewer risk factors (i.e., ≤ 3) than for children who had experienced many risks.

Figure 2 reveals two other noteworthy trends. First, the IQ scores of children who were poor and who received the intervention were higher than those of children who were not poor and who did not receive the intervention across all risk groups. Second, the IQ scores of children who did and did not receive the intervention seemed not to differ as a function of poverty status for those children who experienced 3 or fewer risks.

Children's behavior problems. Regression results for children's behavior problems indicated no treatment effect. Generally, children who were poor and who received the intervention had lower behavior-problem scores than did children who were poor but who did not receive the intervention (results not shown here). A significant main effect of multiple risks for poor, $t = 3.09$, $p < .01$, and nonpoor, $t = 4.62$, $p < .001$ children indicated that as the number of risks increased, incidence of severe behavior problems increased. No Treatment $\times$ Risk interaction was found. However, when the continuous CBCL/2–3 scores, rather than the dichotomized behavior-problem measure, were used, a significant treatment effect was found for children who were raised in poor families, $t = -2.01$, $p < .05$, but not for children who were not poor.

Discussion

As the number of risks increased, child IQ scores decreased. Our findings for IQ were quite similar to those reported by Sameroff et al. (1987) for normal-birthweight children at age 4. With respect to the effects of individual risk factors, maternal education and verbal ability showed significant associations with child IQ, along with maternal depression and stressful life events. These findings are consistent with those for normal-birthweight children (e.g., Garcia-Coll, Vohr, Hoffman, & Oh, 1986; Kopp & McCall, 1981; McCall, 1983; McLoyd & Wilson, 1991; Sameroff et al., 1993).

Poverty not only had a main effect on child IQ, but also had interactive effects with other risk factors. The negative effects of risk factors (being African American or Hispanic American and having a mother with low verbal ability) were greater for children from nonpoor families than for children from poor families, although significant for both. These results may be interpreted as indicating that low income accounts for such a significant portion of the variance in children's outcomes that other factors play a

relatively smaller role than they do in families whose income is higher (Duncan et al., 1994; Spencer, 1983). Alternatively, or additionally, effects of individual risk factors on outcomes are more salient in families who are at a relative advantage.

This study examined the cumulative risks in the context of poverty. It is noted that IQ scores for children who were poor were generally low irrespective of number and existence of risks. Furthermore, children whose families had 2 or more risk factors had IQ scores under 85 (i.e., 1 *SD* below the mean). These results support the pervasively devastating effect of living in poverty over and above the existence of many risk factors (Huston, 1991; McCormick & Brooks-Gunn, 1989).

These results also indicate that although the number of nonpoor families who have experienced multiple risks (especially more than four risks) are small, these families exist and the risk for cognitive deficits of their children is high. Moreover, our results show that the cumulative effects of multiple risks were as great for children who were not poor and experienced six or more risk factors as their poor counterparts who had six or more risk factors. These findings highlight the need for examining within-group heterogeneity (Meisels & Shonkoff, 1990).

Previous studies of the IHDP, or other studies of intervention effects, have not examined the function of early intervention in altering the effects of cumulative risks, nor have they looked at efficacy of early intervention by family poverty. Our results show that participation in the IHDP influenced IQ scores for both poor and nonpoor children. In view of the paucity of empirical evidence that early intervention is beneficial for children from more affluent backgrounds (Brooks-Gunn, Gross, Kraemer, Spiker, & Shapiro, 1992; Farran, 1990; Zigler, 1987), this finding is important.

Concerning the effects of the intervention on poor children's IQ scores, the IHDP program was more likely to benefit poor children who experienced low to moderate ranges of risk factors than those who presented a large number of risks (i.e., significant Risk $\times$ Treatment interaction; see Figure 2). Three-year-old poor LBW children who had experienced three or fewer risks had higher IQ scores than did poor children who experienced the same range of risks but who did not receive the intervention. Being poor and experiencing a large number of other family risk conditions may render it difficult for families to benefit from this particular set of intervention services. The services may need to be more intensive (i.e., with more frequent home visits and parenting classes), more extensive (i.e., provided through age 5 or even longer), or more focused on ameliorating familial risk (i.e., providing job training or education services, housing, etc.); or they may need to provide more support (the parent curriculum was designed to facilitate problem solving skills, not to provide social support or to increase support networks). Further, some combination of these changes may be required. The burden of poverty and multiple family risks may be too great to overcome with a standard set of interventions. More individualized treatment programs are probably necessary for multi-problem families (Meisels & Shonkoff, 1990; Seitz, Rosenbaum, & Apfel, 1985).

As expected, findings for behavior problems were similar to those for IQ (i.e., poor children were rated as having more behavior problems, risk factors had independent effects, and cumulative risks increased problem scores). However, the strength of these associations was lower, overall, than that for IQ. Whether this finding could be due to limitations of maternal report, to the measure of behavior problems used, or to a weaker link between familial risk and behavior problems than between familial risk and cognition is not known.

In contrast to IQ findings, intervention effects on decreasing children's behavior problems were found only for children who were poor. This finding is important, given that preschool behavior problems as rated by mothers have been linked to teachers' ratings of behavior problems in elementary school (Benasich et al., in press; Richman, 1977; Richman & Graham, 1971) and, perhaps, to behavior problems in adolescence (Furstenberg, Brooks-Gunn, & Morgan, 1987; Lerner, Inui, Trupin, & Douglas, 1985). Zigler (1992) recently suggested that programs for poor children may have long-term effects on juvenile delinquency and treatment of aggressive behavior. Early effects on behavior may be one pathway by which adolescent problem behavior is affected.

This study has several implications. First, poor families may be more likely to be exposed to multiple risks, which, in turn, have detrimental effects on child and parent well-being, highlight the importance of looking at cumulative risks rather than focusing on single risk factors. Second, the finding that being classified as above the poverty line does not prevent a family from experiencing risk factors—or prevent the adverse effects of risk factors—suggests that income per se should not be taken as the single criterion for negative outcomes or be used as a marker for a range of family conditions. Third, poverty is, however, a significant predictor of decrements in child well-being; differences between poor and nonpoor children were seen across the cumulative risk spectrum (with the exception of similar cognitive scores at the high end of the risk continuum).

Several points may be raised vis-à-vis designing programs for children. Programs need to consider reducing the number of risks families experience. Programs like the IHDP, as well as programs that provide job training, and high-quality child-care and parenting programs and/or include education and literacy skills (e.g., JOBS programs; Chase-Lansdale & Brooks-Gunn, in press; Clewell, Brooks-Gunn, & Benasich, 1989; Smith, in press), may do well in improving maternal verbal ability and in reducing maternal depression and stress—factors that are associated with behavior problems in children and poorer home environments. Maternal depression, however, may be the most difficult risk factor to influence, although improvement in life conditions, movement out of poverty, and provision of parenting skills all may alter depressive symptoms (Benasich, Brooks-Gunn, & Clewell, 1992). Programs may also need to have closer links to community agencies (providing referrals and support). Community-based programs may themselves alter (or expand) support networks for individual families.

In conclusion, the finding of the ameliorative effect of an early intervention that provides home visiting to parents and center-based early schooling to children on reducing the adverse effects of multiple risks highlights the importance for early intervention programs to focus on both parents and children (Meisels et al., 1993; Meisels & Shonkoff, 1990). Providing poor mothers of LBW infants with social and emotional support and teaching them interactive skills with their children, as well as providing educational services to their child, are some of the strategies to produce positive outcomes in the child by altering the risk status of the family (Smith, in press).

References

Achenbach, T. M., Edelbrock, C. S., & Howell, C. T. (1987). Empirically based assessment of the behavior/emotional problems of 2- and 3-year-old children. *Journal of Abnormal Child Psychology, 15,* 629–650.

Beckwith, L., & Cohen, S. E. (1984). Home environment and cognitive competence in preterm children during the first 5 years. In A. Gottfried (Ed.), *Home environment and early cognitive development* (pp. 235–271). New York: Academic.

Benasich, A. A., Brooks-Gunn, J., & Clewell, B. C. (1992). How do mothers benefit from early intervention programs. *Journal of Applied Developmental Psychology, 13,* 311–362.

Benasich, A. A., Brooks-Gunn, J., & McCormick, M. (in press). Behavioral problems in the two-to-five-year-old: Measurement and prognostic ability. *Journal of Developmental and Behavioral Pediatrics.*

Billings, A. G., & Moos, R. H. (1981). The role of coping response and social resources in attenuating the impact of stressful of life events. *Journal of Behavioral Medicine, 4,* 139–157.

Bronfenbrenner, U. (1975). Is early intervention effective? In M. Guttentag & E. Streuning (Eds.), *Handbook of evaluation research* (Vol. 2, pp. 519–603). Beverly Hills, CA: Sage.

Brooks-Gunn, J. (1990a). Identifying the vulnerable young child. In D. E. Rogers & E. Ginzberg (Eds.), *Improving the life chances of children at risk* (pp. 104–124). Boulder, CO: Westview.

Brooks-Gunn, J. (1990b). Promoting healthy development in young children: What educational interventions work? In D. E. Rogers & E. Ginzberg (Eds.), *Improving the life chances of children at risk* (pp. 125–145). Boulder, CO: Westview.

Brooks-Gunn, J. (in press). Growing up poor: Context, risk and continuity in the Bronfenbrenner tradition. In P. Moen, G. H. Elder, & K. Lusher (Eds.), *Linking lives in contexts: Perspectives on the ecology of human development*. Washington, DC: American Psychological Association.

Brooks-Gunn, J., & Furstenberg, F. F., Jr. (1986). Antecedents and consequences of parenting: The case of adolescent motherhood. In A. Fogel & G. F. Melson (Eds.), *Origins of nurturance*. (pp. 233–258). Hillsdale, NJ: Lawrence Erlbaum Associates, Inc.

Brooks-Gunn, J., Gross, R. T., Kraemer, H. C., Spiker, D., & Shapiro, S. (1992). Enhancing the cognitive outcomes of low-birthweight, premature infants: For whom is the intervention most effective? *Pediatrics, 89,* 1209–1215.

Brooks-Gunn, J., Klebanov, P. K., Liaw, F. R., & Spiker, D. (1993). Enhancing the development of low-birthweight, premature infants: Change in cognition and behavior over the first three years. *Child Development, 64,* 736–753.

Bryant, D. M., & Ramey, C. T. (1987). An analysis of the effectiveness of early intervention programs for environmentally at-risk children. In M. J. Guralnick & F. C. Bennett (Eds.), *The effectiveness of early intervention for at-risk and handicapped children* (pp. 33–78). New York: Academic.

Butler, J. A., Starfield, B., & Stenmark, S. (1984). Child health policy. In H. W. Stevenson & A. E. Siegel (Eds.), *Child development research and social policy* (Vol. 1, pp. 110–188). Chicago: University of Chicago Press.

Chase-Lansdale, P. L., & Brooks-Gunn, J. (Eds.). (in press). *Escape from poverty: What makes a difference for children*. New York: Cambridge University Press.

Chase-Lansdale, P. L., Brooks-Gunn, J., & Zamsky, E. S. (1994). Young African-American multigenerational families in poverty: Quality of mothering and grandmothering. *Child Development, 65,* 373–393.

Clarke-Stewart, K. A., & Fein, G. G. (1983). Early childhood programs. In P. H. Mussen (Series Ed.) & M. M. Haith & J. J. Campos (Vol. Eds.), *Handbook of child psychology: Vol. 2. Infancy and developmental psychology* (4th ed., pp. 917–999). New York: Wiley.

Clewell, B. C., Brooks-Gunn, J., & Benasich, A. A. (1989). Evaluating child-related outcomes of teenage parenting programs. *Family Relations, 38,* 201–209.

Cohen, J., & Cohen, P. (1983). *Applied multiple regression/correlation analysis for the behavioral sciences* (2nd ed.). Hillsdale, NJ: Lawrence Erlbaum Associates, Inc.

Cohen, J. B., & Lazarus, R. S. (1977). *Social support questionnaire*. Berkeley: University of California Press.

Cohen, S., & Parmelee, A. (1983). Prediction of five-year Stanford–Binet scores in preterm infants. *Child Development, 54,* 1242–1253.

Drillien, C. M. (1964). *The growth and development of the prematurely born infant*. Edinburgh, Scotland: Livingstone.

Duncan, G. (1991). The economic environment of childhood. In A. C. Huston (Ed.), *Children in poverty* (pp. 23–50). New York: Cambridge University Press.

Duncan, G., Klebanov, P., & Brooks-Gunn, J. (1994). Economic deprivation and early-childhood development. *Child Development, 65,* 296–318.

Duncan, G., Hill, M. S., & Hoffman, S. D. (1988). Welfare dependence within and across generations. *Science, 1,* 467–471.

Duncan, G., & Rodgers, W. (1988). Longitudinal aspects of childhood poverty. *Journal of Marriage and the Family, 50,* 1007–1021.

Dunn, L. M., & Dunn, L. M. (1981). *Peabody Picture Vocabulary Test–Revised*. Circle Pines, MN: American Guidance Service.

Escalona, S. K. (1982). Babies at double hazard: Early development of infants at biological and social risk. *Pediatrics, 70,* 670–676.

Farran, D. (1990). Effects of intervention with disadvantaged and disabled children: A decade review. In S. J. Meisels & J. P. Shonkoff (Eds.), *Handbook of early childhood intervention* (pp. 501–539). New York: Cambridge University Press.

Field, T. M. (1981). Early development of the preterm offspring of teenage mothers. In K. Scott, T. Field, & E. Robertson (Eds.), *Teenage parents and their offspring* (pp. 145–175). New York: Grune & Stratton.

Field, T. M., Dempsey, J. R., & Shuman, H. H. (1979). Developmental assessments of infants surviving the respiratory distress syndrome. In T. M. Field, A. M. Sostek, C. Goldberg, & H. H. Shuman (Eds.), *Infants born at risk* (pp. 261–280). New York: Spectrum.

Furstenberg, F. F., Jr., Brooks-Gunn, J., & Morgan, S. P. (1987). Adolescent mothers and their children in later life. *Family Planning Perspectives, 19,* 142–151.

Garcia-Coll, C. T. (1988). The consequences of teenage childbearing in traditional Puerto Rican culture. In J. K. Nugent, B. M. Lester, & T. B. Brazelton (Eds.), *The cultural context of infancy* (Vol. 1, pp. 111–132). Norwood, NJ: Ablex.

Garcia-Coll, C. T., Hoffman, J., & Oh, W. (1987). The social ecology and early parenting of Caucasian adolescent mothers. *Child Development, 58,* 955–963.

Garcia-Coll, C., Vohr, B., Hoffman, J., et al. (1986). Maternal and environmental factors affecting developmental outcome of infants of adolescent mothers. *Journal of Developmental and Behavioral Pediatrics, 7,* 230–236.

Garmezy, N., & Rutter, M. (Eds.). (1983). *Stress, coping, and development in children*. New York: McGraw-Hill.

Gibbs, J. (1989). Black American adolescents. In J. Gibbs, L. Huang, & Associates (Eds.), *Children of color: Psychological interventions with minority youth* (pp. 179–223). San Francisco: Jossey-Bass.

Goldberg, S. (1978). Prematurity: Effects of parent–infant interaction. *Journal of Pediatric Psychology, 3,* 137–144.

Gross, R. T., Brooks-Gunn, J., & Spiker, D. (1992). Efficacy of comprehensive early interventions for low birth weight, premature infants and their families: The Infant Health and Development Program. In S. L. Friedman & M. D. Sigman (Eds.), *The psychological development of low birthweight children: Advances in applied developmental psychology* (pp. 411–434). Norwood, NJ: Ablex.

Hack, M., Fanaroff, A. A., & Merkatz, I. R. (1975). The low birthweight infant—Evolution of a changing outlook. *New England Journal of Medicine, 301,* 1162–1165.

Hall, L. A., Williams, C. A., & Greenberg, R. S. (1985). Supports, stressors and depressive symptoms in low-income mothers of young children. *American Journal of Public Health, 75,* 518–522.

Haskins, R. (1989). Beyond metaphor: Efficacy of early childhood education. *American Psychology, 44,* 274–282.

Hunt, J. V. (1983). Environmental risks in fetal and neonatal life as biological determinants of infant intelligence. In M. Lewis (Ed.), *Origins of intelligence* (pp. 255–304). New York: Plenum.

Hunt, J., & Cooper, B. A. B. (1989). Differentiating the risk for high-risk preterm infants. In M. H. Bornstein & N. A. Krasnegor (Eds.), *Stability and continuity in mental development: Behavioral and biological perspectives* (pp. 105–122). Hillsdale, NJ: Lawrence Erlbaum Associates, Inc.

Huston, A. C, (Ed.). (1991). *Children in poverty*. New York: Cambridge University Press.

Infant Health and Development Program. (1990). Enhancing the outcomes of low-birthweight, premature infants. *Journal of the American Medical Association, 263,* 3035–3042.

Institute of Medicine. (1985). *Preventing low birthweight*. Washington, DC: National Academy Press.

Klein, N., Hack, M., & Breslau, N. (1989). Children who were very low birthweight: Development and academic achievement at nine years of age. *Journal of Developmental and Behavioral Pediatrics, 10,* 32–37.

Klein, N., Hack, M., Gallagher, J., & Fanaroff, A. V. (1985). Preschool performance of children with normal intelligence who were very low-birthweight infants. *Pediatrics, 75,* 532–537.

Klerman, L. V. (1991). The health of poor children: Problems and programs. In A. C. Huston (Ed.), *Children in poverty* (pp.

136–157). New York: Cambridge University Press.

Kopp, C. B., & McCall, R. B. (1981). Predicting later mental performance for normal, at-risk, and handicapped infants. In P. B. Baltes & O. G. Brim, Jr. (Eds.), *Life-span development and behavior* (Vol. 4, pp. 33–60). New York: Academic.

Lazar, I., Darlington, R. B., Murray, H., Royce, J., & Snipper, A. (1982). Lasting effects of early education: A report from the Consortium for Longitudinal Studies. *Monographs of the Society for Research in Child Development, 47* (2–3, Serial No. 195).

Lerner, J. A., Inui, T. S., Trupin, E. W., & Douglas, E. (1985). Preschool behavior can predict future psychiatric disorders. *Journal of the American Academy of Child Psychiatry, 24,* 42–48.

Levin, H. M. (1991). Educational acceleration for at-risk children. In A. C. Huston (Ed.), *Children in poverty* (pp. 222–240). New York: Cambridge University Press.

McCall, R. B. (1983). Nature–nurture and the two realms of development: A proposed integration with respect to mental development. *Child Development, 52,* 1–12.

McConaughy, S. H., & Achenbach, T. M. (1989). Empirically based assessment of serious emotional disturbance. *Journal of School Psychology, 27,* 91–117.

McCormick, M. C. (1989). Long-term follow-up of infants discharged from neonatal intensive care units. *Journal of the American Medical Association, 261,* 1767–1772.

McCormick, M. C., & Brooks-Gunn, J. (1989). Health care for children and adolescents. In H. E. Freeman & S. Levine (Eds.), *Handbook of medical sociology* (pp. 347–379). Englewood Cliffs, NJ: Prentice-Hall.

McCormick, M. C., Brooks-Gunn, J., Shorter, T., Wallace, C. Y., Holmes, J. H., & Heagarty, M.C. (1987). The planning of pregnancy among low-income women in central Harlem. *American Journal of Obstetrics and Gynecology, 156,* 145–149.

McCormick, M. C., Brooks-Gunn, J., Workman-Daniels, K., Turner, J., & Peckham, G. (1992). The health and developmental status of very low birthweight children at school age. *Journal of the American Medical Association, 267,* 2204–2208.

McLoyd, V. C. (1990). The impact of economic hardship on Black families and development. *Child Development, 61,* 311–346.

McLoyd, V. C., & Wilson, L. (1991). The strain of living poor: Parenting, social support, and child mental health. In A. C. Huston (Ed.), *Children in poverty* (pp. 105–135). New York: Cambridge University Press.

Meisels, S. J., Dichtelmiller, M., & Liaw, F. R. (1993). A multidimensional analysis of early childhood intervention programs. In C. Zeanah (Ed.), *Handbook of infant mental health.* New York: Guilford.

Meisels, S. J., & Plunkett, J. W. (1988). Developmental consequences of preterm birth: Are there long-term effects? In P. B. Baltes, D. L. Featherman, & R. M. Lerner (Eds.), *Life-span development and behavior* (Vol. 9, pp. 87–128). Hillsdale, NJ: Lawrence Erlbaum Associates, Inc.

Meisels, S. J., Plunkett, J. W., Pasick, P. L., Stiefel, G. S., & Roloff, D. W. (1987). Effects of severity and chronicity of respiratory illness on the cognitive development of preterm infants. *Journal of Pediatric Psychology, 12,* 117–132.

Meisels, S. J., & Shonkoff, J. P. (Eds.). (1990). *Handbook of early childhood intervention.* New York: Cambridge University Press.

Myers, H. F., & King, L. (1983). Mental health issues in the development of the black American child. In G. Powell, J. Yamamoto, A. Romero, & A. Morales (Eds.), *The psychological development of minority group children* (pp. 275–306). New York: Brunner/Mazel.

Neisser, U. (Ed.). (1986). *The school achievement of minority children: New perspectives.* Hillsdale, NJ: Lawrence Erlbaum Associates, Inc.

Oppel, W., & Roystom, A. (1971). Teenage births: Some social, psychological, and physical sequelae. *American Journal of Public Health, 61,* 751–756.

Orvaschel, H., Weissman, M., & Kidd, K. K. (1980). The children of depressed parents: The childhood of depressed patients. *Journal of Affective Disorders, 2,* 1–16.

Parker, S., Greer, S., & Zuckerman, B. (1988). Double jeopardy: The impact of poverty on early child development. *Pediatric Clinics of North America, 35,* 1227–1240.

Ramey, C. T., Bryant, D. M., Wasik, B. H., Sparling, J. J., Fendt, K. H., & LaVange, L. M. (1990). The Infant Health and Development Program for low birthweight, premature infants: Program elements, family participation, and child intelligence. *Pediatrics, 3,* 454–465.

Richman, N. (1977). Behavior problems in pre-school children: Family and social factors. *British Journal of Psychiatry, 131,* 523–527.

Richman, N., & Graham, P. J. (1971). A behavioral screening questionnaire for use with three-year-old children: Preliminary findings. *Journal of Child Psychology and Psychiatry, 12,* 5–33.

Roosa, M. W., Fitzgerald, H. E., & Carlson, N. A. (1982). A comparison of teenage and older mothers: A systems analysis. *Journal of Marriage and the Family, 32,* 367–377.

Sameroff, A. J. (1986). Environmental context of child development. *Journal of Pediatrics, 109,* 192–200.

Sameroff, A. J., & Chandler, M. J. (1975). Reproductive risks and the continuum of caretaking casualty. In F. D. Horowitz, M. Hetherington, S. Scarr-Salapatek, & G. Siegel (Eds.), *Review of child development research* (Vol. 4, pp. 187–244). Chicago: University of Chicago Press.

Sameroff, A. J., & Feil, L. A. (1985). Parental concepts of development. In I. E. Sigel (Ed.), *Parental belief systems: The psychological consequences for children* (pp. 85–105). Hillsdale, NJ: Lawrence Erlbaum Associates, Inc.

Sameroff, A. J., Seifer, R., Baldwin, A., & Baldwin, C. (1993). Stability of intelligence from preschool to adolescence: The influence of social and family risk factors. *Child Development, 64,* 80–97.

Sameroff, A. J., Seifer, R., Barocas, R., Zax, M., & Greenspan, S. (1987). Intelligence quotient scores of 4-year-old children: Social and environmental risk factors. *Pediatrics, 79,* 343–350.

Schorr, E. (1988). *Within our reach.* New York: Anchor.

Scott, D. T., Bauer, C. R., Kraemer, H. C., & Tyson, J. (1989). A neonatal health index for preterm infants. *Pediatric Research, 25,* 263a.

Seitz, V., Rosenbaum, L. K., & Apfel, N. H. (1985). Effects of family support interventions: A ten year follow-up. *Child Development, 56,* 376–391.

Smith, S. (in press). Two-generation program models: A new intervention strategy. In P. L. Chase-Lansdale & J. Brooks-Gunn (Eds.), *Escape from poverty: What makes a difference for children.* New York: Cambridge University Press.

Sparling, J., & Lewis, I. (1985). *Partners for learning.* Lewisville, NC: Kaplan.

Sparling, J., Lewis, I., & Neuwirth, S. (1988). *Early partners* [Curriculum kit]. Lewisville, NC: Kaplan.

Sparling, J., Lewis, I., Ramey, C. T., Wasik, B. H., Bryant, D. M., & LaVange, L. M. (1991). Partners, a curriculum to help premature, low-birthweight infants get to a good start. *Topics in Early Childhood Special Education, 11,* 36–55.

Spencer, M. B. (1983). Children's cultural values and parental child rearing strategies. *Developmental Review, 3,* 351–370.

Spencer, M. B., & McLoyd, V. C. (Eds.). (1990). Minority children [Special issue on child development]. *Child Development, 61.*

Terman, L. M., & Merrill, M. A. (1973). *Stanford–Binet Intelligence Scale: Manual for the third revision, Form L–M.* Boston: Houghton Mifflin.

U.S. Department of Commerce. (1986). *Poverty in the United States 1986: Current population reports. Consumer income* (Series P–60, No. 160). Washington, DC: Author.

Wasik, B. H. (1984). *Coping with parenting through effective problem solving: A handbook for professionals.* Chapel Hill: University of North Carolina, Frank Porter Graham Child Development Center.

Werner, E. E., Bierman, J. M., & French, F. E. (1971). *The children of Kauai: A longitudinal study from the prenatal period to age ten.* Honolulu: University of Hawaii Press.

Werner, E. E., & Smith, R. S. (1982). *Vulnerable but invincible: A longitudinal study of resilient children and youth.* New York: McGraw-Hill.

Wilson, W. J. (1987). *The truly disadvantaged: The inner city, the underclass, and public policy.* Chicago: University of Chicago Press.

Woodhead, M. (1988). When psychology informs public policy: The case of early childhood intervention. *American Psychology, 43,* 443–454.

Zigler, E. (1987). Formal schooling for four-year-olds? No. *American Psychologist, 42,* 254–260.

Zigler, E. (1992). Early childhood intervention: A promising preventative for juvenile delinquency. *American Psychologist, 47,* 997–1006.

Received May 24, 1993
Final revision received December 2, 1993

Journal of Clinical Child Psychology
1994, Vol. 23, 373–381

Behavioral Difficulties in Toddlers:
Impact of Sociocultural and Biological Risk Factors

Christina D. Adams

Louisiana State University, Baton Rouge, and
University of Mississippi Medical Center, Jackson

Nancy Hillman

Woman's Hospital, Baton Rouge

Gerard R. Gaydos

Pinecrest Developmental Center, Alexandria, Louisiana

Evaluated behavioral difficulties in three groups of preschoolers (ages 2 to 4 years): low risk, social risk (e.g., poverty, one-parent families), and dual risk (both biological and social risk conditions). Parents of 238 toddlers completed the Child Behavior Checklist/2–3 (CBCL/2–3) and the Eyberg Child Behavior Inventory (ECBI). Demographic, prenatal, and perinatal information was obtained to determine group status. Results indicated that toddlers in social- and dual-risk groups obtained significantly higher parent ratings on the Internalizing behaviors scale and the Anxious/Depressed, Withdrawn, and Destructive behavior subscales of the CBCL/2–3 when compared to toddlers in the low-risk group. No significant differences were obtained between social- and dual-risk groups or between specific biological risk categories (e.g., prematurity vs. developmental disorder). All ECBI results were nonsignificant. These findings suggest that social risk conditions place a preschooler at greater risk for behavioral difficulties, whether these poor social conditions occur with full-term, healthy infants or with children at biological risk (e.g., prematurity). It is recommended that social risk factors as well as biological risk factors be considered so that early intervention programs may target problematic behavior in their treatment approaches with preschoolers.

Interest in assessment of emotional and behavioral problems of toddlers and preschoolers is relatively new, as either a clinical or research endeavor. Historically, preschool assessment has been confined to cognitive development for the purposes of determining school readiness and assessing efficacy of compensatory education programs (Martin, 1988). Recently, preschool assessment tools have been broadened to include other domains of development (e.g., behavioral, social, motor, communication, and adaptive) in addition to cognitive. The impetus for this shift in assessment has been: (a) the Education of the Handicapped Act of 1986

(Public Law 99–457), which has mandated that eligibility for an array of early intervention services be formally assessed; (b) the increasing number of referrals from preschool teachers for psychological services for young children in group care where behavioral demands are greater than in home care; and (c) a recent increase in scientific interest in the psychological development of preschoolers (Martin, 1988, 1991).

To a greater extent, research interest has focused on investigating risk factors present at birth that compromise children's long-term developmental outcomes. These risk factors are hypothesized to predispose children to developmental delays and behavioral and emotional problems. Lists of biological and environmental variables that may have been correlated with later developmental compromise have appeared as a result of these research efforts (Allen, 1993; Dunst, 1993; Jensen, Bloedau, DeGroot, Ussery, & Davis, 1990). Biological risk factors have included prematurity, low birthweight, physical illness, and central nervous system injury. Environmental risk factors have involved

We express our appreciation to Rose Ann Perez and Michelle Berner for their assistance with the organization of data collection, and to the staff at Earl K. Long Memorial Hospital, The Handicapped Children's Clinic, and local day-care centers in Baton Rouge, Louisiana for their cooperation with subject recruitment.

Requests for reprints should be sent to Christina D. Adams, Department of Clinical and Health Psychology, University of Florida Health Science Center, P.O. Box 100165, Gainesville, FL 32610–0165.

low socioeconomic status (SES), parental psychopathology, parental age, and child temperament, among others. However, some environmental risk factors (e.g., parental psychopathology) may influence parental impression, rather than actual level of child behavior and temperament.

With improvements in neonatal care, survival of very-low- and extremely-low-birthweight infants has increased, thus producing a larger group of infants with biological risk factors (Ornstein, Ohlsson, Edmonds, & Asztalos, 1991). The Infant Health and Development Program (1990) conducted a large, multisite early intervention project with low-birthweight premature infants. Using behavioral rating scales, they found that these children were at risk for difficulties with behavioral adjustment at 2 and 3 years of age. Ornstein et al. (1991) reviewed neonatal follow-up studies from 1980 to 1990 for low birthweight infants and found that the best predictor of long-term outcome was most often environmental factors rather than perinatal factors.

Environmental characteristics associated with social risk include poverty, one-parent families, low educational achievement in parents, parental psychopathology, and negative life events. The relation of poverty and other poor environmental characteristics with poor child health and behavioral maladjustment has been clearly demonstrated (Abidin, Jenkins, & McGaughey, 1992; Earls & Jung, 1987; Jones, 1991; McLloyd, 1990; Needlman, Stevenson, & Zuckerman, 1991; Tarnowski & Blechman, 1991). For example, a large-scale investigation of mental health problems in pediatric practice found that children on Medicaid had significantly higher rates of behavior problems than children from more financially advantaged families (Goldberg, Roghmann, McInerny, & Burke, 1984). The majority of poor children under the age of 6 years live in single-mother families (Jones, 1991), and Goldberg et al. found that the rate of behavioral difficulties in children from one-parent families was twice as great as that of children from intact families. Webster-Stratton (1990) also indicated that single mothers both reported and were observed to experience more deviant and noncompliant child behavior problems than married mothers. Larson, Pless, and Miettinen (1988) found that low SES, low family income, and low maternal education were associated with prevalence of psychopathology in 3-year-old Canadians.

Studies have demonstrated that a combination of environmental and biological risk factors pose a double threat to children's development (Beckwith & Parmelee, 1986; Escalona, 1982; Werner & Smith, 1977). Environmental influences have often been found to be the most important independent predictors of long-term outcome in infants born with medical risk factors (Ornstein et al., 1991). Escalona (1982) studied infants who were born prematurely with significant illness during the neonatal period and who were from impoverished families ("babies at double risk") to determine the interactive effect of biological and social factors on their mental and psychosocial development. Escalona found that 30% of their preschool-age children showed major behavioral adjustment problems by age 4 years. Yet, these findings were limited by the lack of specificity in behavioral assessment and the lack of comparison groups. Indeed, Escalona reported that "whether biologically vulnerable infants are . . . more vulnerable to environmental stress and deprivation . . . remains to be proven" (p. 674) and that further research would be needed to demonstrate "whether full-term, healthy infants respond as drastically to environmental and emotional hazards as was observed in this low birthweight group" (p. 674).

Similarly, a combination of biological and social risk factors (e.g., low SES) has been implicated in difficulties with cognitive, motor, and social development of toddlers (e.g., Zeskind & Ramey, 1978; 1981). By contrast, other researchers (e.g., Gortmaker, Walker, Weitzman, & Sobol, 1990) have found that children with chronic health problems who were from impoverished households were at no greater risk for behavioral difficulties than impoverished children without chronic illness. However, this research was not limited to the preschool age-range.

As a result of these biological and environmental risk factors, recent legislation has encouraged the assessment of emotional and behavioral development in preschoolers. Specifically, the Education of the Handicapped Act (Public Law 99–457, 1986) now mandates the development of early intervention programs for infants and toddlers who are handicapped and/or at risk for developmental delays. This legislation has promoted the development of objective and efficient methods for determining eligibility for programs as well as for assessing program efficacy. Many early intervention programs are conducted in group settings (e.g., learning centers) where more behavioral demands are placed on children and where they are more likely to be compared with their peers. As a result, many preschool teachers have turned to professionals to help them objectively discriminate normal, age-appropriate behavior from troublesome, clinically elevated behavior.

Despite the interest in and need for the behavioral and emotional assessment in preschoolers, the assessment tools are still in their infancy (Martin, 1991). Most available instruments are designed to assess problem behaviors rather than emotional and behavioral competence. Also, because most of the instruments in this area are downward extensions of existing measures for assessing school-age children, many problem behaviors unique to preschoolers may not be tapped by such measures (Martin, 1991). Of the available assessment tools, psychometric adequacy and research support have been lacking.

Two notable exceptions are the Child Behavior Checklist/2–3 (CBCL/2–3; Achenbach & Edelbrock, 1992) and the Eyberg Child Behavior Inventory (ECBI; Eyberg & Ross, 1978). The CBCL/2–3 and the ECBI both represent empirically based, standardized efforts to assess behavior problems in children as young as 2 and 3 years old via parent report. Both of these behavior rating scales have been used in research with preschoolers, children with medical conditions, and children at risk for behavioral and developmental problems (Achenbach, Edelbrock, & Howell, 1987; Eyberg & Robinson, 1982; Eyberg & Ross, 1978).

Because of the level of language and social development in preschoolers, parent and teacher reports of behavioral problems are typically emphasized. Because teachers and substitute caregivers are not always available with preschoolers, parent-report measures assume relatively greater importance than for older school-age children. Research has demonstrated the validity and reliability of parent-report behavior rating scales for preschoolers. For example, one study found that observational data confirmed parent reports (rating scales and interviews) of overactive, inattentive, and impulsive behavior in toddlers (Campbell, Szumowski, Ewing, Gluck, & Breaux, 1982).

In summary, research has indicated that both environmental difficulties (e.g., poverty, one-parent families) and biological risk factors (e.g., prematurity, chronic illness) negatively influence developmental and behavioral outcomes in preschoolers and that environmental risk factors have a greater negative impact than do biological risk factors. Webster-Stratton (1990) recommended that researchers begin to investigate the interaction effects of different variables on developmental outcomes rather than the effects of single variables in isolation. This study seeks to determine the base rates and statistical differences of parent-reported problem behaviors in three samples of toddlers: low risk (no biological or social risk factors), social risk (social risk factors such as low income and low maternal education; no biological risk factors), and dual risk (social and medical risk factors). By including a low-risk control group and a social-risk group, this study intends to address those questions generated by Escalona's (1982) research. Specifically, are biologically vulnerable infants more negatively influenced by environmental difficulties than are normal, healthy infants as reflected in their preschool behavioral outcome?

Method

Participants

Participants included 238 toddlers and their parent (222 mothers, 16 fathers). Families were recruited from Baton Rouge area day-care centers, pediatric clinics, and clinics at a handicapped children's medical facility. In addition, undergraduate university students obtained extra credit in psychology classes for recruiting families with toddlers to participate in this study. The toddlers' ages ranged from 2 to 4 years ($M = 2.79$ years, $SD = 0.85$ years). The sample was composed of 128 males (54%) and 109 females (46%). Ninety-one toddlers were Caucasian (38%) and 147 were non-Caucasian (62%); the majority of the non-Caucasian children were African American.

Children were placed in one of three groups: dual risk ($n = 78$), social risk ($n = 79$), and low risk ($n = 81$). The dual-risk sample consisted of children who were from low-SES families and who were born with congenital medical conditions. The social-risk group included toddlers who were from low-SES families. Finally, the low-risk group included children from middle to upper SES families. All children in the social-risk and low-risk groups were born without complications or congenital medical conditions.

SES was classified by annual income and receipt of government-assisted income programs (e.g., Aid to Families With Dependent Children or food stamps). Socioeconomic risk (e.g., social-risk and dual-risk groups) was considered when the family had an annual income less than $20,000 and received at least one government-assisted income program. Low-risk-group families earned annual incomes greater than $25,000 and did not receive any government-assisted income programs. One family was an exception to the annual income standard (making $20,000 to $24,999); this subject was placed into the social-risk group having given consideration to the large family size and the family's receipt of income assistance.

Congenital medical conditions for the dual-risk group included: (a) premature delivery (< 33 weeks gestation) with neonatal intensive care unit (NICU) stay ($M = 41.6$ days; $SD = 49.1$ days; 63%), (b) full-term delivery with a congenital neurological (e.g., spina bifida, cerebral palsy, or neurosyphilis) or a developmental disorder (e.g., Trisomy 13, cleft lip disorder; 29%), or (c) full-term delivery with a chronic illness (e.g., sickle-cell anemia or red-cell aplasia; 8%). Medical complications associated with prematurity in the dual-risk group included birth asphyxia, intraventricular hemorrhage, hypoxia, respiratory distress syndrome, microcephaly, hydrocephalus, and the requirement of ventilator support.

Procedure and Measures

Parents who provided informed consent were interviewed and completed two behavior rating scales. The interview obtained information with regard to family demographic characteristics, as well as brief prenatal and perinatal history of the toddler. After the interview, parents completed the ECBI and the CBCL/2–3. Assistance in reading and answering questions was given to participants having reading difficulties.

ECBI. The ECBI is a 36-item parent-report questionnaire that assesses behavior problems (e.g., oppositional behavior, conduct problems) in children between the ages of 2 and 17 years (Eyberg & Ross, 1978; Robinson, Eyberg, & Ross, 1980). The informant is instructed to indicate how often each problem behavior occurs on a 7-point Likert scale ranging from *never* (1) to *always* (7). In addition, the informant indicates whether the behavior item is a problem or not (yes–no response). Two scores are obtained from this questionnaire: Intensity (sum of Likert-scale responses across all items) and Problem (sum of items endorsed as a problem by the parent). Adequate reliability and validity have been demonstrated for this scale (Barkley, 1990; Boggs, Eyberg, & Reynolds, 1990).

CBCL/2–3. The CBCL/2–3 is a parent-report measure of general psychopathology in children between the ages of 2 and 3 years (Achenbach & Edelbrock, 1992). The questionnaire contains 100 behavior problem items which are rated on a 3-point Likert scale ranging from *not true* (0) to *very true* (2). Results produce scores on two broad-band scales (Internalizing, Externalizing) and six narrow-band subscales (Anxious/Depressed, Withdrawn, Somatic Problems, Sleep Problems, Aggressive Behavior, Destructive Behavior). As recommended in the manual (Achenbach & Edelbrock, 1992), total raw scores on each of the aforementioned broad-band and narrow-band scales were used in data analyses because *T*-scores have a limited floor (extending downward to 50 only). To maintain consistency across subject assessment, the use of the questionnaire was extended to 4-year-olds despite the absence of normative data for this age group.

Results

Group Differences in Demographic Characteristics

To assess for group differences in demographic characteristics, two types of analyses were conducted. Chi-square analyses were performed between groups for the following dichotomous demographic variables: toddler sex, toddler race, parent category, parent sex, parent marital status, annual income category, maternal education level, and special education. One-way analyses of variance (ANOVAs) were conducted for the following continuous demographic variables: toddler age, parent age, number of adults in the home, number of children in the home, and number of income-based government assistance programs received. Using Bonferroni's correction to control Type I error rate, an alpha level of .003 or below was considered to be significant. Descriptive information for significant group differences in demographic characteristics is provided in Table 1.

With respect to toddler sex and age, the three groups did not significantly differ from one another ($p > .003$). However, chi-square analyses produced a significant group effect for toddler race, $\chi^2(2, N = 238) = 154.6$, $p < .001$. Post-hoc chi-square analyses indicated that the low-risk group consisted of more Caucasian children and fewer non-Caucasian children when compared to the social-risk group and dual-risk group.

Significant group differences were obtained for parent marital status, $\chi^2(4, N = 237) = 91.3$; $p < .001$; maternal education, $\chi^2(12, N = 236) = 113.4$, $p < .001$; and annual income level, $\chi^2(16, N = 234) = 241.4$, $p < .001$. Post-hoc chi-square analyses indicated that the low-risk group had significantly higher rates of intact families and lower rates of single parents, higher levels of maternal education, and higher levels of income when compared to the two other risk groups (which did not differ significantly from each other). In addition, ANOVA results for the number of government assistance programs indicated a significant main effect for group, $F(2, 233) = 100.5$, $p < .001$. Post-hoc Tukey tests revealed that the low-risk group received fewer assistance programs than the two other risk groups. The social-risk and dual-risk groups did not differ significantly from one another with respect to income assistance programs.

Significant group differences were also obtained for parent category, $\chi^2(2, N = 237) = 16.6$, $p < .001$. Post-hoc chi-square analyses indicated that the dual-risk group had more caregivers who were not the toddler's natural parent (e.g., foster parent, grandparent) than did the low-risk group. Additionally, a significant main effect for group was obtained for parent age, $F(2, 234) = 6.1$, $p < .003$, and number of children in the family, $F(2, 237) = 6.8$, $p < .002$. Post-hoc Tukey Honestly Significant Differences (HSD) procedures revealed that the low-risk group consisted of older parents when compared to the social-risk group and more children when compared to the dual-risk group. Finally, chi-square results indicated a significant group effect for use of special education services $\chi^2(2, N = 235) = 76.6$, $p < .001$. Post hoc analyses indicated that the dual-risk group had a higher rate of special education services when compared to the other two groups, and the social-risk group had higher rates than the low-risk group. Results for parent sex and number of adults in the family were not significant.

In summary, significant group differences were consistently obtained between the low-risk group and the social-risk and dual-risk groups regarding those demographic characteristics representing social risk factors (e.g., annual income, maternal education, marital status). Furthermore, the social-risk and dual-risk groups did not differ signficantly on these variables. These findings support the presence of significant socioeconomic differences for the two higher risk groups as compared to the low-risk group.

Significant group differences were also obtained with toddler race. In this population sample, toddler race correlated with group membership just as the other sociocultural risk factors did, and therefore acted as a mediator variable. Using toddler race or socioeconomic variables as covariates in further analyses would be ineffective and meaningless. Specifically, using them as covariates to correct for group differences would also correct for sociocultural differences, thus inadvertently failing to reject the null hypothesis. Therefore, these variables were not covaried out of subsequent data analyses.

Group Differences on Dependent Measures

Three separate 3 (Group) × 3 (Age: 2, 3, or 4 years) × 2 (Sex) multivariate analyses of variance (MANOVAs) were conducted on the following data: (a) two CBCL/2–3 broad-band factors (Internalizing, Externalizing), (b) six CBCL/2–3 narrow-band scores (Anxious/Depressed, Withdrawn, Somatic Problems, Sleep Problems, Aggressive Behavior, Destructive Behavior), and (c) two ECBI scores (Problem and Intensity). Univariate ANOVAs were performed only if the multivariate test yielded a significant effect. Bonferroni's correction was utilized to control for experimentwise error with univariate tests. A significant ANOVA was then followed by Tukey's HSD procedure to contrast groups through pairwise comparisons. Table 2 presents ECBI and CBCL/2–3 mean scores by group along with normative data.

MANOVA results for the CBCL/2–3 broad-band factors produced a significant main effect for group,

Table 1. *Significant Demographic Characteristics by Group*

Demographic	Low Risk		Social Risk		Dual Risk	
Race						
Caucasian	75	(93%)	5	(6%)	11	(14%)
Non-Caucasian	6	(7%)	74	(94%)	67	(86%)
Parent Category						
Natural Parent	80	(99%)	77	(97%)	65	(84%)
Other	1	(1%)	2	(3%)	12	(16%)
Parent Age						
M (*SD*) in years	32.0	(6.5)	27.9	(6.2)	30.3	(9.6)
Marital Status						
With Child's Parent[a]	73	(91%)	21	(27%)	21	(27%)
With Other Adult[b]	3	(4%)	5	(6%)	3	(4%)
Single Parent	4	(5%)	53	(67%)	54	(69%)
Annual Income Level						
Under $5,000	0	(0%)	27	(35%)	26	(34%)
$5,000 to $9,999	0	(0%)	24	(31%)	26	(34%)
$10,000 to $14,999	0	(0%)	23	(30%)	16	(21%)
$15,000 to $19,999	0	(0%)	2	(3%)	9	(12%)
$20,000 to $24,999	1	(1%)	1	(1%)	0	(0%)
$25,000 to $34,999	19	(24%)	0	(0%)	0	(0%)
$35,000 to $49,999	27	(34%)	0	(0%)	0	(0%)
$50,000 to $74,999	24	(30%)	0	(0%)	0	(0%)
$75,000 or more	9	(11%)	0	(0%)	0	(0%)
Government Assistance Programs						
M (*SD*)	0.0	(0.0)	1.6	(1.1)	2.1	(1.0)
Range	0 to 0		0 to 4		1 to 4	
Maternal Education						
Less than High School	2	(2%)	20	(26%)	29	(37%)
High School Graduate	11	(15%)	30	(38%)	26	(34%)
Some College/Vocational	18	(24%)	26	(33%)	21	(27%)
University Graduate	44	(59%)	2	(3%)	1	(1%)
Children in Family						
M (*SD*)	2.1	(0.9)	2.5	(1.3)	2.9	(1.8)
Current Special Education[c]						
Yes	0	(0%)	6	(8%)	37	(49%)
No	80	(100%)	73	(92%)	39	(51%)

Note: For categorical variables, numbers and percentages are given by category. For continuous variables, statistics are as noted.
[a]Married to or living with the child's other natural parent. [b]Married to or living with another adult who is not the child's natural parent (e.g., stepparent). [c]Special education services (e.g., early intervention program) currently being provided to the toddler participant.

Table 2. *Mean Total Scores for CBCL/2–3 and ECBI by Group*

Measure	Low Risk		Social Risk		Dual Risk		Normative[a]	
	M	*SD*	*M*	*SD*	*M*	*SD*	*M*	*SD*
CBCL/2–3								
Internalizing	7.2	4.8	11.5	8.9	12.9	7.6	8.2	5.2
Externalizing	11.7	7.6	14.1	10.3	15.4	9.0	12.9	8.2
Anxious/Depressed	4.2	3.1	5.9	4.1	6.4	3.7	4.7	3.1
Withdrawn	3.0	2.4	5.6	5.2	6.6	4.6	3.5	2.8
Sleep Problems	3.6	3.0	4.1	3.2	4.4	3.3	3.3	2.8
Somatic Problems	2.9	3.1	3.7	3.5	4.1	3.3	2.4	2.4
Aggressive Behavior	8.9	7.1	9.0	6.9	9.8	5.7	8.7	5.7
Destructive Behavior	3.2	2.5	5.2	4.3	5.7	3.9	4.2	3.3
ECBI								
Problem Score	6.4	6.2	7.7	8.7	5.3	6.5	7.0	7.8
Intensity Score	101.0	29.8	95.3	46.0	93.4	38.4	103.8	34.6

[a]Normative data were derived from Achenbach and Edelbrock (1992) for the CBCL/2–3 and Robinson, Eyberg, and Ross (1980) for the ECBI.

Wilks's lambda (4, 426) = .89, $p < .001$. Univariate tests for each independent variable indicated a significant main effect for group for Internalizing Behaviors, $F(2, 214) = 11.5$, $p < .001$, but not for Externalizing Behaviors ($p > .02$). Tukey's HSD procedure revealed that the dual-risk and social-risk groups displayed higher levels of Internalizing behaviors than did the low-risk group. The two higher risk groups did not differ significantly. Additionally, the low-risk-group means across all CBCL subscales were quite similar to those obtained in the normative sample (Achenbach & Edelbrock, 1992), thus suggesting that the low-risk means were not significantly skewed.

For the CBCL/2–3 narrow-band scales, MANOVA results revealed a significant main effect for group, Wilks's lambda (12, 404) = .82, $p < .002$. Univariate F tests showed significant group effects for the following subscales: Anxious/Depressed, $F(2, 14) = 6.9$, $p < .005$; Withdrawn, $F(2, 14) = 12.7$, $p < .001$; and Destructive Behavior, $F(2, 14) = 13.1$, $p < .001$. Across these three subscales, Tukey's HSD procedure indicated that the dual-risk and social-risk groups obtained higher scores than did the low-risk group. Again, the two higher risk groups did not differ significantly on these subscale scores. Univariate results for Sleep Problems, Somatic Problems, and Aggressive Behavior were not significant. MANOVA results for ECBI scores were not statistically significant.

Because the CBCL/2–3 was not standardized for use with 4-year-olds, MANOVA analyses were repeated using only 2- and 3-year-old subjects to demonstrate consistency in findings. Indeed, significant results with the broad-band and narrow-band scales were identical to those presented for the full sample (ages 2 to 4 years).

Risk Category Differences on Dependent Measures

To examine differences between types of biological risk factors in children with social-risk conditions, three

additional one-way MANOVAs were conducted. Only subjects from the social-risk and dual-risk groups were utilized. As such, potentially significant results could not be attributed to the addition of subjects who were without social risk factors as well as biological risk factors. The independent variables consisted of three categories of biological risk factors: *normal* (no biological risk factors; $n = 80$), *premature risk* (delivery at fewer than 33 weeks gestation with a NICU stay; $n = 49$), and full-term risk (full-term delivery with neurological, developmental, or chronic illness complications; $n = 29$). Dependent measures for the analyses were the same as those used previously (CBCL/2–3 broad-band factors, CBCL/2–3 narrow-band scores, and ECBI scores). MANOVA results for all three analyses were not significant ($p > .05$).

Discussion

This study investigated parent-reported behavior problems in three samples of toddlers (ages 2 to 4 years): low risk, social risk, and dual risk. The purpose of this investigation was to determine whether children who were born with biological and social risk factors (dual-risk group) displayed significantly more behavior problems than children born with social risk factors alone (social-risk group). Additionally, a low-risk sample of toddlers was included as a control comparison.

Results consistently demonstrated that parents of both higher risk groups (social and dual) reported that their toddlers exhibited significantly more behavior problems than did the low-risk control group. Specifically, group differences were found with Internalizing, Anxious/Depressed, Withdrawn, and Destructive Behaviors as measured with the CBCL/2–3. These results indicate that both biological and social risk factors are associated with behavior difficulties in preschoolers. However, these two risk groups did not differ significantly from one another with respect to parent-reported behavior problems. Therefore, our findings suggest that children who experience both biological and social risk factors as measured in the current study do not display significantly more behavioral adjustment problems than children with only social risk factors. Additionally, analyses conducted among subjects experiencing social risk conditions indicated no significant differences in parent-reported behavioral difficulties between groups based on specific categories of biological risk factors.

These findings correspond with previous studies (e.g., Escalona, 1982; Gortmaker et al., 1990) in that the addition of biological risk factors to social risk factors does not appear to place toddlers at greater risk for behavioral difficulties than do social risk factors alone. The present results also correspond with the Escalona's (1982) findings that a "double hazard" (with both biological and social risk factors) preschool sample exhibited significant behavioral adjustment problems. However, because Escalona's study did not utilize comparison groups (e.g., social risk factors alone), it was not possible to determine whether "double hazard" characteristics placed children at *greater* risk for behavioral difficulties than either risk factor alone.

The present study improved on research by utilizing a social-risk comparison sample. Our research evaluated whether full-term, healthy infants born with social risk factors (e.g., poverty) also exhibit significant behavioral problems as preschoolers when compared to infants born with both biological (e.g., prematurity) and social risk factors. It appears from our data that relative risk is primarily associated with certain identifiable social conditions such as poverty, low maternal education, and single parenthood, rather than a combination of biological and social risk conditions. In other words, the *additional* presence of perinatal complications as sampled in the current study does not necessarily predispose a child to increased risk of behavioral maladjustment above that of social complications alone. Given the lack of a biological risk group, it could not be determined whether a combination of risk factors predisposed the preschoolers to increased risk above and beyond biological risk factors alone.

In addition, the present study improved upon Escalona's (1982) methods of assessing behavioral adjustment. Escalona (1982) did not clearly specify exact assessment procedures for measuring maladjustment, but appeared to use clinician judgment ("maladjusted" vs. "not overtly maladjusted") as opposed to standardized assessment tools. This bivariate rating also limited the specificity of behavioral description for participants. By contrast, we used well-established, standardized, parent-reported behavior rating scales commonly used with preschoolers. The CBCL/2–3 produces scores across various subscales, whereas the ECBI

yields scores for both the frequency and intensity behavior problems. The presence of multiple scores and normative data enhances the interpretation of our results both descriptively and quantitatively. For example, all three groups obtained scores comparable to those of the normative sample on both the CBCL/2–3 and ECBI. Although a statistically significant group difference was found, it could be argued that these differences were not clinically significant. Further research would be needed to support such an argument.

With respect to behavior rating scales for preschoolers, our results may suggest that it is more effective to use comprehensive measures specifically developed for this age population. Significant results were obtained only with the CBCL/2–3 and not the ECBI. The CBCL/2–3 was designed to assess various behavioral difficulties in young toddlers. The ECBI has been used extensively with preschoolers suspected of conduct disturbances and it is relatively more sensitive to externalizing than to internalizing behaviors. Therefore, it does not adequately assess internalizing behavior problems. This limitation in the ECBI may explain the lack of significant results obtained with this measure in our study. All but one of the significant group differences found with the CBCL/2–3 were Internalizing subscales or behaviors.

Additionally, it should be noted that across all results, raw scores on the dependent measures for each of the three groups were comparable to those of the normative sample. As such, our results suggest that although statistically significant differences were obtained between risk groups on behavioral measures, these differences may not be clinically significant. Perhaps these findings suggest that at-risk preschoolers actually demonstrated good behavioral and emotional adjustment. Conversely, the dependent measures may not have been sensitive to actual differences between the three risk samples. Further research is needed to explain whether our results demonstrate behavioral and emotional resiliency of at-risk toddlers or an inadequacy of criterion variables.

Despite methodological improvements over previous research, the findings of this study are somewhat limited. First, only one informant (parent) was utilized in assessing each of the preschooler's behavior. However, many of these children did not have another parent, substitute caregiver, or teacher who could have served as a second informant. This is not surprising given that these children are not school age and the majority of families were socioeconomically disadvantaged. Second, only one method of assessment, behavior rating scales, was utilized. Group differences could be secondary to either true differences in children's behavior or to differences in how parents report the children's behavior. Although it has been well-established that parent-report data with preschooler behavior problems appears reliable and valid (e.g., Campbell et al., 1982), our findings would have been strengthened had observational data or monitoring data been included. Third, maternal depression has been shown to affect parent ratings of child behavior (e.g., Brody & Forehand, 1986); yet, this was not evaluated in the current study. Fourth, the impact of biological risk factors alone was not determined. Another comparison sample of infants born with biological risk factors and without social risk factors would have been needed to address their particular risk. This had been the original intent of the study, but locating a sufficient number of children to complete this fourth group proved impossible given data collection procedures and sites utilized (e.g., biological risk factors were typically found in social-risk samples). Future research endeavors should attempt to include several groups comparing both individual and various combinations of biological and social risk factors.

In review, our study found that preschoolers with only social risk factors and preschoolers with both biological and social risk conditions are reported by parents to exhibit significantly more behavior problems than toddlers in a low-risk control sample. Our social-risk and dual-risk groups did not differ, however, suggesting that the *addition* of biological factors does not necessarily increase the risk association above and beyond social factors alone. The relation between risk factors and behavioral adjustment does not appear to be additive. Furthermore, results comparing different types of biological risk factors in socially disadvantaged preschoolers were not significant. Sample sizes precluded the comparison of individual biological risk factors (e.g., neurological complication vs. chronic illness); thus, further research is needed to clarify the contribution of each biological risk factor to the behavioral development of children.

From a preventive focus, our results indicate that early intervention programs should consider targeting socioculturally disadvantaged, healthy infants and toddlers as well as infants and toddlers at biological risk regardless of social risk factors. Our data suggest that in the Baton Rouge area, children born with biological risk factors are more likely to receive intervention services than are socioculturally disadvantaged children. Specifically, our dual-risk group had a significantly higher rate of special education services (e.g., early intervention programs) than did the other two groups. This finding indicates that our social-risk group has not received an equivalent rate of intervention services when compared to children who were born with additional biological risks. Exposure to early intervention services may have been a confounding variable. It is interesting to speculate about whether potential significant differences between the social-risk and dual-risk groups were affected by the inequitable distribution of intervention services. In short, the receipt of services by the dual-risk group may have

ameliorated possible differences in the two risk groups.

Research has typically demonstrated a relation between social risk conditions and poor behavioral adjustment in children with and without biological compromise (Tarnowski, 1991). Despite our understanding of this relation, effective identification and treatment strategies for behavioral difficulties in socially disadvantaged children remains largely unrealized. Recently, research has begun to demonstrate the efficacy of early intervention services for children identified at birth as being at "high risk" based on social and economic variables (e.g., Horacek, Ramey, Campbell, Hoffmann, & Fletcher, 1987). Indeed, the House Select Committee on Children, Youth, and Families stated in 1986 that early intervention and Head Start studies have led the agency "to estimate that every $1.00 spent on preschool education saves at least $4.75 in later educational and social costs" (cited in Parker, Greer, & Zuckerman, 1988).

References

Abidin, R. R., Jenkins, C. L., & McGaughey, M. C. (1992). The relationship of early family variables to children's subsequent behavioral adjustment. *Journal of Clinical Child Psychology, 21,* 60–69.

Achenbach, T. M., & Edelbrock, C. (1992). *Manual for the Child Behavior Checklist/2–3 and 1992 Profile.* Burlington: University of Vermont, Department of Psychiatry.

Achenbach, T. M., Edelbrock, C., & Howell, C. T. (1987). Empirically based assessment of the behavioral/emotional problems of 2- and 3-year-old children. *Journal of Abnormal Child Psychology, 15,* 629–650.

Allen, M. C. (1993). The high-risk infant. *Pediatric Clinics of North America, 40,* 479–490.

Barkley, R. A. (1990). *Attention deficit hyperactivity disorder: A handbook for diagnosis and treatment.* New York: Guilford.

Beckwith, L., & Parmelee, A. (1986). EEG patterns of preterm infants, home environment, and later IQ. *Child Development, 57,* 777–789.

Boggs, S. R., Eyberg, S., & Reynolds, L. A. (1990). Concurrent validity of the Eyberg Child Behavior Inventory. *Journal of Clinical Child Psychology, 19,* 75–78.

Brody, G. H., & Forehand, R. (1986). Maternal perceptions of child maladjustment as a function of the combined influence of child behavior and maternal depression. *Journal of Consulting and Clinical Psychology, 54,* 237–240.

Campbell, S. B., Szumowski, E. K., Ewing, L. J., Gluck, D. S., & Breaux, A. M. (1982). A multidimensional assessment of parent-identified behavior problem toddlers. *Journal of Abnormal Child Psychology, 10,* 569–592.

Dunst, C. J. (1993). Implications of risk and opportunity factors for assessment and intervention practices. *Topics in Early Childhood Special Education, 12,* 143–153.

Earls, F., & Jung, K. G. (1987). Temperament and home environment characteristics as causal factors in the early development of childhood psychopathology. *Journal of the American Academy of Child and Adolescent Psychiatry, 26,* 491–498.

Escalona, S. K. (1982). Babies at double hazard: Early development of infants at biologic and social risk. *Pediatrics, 70,* 670–676.

Eyberg, S. M., & Robinson, E. A. (1982). Parent–child interaction training: Effects on family functioning. *Journal of Clinical Child Psychology, 11,* 130–137.

Eyberg, S. M., & Ross, A. W. (1978). Assessment of child behavior problems: The validation of a new inventory. *Journal of Clinical Child Psychology, 7,* 113–116.

Goldberg, I. D., Roghmann, K. J., McInerny, T. K., & Burke, J. D. (1984). Mental health problems among children seen in pediatric practice: Prevalence and management. *Pediatrics, 73,* 278–293.

Gortmaker, S. L., Walker, D. K., Weitzman, M., & Sobol, A. M. (1990). Chronic conditions, socioeconomic risks, and behavioral problems in children and adolescents. *Pediatrics, 85,* 267–276.

Horacek, H. J., Ramey, C. T., Campbell, F. A., Hoffmann, K. P., & Fletcher, R. H. (1987). Predicting school failure and assessing early intervention with high-risk children. *Journal of the American Academy of Child and Adolescent Psychiatry, 26,* 758–763.

Infant Health and Development Program. (1990). Enhancing the outcomes of low-birth-weight, premature infants. *Journal of the American Medical Association, 263,* 3035–3042.

Jensen, P. S., Bloedau, L., DeGroot, J., Ussery, T., & Davis, H. (1990). Children at risk: I. Risk factors and child symptomatology. *Journal of the American Academy of Child and Adolescent Psychiatry, 29,* 51–59.

Jones, J. E. (1991). Statistics on children at risk. *Journal of Health Care for the Poor and Underserved, 2,* 26–39.

Larson, C. P., Pless, I. B., & Miettinen, O. (1988). Preschool behavior disorders: Their prevalence in relation to determinants. *Journal of Pediatrics, 113,* 278–285.

Martin, R. (1988). *Assessment of personality and behavior problems: Infancy through adolescence.* New York: Guilford.

Martin, R. (1991). Assessment of social and emotional behavior. In B. A. Bracken (Ed.), *Psychoeducational assessment of preschool children* (pp. 450–464). Boston: Allyn & Bacon.

McLloyd, V. C. (1990). The impact of economic hardship on black families and children: Psychological distress, parenting, and socio-emotional development. *Child Development, 61,* 311–346.

Needlman, R., Stevenson, J., & Zuckerman, B. (1991). Psychosocial correlates of severe temper tantrums. *Developmental and Behavioral Pediatrics, 12,* 77–83.

Ornstein, M., Ohlsson, A., Edmonds, J., & Asztalos, E. (1991). Neonatal follow-up of very low birthweight/extremely low birthweight infants to school age: A critical overview. *Acta Paediatrica Scandinavica, 80,* 741–748.

Parker, S., Greer, S., & Zuckerman, B. (1988). Double jeopardy: The impact of poverty on early child development. *Pediatric Clinics of North America, 35,* 1227–1240.

Public Law 99–457. (1986). *Education of the Handicapped Act Amendments of 1986* (Rep. No. 99–860). Washington, DC: U.S. Government Printing Office.

Robinson, E. A., Eyberg, S. M., & Ross, A. W. (1980). The standardization of an inventory of child conduct problem behaviors. *Journal of Clinical Child Psychology, 9,* 22–29.

Tarnowski, K. J. (1991). Disadvantaged children and families in pediatric primary care settings: I. Broadening the scope of integrated mental health service. *Journal of Clinical Child Psychology, 20,* 351–359.

Tarnowski, K. J., & Blechman, E. A. (1991). Introduction to the special section: Disadvantaged children and families. *Journal of Clinical Child Psychology, 20,* 338–339.

Webster-Stratton, C. (1990). Stress: A potential disrupter of parent perceptions and family interactions. *Journal of Clinical Child Psychology, 19,* 302–312.

Werner, E., & Smith, R. (1977). *Kauai's children come of age.* Honolulu: University of Hawaii Press.

Zeskind, P. S., & Ramey, C. T. (1978). Fetal malnutrition: An experimental study of its consequences on infant development in two caregiving environments. *Child Development, 49,* 1155–1162.

Zeskind, P. S., & Ramey, C. T. (1981). Preventing intellectual and interactional sequelae of fetal malnutrition: A longitudinal, transactional, and synergistic approach to development. *Child Development, 52,* 213–218.

Received August 11, 1993
Final revision received May 16, 1994

Journal of Clinical Child Psychology
1994, Vol. 23, 382–390

Aggressive, Assertive, and Submissive Behaviors in Disadvantaged, Inner-City Preschool Children

Judith E. Wall

University of Maryland at Baltimore County

E. Wayne Holden

Department of Pediatrics
University of Maryland School of Medicine

Measured the frequency of socioeconomically disadvantaged preschool children's aggressive, assertive, and submissive behaviors in play interaction with their mothers. Boys were significantly more assertive but not more aggressive or submissive than girls. Sociofamilial predictors including maternal depression, maternal anger, parenting stress, family life stress, and maternal perceptions of children's aggressive behavior were examined. Sex of the child interacted with (a) maternal depression to predict aggressive and assertive behavior and (b) maternal anger to predict submissive behavior. In all cases where child's sex exerted a significant moderating influence, boys' behavior was more vulnerable to differences in levels of maternal depression and anger, with lower rates of boys' behavior associated with higher levels of maternal distress.

Despite evidence that impoverished children risk greater sociofamilial stress and behavioral or psychological maladjustment than do their more socioeconomically advantaged counterparts (Garmezy & Tellegen, 1984; Huston, 1991), relatively little is known about the unique relations between sociofamilial stressors and specific aspects of behavioral adjustment for disadvantaged children. For example, although some investigators have identified lower socioeconomic status (SES) as a correlate of children's aggressive/disruptive behavior (Campbell, Breaux, Ewing, & Szumowski, 1986; Farrington, 1989), relatively few have examined specific predictors of aggression and related behaviors within impoverished samples.

Based on a review of the literature on the effects of poverty and economic loss on parenting behavior and family processes, McLoyd (1990) argued that economic hardship renders parents less capable of employing consistent, supportive, and involved parenting and more vulnerable to the effects of stressful life events. The negative effects of economic disadvantage on children's socioemotional functioning occur in part through its impact on parent-to-child behaviors and are likely mediated by psychological distress accruing to parents by virtue of "an excess of negative life events, undesirable chronic conditions, and the absence and disruption of marital bonds" (McLoyd, 1990, p. 311). Specifically, McLoyd reported that economic disadvantage promotes increased levels of parental anxiety, irritability, and depression which generally result in less nurturant and more punitive parenting behaviors. According to this model, the effects of poverty on children's socioemotional functioning are mediated by parental psychological distress with specific child characteristics interacting with parental characteristics to influence outcomes.

Empirical evidence generally indicates that sociofamilial stress is associated with increased externalizing behaviors, at least for boys. Offord (1989) and others have suggested that boys may be differentially more vulnerable to parental psychopathology, family upset, and marital discord than girls, possibly due to parents' efforts to protect daughters more than sons from exposure to family distress. In general, however, such theories were based on the results of research utilizing nonimpoverished, school-age samples. An important, yet little-explored question involves whether the trend of boys' greater emotional/behavioral reactivity in the direction of increased externalizing symptoms generalizes from nonimpoverished, school-age samples to socioeconomically disadvantaged preschoolers.

This study represents portions of Judith Wall's master's thesis in the Department of Psychology at the University of Maryland at Baltimore County. E. Wayne Holden's work on this study was supported by National Institute of Mental Health Grant MH–19182.

We acknowledge the contributions of Elaine Zerhusen, Loreto Martinez, Robert Deluty, Doug Teti, and Eliot Shimoff to this project.

Requests for reprints should be sent to E. Wayne Holden, Department of Pediatrics, University of Maryland School of Medicine, Room 5–678, 630 West Fayette Street, Baltimore, MD 21201.

Specifically, understanding the nature and correlates of aggression and related behaviors in preschool-age children is hindered by the fact that behavioral disorders in preschoolers remain a relatively neglected area of research. There are compelling reasons why such research should be undertaken. Rutter (1988) suggested that the age at which children are exposed to risk factors is an important determinant of whether and in what form disordered behavior will be manifested. Empirical evidence belies the assumption that disturbances in the young are transient and trivial, suggesting instead that behavioral problems in both school-age and preschool children do predict later behavioral disturbance. Stevenson, Richman, and Graham (1985) found a strong, sex-moderated relation between in-home behavioral deviance at age 3 and in-school behavioral deviance at age 8; boys, but not girls, who were identified as behaviorally deviant at age 3 showed significantly greater behavioral deviance at age 8 than did initially nondisturbed controls. Campbell (1990) reported that children whose behavior was identified as problematic by parent report and laboratory measures at age 3 continued to be rated as more aggressive and hyperactive relative to controls at age 4; additionally, problematic 3-year-olds tended to maintain their rank order 1 year later.

That preschool-age children are an important target for study in their own right is illustrated by findings concerning the role of child's sex in moderating children's aggression. Indeed, the importance of sex in moderating the relations among variables associated with aggression and other childhood behavioral disorders for school-age children has received immense support in the epidemiological and clinical literatures. Offord (1989) suggested the apparently greater vulnerability of boys to family upset and marital discord (Rutter & Giller, 1983) as one mechanism whereby sex influences disordered conduct in school-aged children. For younger children, however, evidence of sex-moderated differences in aggressive behavior is more ambiguous. Offord (1989) cautioned that whereas the finding of a male preponderance of conduct disorder applies strongly to school-age children—whether data are based on self-, parent, or teacher reports or on official delinquency statistics (Offord, Alder, & Boyle, 1986; Rutter & Giller, 1983)—it is not as firmly established for preschool children.

The generalization of findings about correlates of aggression in school-age children to preschool-age children cannot be automatically assumed. In fact, there is some evidence that very young boys and girls tend to inhibit rather than express aggressive tendencies in the presence of sociofamilial stress. Zahn-Waxler, McKnew, Cummings, Davenport, and Radke-Yarrow (1984) found 2-year-old offspring of depressed mothers to be more emotionally inhibited in the presence of frustration, less aggressive toward peers, and no more aggressive toward an adult than the young children of nondepressed mothers, with no sex differences noted. It may be that sex differences in the direction of boy's greater aggressiveness and other externalizing behaviors do not begin to emerge until around the age of 5 (Stevenson et al., 1985).

Existing research on children's aggressiveness is complicated by the widespread use of measures that confound aggressive and assertive behaviors, despite evidence that aggressiveness, assertiveness, and submissiveness exist as distinct behavioral classes (Deluty, 1985). Thus, although many research findings converge in identifying school-age boys as differentially more aggressive than female peers, it may be that identified sex differences, if generalizable to preschoolers, have more to do with assertive than aggressive behavior. Research that specifically defines aggressive behavior and simultaneously examines related behavioral classes such as assertiveness and submissiveness is clearly needed.

Our study was conducted to investigate the role of parent, family, and child variables as predictors of preschool-age children's aggressive, assertive, and submissive behaviors in disadvantaged, inner-city families. It was hypothesized that disadvantaged mothers would display normatively high levels of depression, anger, and stress. In addition, for disadvantaged preschool children, it was hypothesized that aggressiveness and assertiveness would be associated with higher levels of maternal distress. Furthermore, it was hypothesized that relations among predictor variables and behavioral classes would be moderated by sex of the child. Because of the inherent confounding of aggressiveness and assertiveness in the existing literature, hypotheses about how aggressive, assertive, and submissive behaviors might be differentially predicted by variables previously found to be associated with aggression were withheld.

Method

Participants

Participants were 85 mother–child dyads who were recruited for a study of family factors and behavior in preschool children at a pediatric primary-care clinic serving an inner-city population. The clinic is a state medical assistance–supported facility in inner-city Baltimore that serves several census tracts densely populated with impoverished families. The facility is the major ambulatory-care training clinic for pediatric residents at the University of Maryland School of Medicine.

The sample was 94% African American. The mean age of mothers was 26.6 years ($SD = 4.6$ years), and the mean age of children was 57 months ($SD = 6.7$, range

= 48 to 71 months). Sixty-seven percent of mothers were single parents. Sixty-eight percent of mothers were unemployed at the time of their participation in the study, and more than 53% of mothers reported an annual family income below poverty level for a family of four. The mean number of siblings in each family was 1.54 (SD = 1.25). Fifty-seven percent of the children in the study were girls. Age did not differ significantly between boys and girls who participated in the study. Sixty-seven percent of mothers reported that they received monthly Aid to Families With Dependent Children (AFDC) payments, and the majority of mothers reported that their children's health care was paid by state medical assistance or that their child did not have health insurance.

The mean SES level based on the Hollingshead Four-Factor Index (Hollingshead, 1975) was 23.7 (SD = 10.4). Although over 75% of the families scored within the two lowest SES strata, some variability was displayed across the SES measure, which is a composite score based on parental education and occupation. The following distribution was obtained across the five categories of the Hollingshead index: Level I (1.2%), Level II (8.2%), Level III (15.3%), Level IV (28.2%), and Level V (47.1%). It should be noted, however, that measures such as the Hollingshead index are only approximate estimates that may tend to overestimate SES levels, especially in inner-city populations (Liberatos, Link, & Kelsey, 1988). We continued to include all subjects in the study, regardless of their assessed SES, because of their attendance at a primary-care clinic specifically designated for poor, inner-city families.

Maternal Report Measures

Several measures were used to assess maternal distress, family stress levels, and perceptions of children's behaviors. Maternal depression was measured using the Beck Depression Inventory (BDI; Beck, Ward, Mendelson, Mock, & Erbaugh, 1961), a 21-item inventory assessing the presence and intensity of depression. Beck, Steer, and Garbin (1988) reported high internal consistency, high test–retest reliability, and high concurrent validity in reviewing the use of the BDI over 15 years of research.

Maternal anger was measured using the Multidimensional Anger Inventory (MAI; Siegel, 1986), a self-report measure which evaluates anger along dimensions of Anger-Arousal, Range of Anger-Eliciting Situations, Hostile Outlook, and Mode of Anger Expression. High internal consistency and test–retest reliability as well as acceptable concurrent validity have been reported for this instrument (Siegel, 1986).

Level of family stress was assessed using the Family Inventory of Life Events (FILE; McCubbin & Patterson, 1981), a 71-item measure on which examinees respond either *yes* or *no* to items reflecting recent (within the past 12 months) family stress in nine areas. McCubbin and Thompson (1991) reported acceptable internal consistency, high test–retest reliability, and acceptable concurrent validity for this measure.

Sources and magnitude of stress in the parent-child relationship were measured using the Parenting Stress Index (PSI; Abidin, 1990), a 120-item questionnaire aimed at uncovering mothers' perceptions of their child's characteristics as well as situational or demographic life stressors. This multidimensional measure has demonstrated acceptable reliability and validity across numerous investigations (Abidin, 1990).

The raw score on the Aggression factor of the parent version of the Child Behavior Checklist (CBCL; Achenbach & Edelbrock, 1983) was employed as a measure of mothers' perceptions of their children's aggressive behaviors. The CBCL is the most widely used child behavior rating scale in research and clinical settings, with substantial evidence available for its reliability, concurrent validity, and factorial validity (Achenbach & Edelbrock, 1983).

Observational Measure

Children's aggressive, assertive, and submissive behaviors in 21-min videotaped play sessions were rated using a Behavior Checklist developed by Deluty (1985) to which minor modifications were made to accommodate observation of parent–child, as opposed to in-school interactions (for modified Behavior Checklist, see Table 1). Although the Behavior Checklist represents a compilation of items that were generally standardized on an older (i.e., school-age) population, the checklist was judged to be suitable as well for use with preschool-age children because it includes major behavioral domains examined in representative studies of aggressiveness in 4- to 6-year-old children.

One of us (Wall) received training and consultation on the use of the Behavior Checklist including detailed descriptions of the target behaviors and instructions for completing the checklist. Interrater reliability was established prior to data collection by comparing Wall's ratings with the coding generated by a similarly trained adult volunteer while observing four structured-play-session videotapes designated for training purposes. Both scorers' Behavior Checklists were compared for number of agreements across aggressive, assertive, and submissive categories in each 1-min interval. Consistent with Crockenberg and Litman (1990), interrater reliability was calculated by dividing [(number of agreements)/(number of agreements + disagreements)] × 100. Interrater reliability was greater than 85% for each of the three behavioral classes.

Table 1. *Behaviors Constituting the Modified Behavior Checklist*

Submissive
  Failing to make requests
  Failing to refuse unreasonable requests
  Failing to object to unreasonable requests
  Reacting oversensitively to criticism
  Inappropriate crying (not a passive–aggressive manipulation)
  Exhibiting difficulty expressing emotions (feelings)
Assertive
  Standing one's ground in an argument (without any form of aggression)
  Making requests for behavior
  Resisting an unfair demand in a nonhostile manner
  Giving/accepting compliments
  Expressing thoughts/feelings in a nonhostile, noncoercive manner in response to frustration or provocation
  Appropriately initiating, maintaining, or terminating a social interaction
  Deciding for self (not at the expense of others)
  Appropriate questioning (vs. whining)
  Appropriate seeking of attention (vs. yelling and screaming for attention)
Aggressive
  Physical attack (e.g., hitting, biting, and pushing)
  Verbal attack (e.g., teasing and ridiculing)
  Gestural disapproval of another (e.g., sticking out tongue)
  Infringement of property (destructiveness)
  Invasion of territory (i.e., making physical contact with another's person or property without being asked)
  Threatening to hurt others
  Choosing for self at the expense of others
  Putting up an argument (screaming, ranting, etc.) when told to do or not to do something
  Bossing
  Not taking orders
  Making unreasonable or unnecessary requests
  Engaging in an aversive, *repetitive* behavior (e.g., banging on table and scraping chair along floor)
  Shouting, yelling, or talking loudly at inappropriate times
  Behaving in a coercive manner to get mother's attention (e.g., shaking arm wildly while leaning toward mother)
  Engaging in a passive, yet coercive and manipulative behavior

Once interrater reliability was established, the remaining videotaped play sessions were scored. To guard against observer drift, weekly reliability checks were made by comparing the scorings of the primary coder and the trained volunteer on a randomly selected 15% of those tapes. As recommended by Gelfand and Hartmann (1984), we calculated reliability statistics for the dependent variables that were used in subsequent statistical analyses—the molar categories of assertiveness, aggressiveness, and submissiveness—rather than the specific molecular categories making up the Behavior Checklist. Because the observational data were collected as frequency of occurrence of behavior class per 1-min interval, interrater reliability was calculated as [(number of agreements per 1-min interval)/(number of agreements per 1-min interval + number of disagreements per 1-min interval)] × 100. For the scoring of aggressive behaviors, interrater reliabilities ranged

from 83% to 100% ($M = 91\%$). For assertive behaviors, they ranged from 65% to 100% ($M = 82\%$), and for submissive behaviors, from 96% to 100% ($M = 99\%$). Our interrater agreement statistics were relatively high, but may have been somewhat inflated because we were unable to use computational procedures that control for chance agreement with our frequency-dependent data.

Procedure

Parent–child dyads were recruited for participation in this study directly from the waiting room at the pediatric primary-care clinic. Parents of 4- to 5-year-old children were approached regarding participation. Children having a diagnosed developmental disability, participating in preschool special-education programs, or having a chronic physical illness other than asthma were excluded from participation. Appointments were scheduled for interested parents to participate in the study following their medical visit. Assessment of each mother–child dyad lasted approximately 2 hr, with each mother being reimbursed $20.00 for expenses associated with participation in the research.

Once consent was obtained from the parent, each mother participated in a structured interview concerning demographic information and completed the parent-report measures prior to participating with her child in a videotaped, structured-play session. A small play area (measuring approximately 10 ft × 12 ft) in a larger room was used for the observation. The play area was carpeted and contained shelves for toys as well as a small table and two chairs. A videotape camera with a wide-angle lens was mounted on a tripod in an adjacent corner of the room and used to record individual play sessions.

Play sessions lasted a total of 21 min and were structured as follows. A research assistant escorted each mother–child dyad to the play area which was stocked with a variety of age-appropriate toys. Both mother and child were asked to play within the confines of the play area which was clearly marked on the floor. Initial instructions were for the mother and child to play freely with any of the toys in the room for a 5-min period. At 5 min into the observation session, the mother was asked to engage in instructional play with her child for 7 min. She was specifically directed to teach the child to complete a set of puzzles that varied in complexity, but were sequenced to teach numerical concepts. At 12 min into the observation, the mother was instructed to engage in competitive play with her child for 7 min. She was specifically asked either to play a miniature basketball game or a competitive board game and to keep track of who was winning on a small chalk board on the wall. Finally, the mother was asked to direct the child to clean the room for the final 3 min of the observation period.

Results

Table 2 provides descriptive statistics for maternal report and observational measures. Differences between the data obtained in this study and published normative data on the maternal-report measures were evaluated by computing t tests. Significantly higher levels of parenting stress, life stress, and anger were found in comparison to norms. Although mean scores were higher in the areas of child aggression and maternal depression, significant differences were not displayed. Zero-order correlations of each dependent variable with SES, family size, child's age, and marital status, considered as possible covariates, were computed. In all cases correlations were weak and, except for submissive behavior and family size ($r = .25, p < .05$), correlation coefficients were nonsignificant. Based on the weakness of the associations, SES, child's age, family size, and marital status were not entered as covariates in multiple-regression analyses.

A series of multiple-regression analyses were conducted to examine the differential influence of demographic and maternal self-report variables on children's aggressive, assertive, and submissive behaviors. Each outcome variable was regressed on the following six predictor variables: mother's perceptions of their children's aggressive behaviors, sex, maternal anger, family life stress, overall parenting stress, and maternal depression. Because there was no clear reason to expect differential predictive power among these independent variables, they were entered individually in stepwise fashion.

A main effect of sex on children's assertive behavior was found: Boys were significantly more assertive than girls, $F(1, 63) = 6.01, p < .05$. No other individual variables contributed significantly to children's aggressive, assertive, or submissive behaviors.

Interactions of Child's Sex and Maternal Distress

To examine the role of child's sex in moderating the effects of maternal anger on children's aggressive, as-

Table 2. *Descriptive Statistics for Parent-Report and Observational Measures*

Measure	M	SD
Parent Report		
CBCL Aggressiveness[a]	9.26	8.00
Maternal Anger[b]	108.38	20.14
Family Life Stress[c]	11.78	8.81
Parenting Stress[d]	238.52	40.06
Maternal Depression[e]	9.15	8.93
Observations		
Aggressive Behaviors	9.64	9.78
Assertive Behaviors	30.47	13.40
Submissive Behaviors	0.45	1.22

Note: $N = 85$.
[a]$t(153) = 1.3$, ns; normative $M = 7.82$ (Achenbach & Edelbrock, 1983). [b]$t(168) = 14.2, p < .001$; normative $M = 71.2$ (Siegel, 1986). [c]$t(2,080) = 3.1, p < .003$; normative $M = 8.8$ (McCubbin & Thompson, 1991). [d]$t(163) = 3.57, p < .0004$; normative $M = 222.8$ (Abidin, 1990). [e]$t(233) = 1.57$, ns; normative $M = 7.5$ (Gould, 1982).

sertive, and submissive behaviors, multiple-regression analyses were performed in which children's (modified) Behavior Checklist aggressive, assertive, and submissive behavior scores were regressed upon the following independent variables: (a) maternal anger and sex of child, entered as a set; and (b) Maternal Anger × Sex of Child. Similar regression analyses were performed to explore the role of child's sex in moderating the effects of life stress on children's aggressive, assertive, and submissive behaviors. Finally, regression analyses were also performed to explore the role of child's sex in moderating the effects of maternal depression and of overall parenting stress on the children's behavior.

Results from these analyses, presented in Table 3, revealed that sex of child moderated the relations between several predictor variables and behavioral class, specifically: (a) maternal depression and children's aggressive behavior, $F(1, 80) = 5.18, p < .05$; (b) maternal depression and children's assertive behavior, $F(1, 80) = 5.27, p < .05$; and (c) maternal anger and children's submissive behavior, $F(1, 80) = 5.10, p < .05$. These significant interactions were probed in the manner suggested by Cohen and Cohen (1983) and are addressed in turn. (*High, medium,* and *low* designations

Table 3. *Sex-Moderated Predictors of Children's Aggressiveness, Assertiveness, and Submissiveness*

	Aggressiveness			Assertiveness			Submissiveness		
Interaction	R^2	df	F	R^2	df	F	R^2	df	F
Maternal Anger × Sex	.00	3, 80	0.30	.01	3, 80	0.64	.06	3, 80	5.10*
Maternal Depression × Sex	.06	3, 80	5.20*	.06	3, 80	5.30*	.03	3, 80	2.20
Family Life Stress × Sex	.01	3, 75	0.36	.01	3, 75	0.73	.04	3, 75	2.90
Parenting Stress × Sex	.04	3, 65	3.00	.01	3, 65	0.40	.03	3, 65	2.10

*$p < .05$.

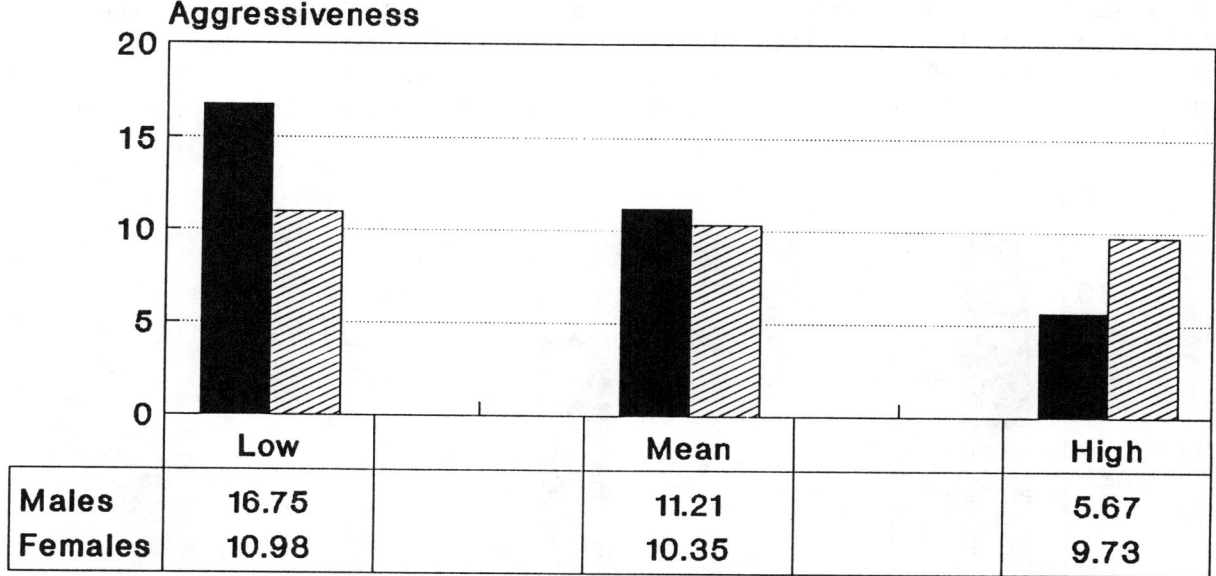

	Low		Mean		High
Males	16.75		11.21		5.67
Females	10.98		10.35		9.73

Maternal Depression Level

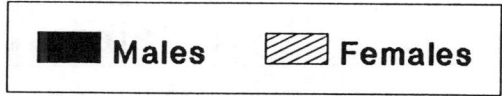

Figure 1.   Sex-moderated influence of maternal depression on rates of preschoolers' aggressive behavior.

represent values 1 *SD* above the mean, at the mean, and 1 *SD* below the mean, respectively.)

The significant Maternal Depression × Sex of Child interactions demonstrated differential effects of maternal depression as a function of children's sex on both children's aggressive and assertive behavior. First, sex of child moderated the effect of maternal depression on children's aggression in the following manner: Boys were less aggressive at higher levels of maternal depression, whereas girls' aggressiveness was essentially constant across levels of maternal depression (see Figure 1). Furthermore, boys were more aggressive than girls at low levels of maternal depression, but they were less aggressive than girls when maternal depression equaled and exceeded mean levels.

Second, sex of child also moderated the effect of maternal depression on children's assertive behavior in the following manner: Boys were less assertive at higher levels of maternal depression, whereas girls evidenced similar levels of assertiveness across levels of maternal depression (see Figure 2). Again, boys were more assertive than girls at low levels of maternal depression and less assertive than girls when maternal depression exceeded mean levels.

Child's sex also moderated the effect of maternal anger on children's submissive behavior (see Figure 3). Boys were less submissive at high levels of maternal anger, whereas girls evidenced similar rates of submissive behaviors across levels of maternal anger. Boys were more submissive than girls at low levels of mater-

nal anger, but were less submissive than girls for levels of maternal anger that approached and exceeded the mean.

Discussion

This study differs from most studies of children's aggressive behavior in several important respects. First, whereas most such studies have examined school-age children, we studied a preschool-age population. Second, unlike many studies that have utilized European-American, middle-SES, or heterogeneous samples, this study employed a sample that was predominantly impoverished and African American. Third, whereas it has been argued that most studies of aggressive and/or assertive behavior are compromised by the use of measures confounding those two variables, our study employed a behavior rating scale to reliably distinguish aggressive from assertive behaviors and thereby examine each (along with submissive behavior) as separate constructs. Interpretation of findings must consider that, in these ways, this study represents a major departure from representative studies on aggressive behavior in children.

Results from this study provide only partial confirmation for the hypothesis that maternal perceptions, maternal anger, maternal depression, SES, family life stress, sex of child, and family size are associated with different patterns of aggressive, assertive, and submissive behavior in preschool-age children from lower

SES families. Of those variables, only children's sex was significant in directly predicting behavioral class, contributing approximately 9% of the variance to children's assertiveness. SES, consistently reported in the literature as being associated with children's aggressive behavior, failed to contribute significant variance in this study, presumably due to the restricted range of SES variability among this predominantly

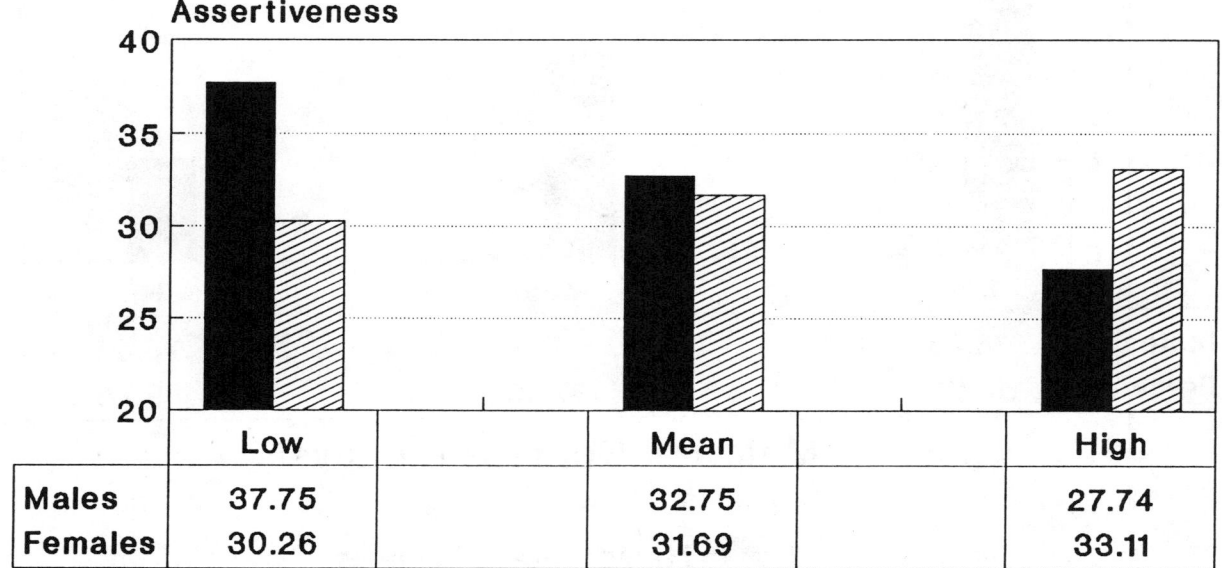

Assertiveness

	Low		Mean		High
Males	37.75		32.75		27.74
Females	30.26		31.69		33.11

Maternal Depression Level

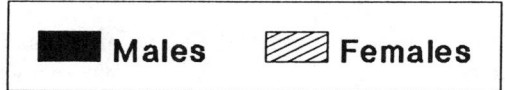

Figure 2.   Sex-moderated influence of maternal depression on rates of preschoolers' assertive behavior.

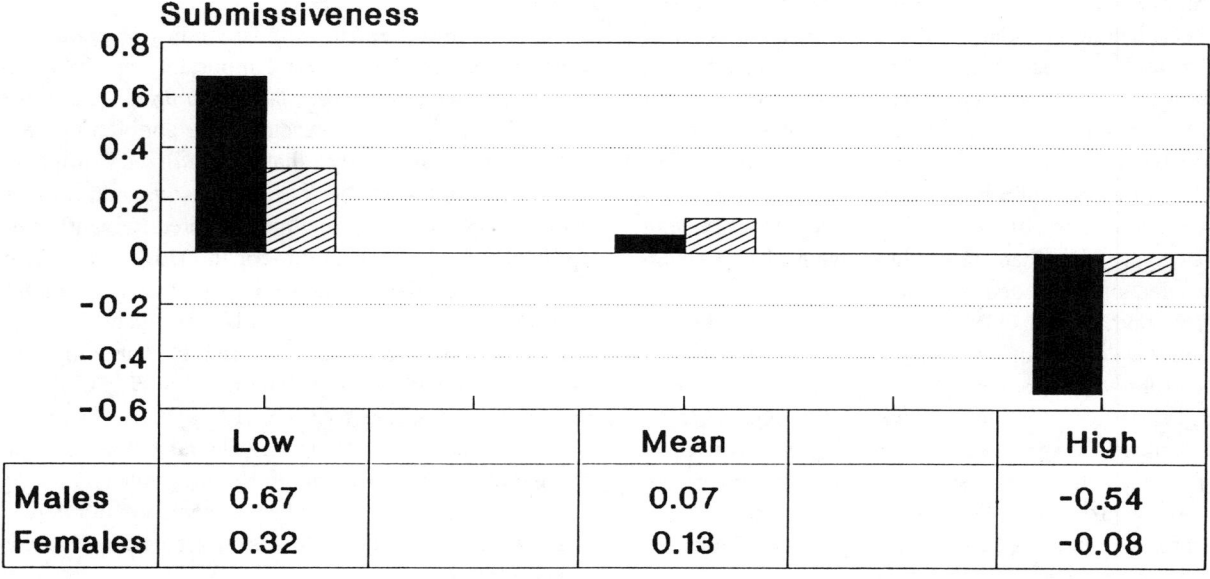

Submissiveness

	Low		Mean		High
Males	0.67		0.07		-0.54
Females	0.32		0.13		-0.08

Maternal Anger Level

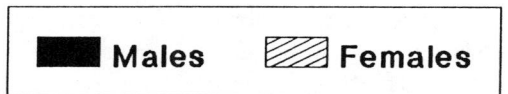

Figure 3.   Sex-moderated influence of maternal anger on rates of preschoolers' submissive behavior.

impoverished, inner-city sample. The most remarkable findings from this study involved the role of children's sex in moderating relations between various maternal and/or family characteristics and children's behavior. Although no maternal or family characteristic independently predicted children's aggressive, assertive, or submissive behavior, children's behavior was significantly affected by the interaction of specific maternal and family characteristics with children's sex. The significant interaction effects that were obtained provide support for McLoyd's (1990) contention that parent distress and child characteristics interact to influence child behavioral outcomes in disadvantaged families.

The results of this study add to a substantial body of literature documenting males' reactivity to a variety of sociofamilial stressors while presenting new evidence suggesting that, at least for low-SES preschoolers, the manner in which males' vulnerability manifests may differ from prior expectations. Employing a measurement system that distinguished aggressiveness, assertiveness, and submissiveness as distinct behavioral classes, this study showed boys to be significantly more assertive but not more aggressive than girls. Sex moderated relations between two sociofamilial variables (maternal depression and anger) and specific behavioral classes: Boys demonstrated lower levels of both aggressive and assertive behaviors for higher levels of maternal depression. Further, higher levels of maternal anger were associated with lower rates of submissive behaviors in boys, although difficulties with the measurement of submissiveness inhibit a clear interpretation of those findings.

The nature of results related to boys' aggressive and assertive behavior suggests some support for the notion that preschool-age sons of depressed, low-SES mothers suppress not only some frustration-induced emotions but also behaviors that would promote their own interests or needs. This goes beyond the findings of Zahn-Waxler et al. (1984) who found 2-year-old sons of a more socioeconomically diverse group of depressed mothers to be more emotionally inhibited in the presence of frustration but no more aggressive toward an adult than control children. Although it is not possible to account for differences in boys' aggression across the two studies, the fact that we examined an older and more impoverished group of preschool children suggests the possibility that age and socioeconomic characteristics may mediate the effects of maternal depression on preschool-age boys' aggressive behaviors. Future studies will benefit from directly examining the relation between maternal depression and children's aggressive and assertive behavior across age and socioeconomic status levels.

That boys but not girls differed in rates of aggressive, assertive, and submissive behaviors as a function of specific maternal or sociofamilial characteristics is a finding that, although consistent with much prior reported literature, defies easy explanation. Rutter (1989) suggested that it may be misleading to characterize such findings as a "male vulnerability," suggesting that females may be equally susceptible to the effects of some yet-to-be-identified stressors or that females may manifest their distress in ways that have not so easily lent themselves to experimental investigation. For example, noting that most studies of children's responses to sociofamilial stress utilized school-age subject pools, Rutter (1989) speculated that females may in fact develop certain compensatory responses at a younger age and therefore demonstrate no appreciable behavioral changes during the time of empirical investigation. Continued mixed-sex studies of the relations among a variety of sociofamilial stressors and behavioral responses of preschoolers, as well as longitudinal studies investigating the development of stress responses over time, should shed more light on ways in which females are affected by stress in lower SES, disadvantaged environments.

These results should be interpreted cautiously because of several limitations of this study. First, the heterogeneity in SES levels displayed across the sample represents a potential factor that could have biased our results. Given the difficulties with descriptively and demographically defining poverty (Huston, 1991; Liberatos et al., 1988), we chose to include families attending a pediatric primary care clinic serving an inner-city, indigent population, despite some variability across our SES measure. It should be noted, however, that over three fourths of our families were within the lower two SES strata on the Hollingshead index and the majority of the mothers were unemployed, receiving AFDC and on state medical assistance. The absence of a statistically significant relation between SES levels and our outcome variables further suggests that the impact of maintaining our original sampling frame may have minimally affected our results. Second, although we detected several statistically significant interaction effects, relatively small amounts of variance were accounted for in the children's observable behavior. It is likely that other sociofamilial stressors as well as specific observable parenting behaviors are important variables that also predict preschoolers' behavior. Interactions between different forms of maternal distress and child sex likely represent only one set of factors among many within the context of poverty and social disadvantage that affect children's development. Finally, the cross-sectional methodology employed in this study prevents us from making any inferences regarding causal associations between parental characteristics and preschoolers' behavior. Longitudinal methodologies are clearly needed in this area to understand the ultimate impact of maternal distress and child's sex on the development of aggressive, assertive, and submissive behavior in preschool children from disadvantaged families.

References

Abidin, R. R. (1990). *Parenting Stress Index manual.* Charlottesville, Virginia: Pediatric Psychology Press.

Achenbach, T. M., & Edelbrock, C. S. (1983). *Manual for the Child Behavior Checklist and the Revised Child Behavior Profile.* Burlington, VT: University Associates in Psychiatry.

Beck, A. T., Steer, R. A., & Garbin, M. G. (1988). Psychometric properties of the Beck Depression Inventory: Twenty-five years of evaluation. *Clinical Psychology Review, 8,* 77–100.

Beck, A. T., Ward, C. H., Mendelson, M. M., Mock, J., & Erbaugh, J. (1961). An inventory for measuring depression. *Archives of General Psychiatry, 4,* 561–571.

Campbell, S. B. (1990). *Behavior problems in preschool children.* New York: Guilford.

Campbell, S. B., Breaux, A. M., Ewing, J. L., & Szumowski, E. K. (1986). Correlations and predictors of hyperactivity and aggression: A longitudinal study of parent-referred problem preschoolers. *Journal of Abnormal Child Psychology, 14,* 217–234.

Cohen, J., & Cohen, P. (1983). *Applied multiple regression/correlation analysis for the behavioral sciences* (2nd ed.). Hillsdale, NJ: Lawrence Erlbaum Associates, Inc.

Crockenberg, S., & Litman, C. (1990). Autonomy as competence in 2 year olds: Maternal correlates of child defiance, compliance, and self assertion. *Developmental Psychopathology, 26,* 961–971.

Deluty, R. H. (1985). Consistency of assertive, aggressive, and submissive behavior for children. *Journal of Personality and Social Psychology, 49,* 1054–1065.

Farrington, D. P. (1989). Early predictors of adolescent aggression and adult violence. *Violence and Victims, 4,* 79–99.

Garmezy, N., & Tellegen, A. (1984). Studies of stress resistant children: Methods, variables, and preliminary findings. In F. Morrison, C. Lord, & D. Keating (Eds.), *Advances in applied developmental psychology* (Vol. 1, pp. 231–287). New York: Academic.

Gelfand, D. M., & Hartmann, D. P. (1984). Reliability. In D. M. Gelfand & D. P. Hartmann (Eds.), *Child behavior analysis and therapy* (pp. 168–187). New York: Pergamon.

Gould, M. (1982). A psychometric investigation of the standard and short form Beck Depression Inventory. *Psychological Reports, 51,* 1167–1170.

Hollingshead, A. B. (1975). *Four-Factor Index of Social Status.* Unpublished manuscript, Yale University, Department of Sociology, New Haven, CT.

Huston, A. C. (Ed.). (1991). *Children in poverty.* New York: Cambridge University Press.

Liberatos, P., Link, B. G., & Kelsey, J. L. (1988). The measurement of social class in epidemiology. *Epidemiologic Reviews, 10,* 87–121.

McCubbin, H. M., & Patterson, J. (1981). *Family Inventory of Life Events (FILE).* Madison: University of Wisconsin Press.

McCubbin, H. M., & Thompson, A. (1991). *Family assessment inventories for research and practice* (2nd ed.). Madison: University of Wisconsin, Family Stress, Coping, and Health Project.

McLoyd, V. (1990). The impact of economic hardship on black families and children: Psychological distress, parenting, and socioemotional development. *Child Development, 61,* 311–346.

Offord, D. R. (1989). Conduct disorder: Risk factors and prevention. In D. Shaffer (Ed.), *Prevention of mental disorders, alcohol, and other drug use in children and adolescents* (pp. 273–307). Rockville, MD: Office of Substance Abuse Prevention.

Offord, D. R., Alder, R. J., & Boyle, M. H. (1986). Prevalence and sociodemographic correlates of conduct disorder. *American Journal of Social Psychiatry, 6,* 272–278.

Rutter, M. (1988). Epidemiological approaches to developmental psychopathology. *Archives of General Psychiatry, 45,* 486–495.

Rutter, M. (1989). Isle of Wight revisited: Twenty-five years of child psychiatric epidemiology. *Journal of the American Academy of Child and Adolescent Psychiatry, 28,* 633–653.

Rutter, M., & Giller, H. (1983). *Juvenile delinquency: Trends and perspectives.* New York: Penguin.

Siegel, J. M. (1986). Multidimensional Anger Inventory. *Journal of Personality and Social Psychology, 51,* 191–200.

Stevenson, J., Richman, N., & Graham, P. (1985). Behavior problems and language abilities at three years and behavioral deviance at eight years. *Journal of Child Psychology and Psychiatry, 26,* 215–230.

Zahn-Waxler, C., McKnew, D. H., Cummings, E. M., Davenport, Y. B., & Radke-Yarrow, M. (1984). Problem behaviors and peer interactions of young children with a manic-depressive parent. *American Journal of Psychiatry, 141,* 236–240.

Received August 16, 1993
Final revision received February 25, 1994

Journal of Clinical Child Psychology
1994, Vol. 23, 391–400

Neighborhood Disadvantage, Stressful Life Events, and Adjustment in Urban Elementary-School Children

Beth K. Attar, Nancy G. Guerra, and Patrick H. Tolan
University of Illinois at Chicago

Assessed the occurrence of three types of stressful life events among African-American and Hispanic children living in urban neighborhoods, and examined the concurrent and prospective relations between stressful life events and adjustment. Younger children and children living in the most disadvantaged neighborhoods experienced more stressful life events. Stressful life events were significantly related to higher concurrent levels of aggression and predicted increases in aggression 1 year later. Life transitions and exposure to violence predicted concurrent aggression, but circumscribed events served as the strongest predictor of aggression 1 year later. Total number of stressful events and exposure to violence significantly interacted with neighborhood disadvantage, such that effects were only apparent under conditions of high neighborhood disadvantage.

Over the past two decades there has been much interest in the relation between exposure to stress and emotional and behavioral maladjustment in children and youth. In general, cumulative exposure to stressors is predictive of a range of adjustment problems, although the relations are somewhat modest in size (for reviews, see Compas, 1987; Johnson, 1986). Many of the studies of the stress–adjustment relation can be classified into one of two groups: (a) those focusing on the role of chronic stressors and (b) those examining the impact of discrete stressful life events.

Chronic stressors are ongoing and persistent. One type of chronic stress that has been investigated in relation to children's development is *neighborhood disadvantage* (ND), as determined by the presence of a number of community-level stressors such as poverty, unemployment or underemployment, limited resources, substandard housing, and high crime rates. Such stress is chronic, and affects all individuals in a given setting. For example, a person who earns above the national median income but lives in a disadvantaged neighborhood would experience ND effects (limited community resources, fear of crime, etc.) even though he or she would not be considered economically disadvantaged according to individual-level data. In the United States at this time, many urban communities are

characterized by high ND levels (Wilson, 1987). This type of chronic environmental stress also disproportionately affects members of ethnic minority groups, because they are overrepresented in urban communities.

Studies focusing primarily on the relation between ND within an urban context and psychological adjustment have found that children who face these high levels of hazardous environmental conditions are more likely than children growing up under more favorable circumstances to evidence a variety of behavioral and emotional difficulties (McLoyd, 1990; Wyman, Cowan, Work, & Parker, 1991). In the most extreme cases, it has been suggested that these environmental conditions contribute to psychological symptomatology, specifically posttraumatic stress disorder (Garbarino, Kostelny, & DuBrow, 1991).

In contrast to chronic stressors such as ND, discrete stressful life events occur at the level of an individual's immediate interpersonal context and include both *negative life events* and *daily hassles*. Negative life events can be differentiated further according to the type of readjustment they require. For example, Felner, Farber, and Primavera (1983) and Tolan, Miller, and Thomas (1988) have distinguished *circumscribed* or *discrete traumatic events* (e.g., death of a relative) from stressors associated with the onset of a *life transition* (e.g., parental divorce). Daily hassles are described as ongoing, daily frustrations and demands found in everyday situations (e.g., feeling pressured by friends, arguments with parents, or school demands). In studies examining the relative weightings of these different

This research was partially supported by National Institute of Mental Health Grant MH–48034.

We thank L. R. Huesmann for his assistance with the data analysis.

Requests for reprints should be sent to Nancy G. Guerra, Department of Psychology, University of Illinois at Chicago, P.O. Box 4348, MC 285, Chicago, IL 60680.

types of stressors, circumscribed events and life transitions are rated as more stressful than daily hassles (e.g., Tolan et al., 1988).

Experiencing several of major negative life events has been linked with a range of adjustment problems, including social withdrawal (Rutter, 1983), school adjustment problems (Pryor-Brown & Cohen, 1989), self-reported delinquency (Tolan, 1988; Vaux & Ruggerio; 1983), and psychological distress, including depression and anxiety (Compas, Howell, Phares, Williams, & Giunta, 1989; Dubois, Felner, Brand, Adan, & Evans, 1992; Wagner, Compas, & Howell, 1988). Similarly, several studies have found support for a relation between daily hassles and adjustment problems, even when the degree to which these hassles co-occur with negative life events is controlled (Rowlison & Felner, 1988).

In addition, research has pointed to the effects of multiple stressors on children's coping and adjustment. Studies have consistently found that the presence of one stressor is not sufficient to lead to pronounced maladjustment; rather, exposure to a combination of stressors is necessary for a child to develop serious emotional or behavioral problems (Forehand, Middleton, & Long, 1987; Garmezy, 1987; Rutter, 1989; Seifer & Sameroff, 1987). Furthermore, the effect is not additive, but multiplicative. As Garmezy (1987) pointed out, "Two risk factors . . . provided a four-fold increase in the likelihood of a psychiatric disorder; four factors increased the risk ten-fold" (p. 165).

If the effects of stressors are indeed multiplicative, then living under conditions of heightened ND should increase risk for all children, and particularly for children who also experience more stressful life events. As DuBois et al. (1992) noted, "Youth faced with these kinds of contextual conditions may well exhibit greater vulnerability to stressful events that occur in their lives than do youth in more resource-enriched environments" (p. 553). Yet, most investigations of the stress–adjustment relation have not disentangled the relations between chronic environmental stressors such as ND and stressful life events within a single study. It is therefore difficult to determine whether the effects of stressful life events on behavior vary in relation to differing ND levels.

The first aim of our research was to examine the occurrence of three types of negative life events among African-American and Hispanic elementary-school-age boys and girls living in urban communities characterized by varying levels of ND (high vs. moderate). In addition to circumscribed events and life transitions, children's observation of violent events was also of interest; thus, *exposure to violence* was identified as an additional category of stressful negative life events. It was expected that children in the high-environmental-stress condition would report experiencing more life transitions and circumscribed events and would report

witnessing more violence than children in the moderate-stress condition.

The second aim of this study was to examine the concurrent relations between ND level, negative life events, and two indices of psychological adjustment—aggression and depression/anxiety. It was predicted that there would be a positive relation between total number of stressful events and both aggression and depression/anxiety, and that this relation would be stronger under high-ND conditions. In addition, the relations between the three types of negative life events (transitions, circumscribed events, witnessing violence) on each measure of adjustment were of interest. Despite our current understanding of the impact of various stressful life events on adjustment, most studies generally have not examined the differential effects of specific types of stressful events vis-à-vis specific behavioral and emotional outcomes. In addition, many of the stress–adjustment studies have focused on depression/anxiety and have relied primarily on self-report measures of both stress and depression, raising concerns over common-method variance.

Related to the second aim, the study also sought to explore whether the stress–adjustment relation was moderated by sex, grade, and ethnicity. For instance, a child's behavioral response to stressful events may reflect an amplification of sex-stereotypic behaviors, whereby girls may be more likely to respond to stress with increased depression and anxiety and boys may be more likely to respond with increased aggression. Previous studies have, in fact, found sex differences in the types of behaviors coinciding with or follow the occurrence of stressful events. For example, following parental divorce, boys tend to exhibit more aggressive and acting-out behaviors than do girls (Hetherington, 1989). Generally, however, studies have not tested a link between age and ethnicity and the stress–adjustment relation.

Finally, the third aim of this study was to examine the relation of stress to subsequent aggression and school achievement. With some exceptions (e.g., Dubow, Tisak, Causey, Hryshko, & Reid, 1991), there have been few prospective studies of the relation between stress and behavioral adjustment in elementary-school children. Most prospective studies have sampled adolescents and have focused on depression/anxiety as an index of psychological adjustment, although school achievement has frequently been assessed. In general, long-term effects of stressors on these variables have been reported. For example, DuBois et al. (1992) found that major negative life events contributed significantly to the prediction of a subsequent decline in grade-point average and an increase in depression/anxiety among adolescents, even after controlling for initial levels of these variables. Little is known, however, about the longitudinal relations between stressful life events and aggression in children, and even less about this relation in the context of varying ND levels.

Method

Participants

The initial (Time 1) participants were 384 first-, second-, and fourth-grade African-American ($n = 220$) and Hispanic ($n = 164$; predominantly of Mexican descent) children from six schools in a large midwestern city. Because the stress–adjustment relation among ethnic minority children was of primary interest, and because there were relatively few nonminority children (approximately 12%), these nonminority children were not included in the present study. Participants were all African-American and Hispanic children from these grades in the six schools from classrooms where teachers had agreed to participate and for whom parental permission had been obtained (86%). As shown in Table 1, the sample was approximately equally divided between boys and girls, and approximately equally distributed across grade levels. All public schools in this particular city were considered as located in communities that were at least moderate in ND by virtue of citywide statistics on crime, income level, housing, and employment. For example, average city violent-crime rates were 10 times higher than for surrounding communities, and were the fourth highest in the United States (Federal Bureau of Investigation, 1990). Additionally, 25% of city residents receive some form of public aid (Illinois Department of Public Aid, 1992). Of the initial (Time 1) sample of 384 children, 1-year follow-up (Time 2) achievement data were available for 243 children (63% of original sample) and aggression data were available for 196 children (51% of original sample). Of the subjects who dropped out of the study between Time 1 and Time 2, approximately 20% had left their school and could not be located; data on the other subjects were unavailable due to teacher noncompliance in completing behavioral checklists and lack of comparable norms for the Spanish language achievement tests. According to *t* tests, subjects for whom achievement and aggression

data were available at both Time 1 and Time 2 did not differ significantly on initial levels of aggression from subjects who had dropped out after Time 1, although subjects who had dropped out were rated as significantly less anxious/depressed and reported fewer stressful life events at Time 1.

Measures and Assessment Procedures

Time 1 assessments were collected in the spring of 1991 and included self-report data on stressful life events, peer ratings of aggression, teacher ratings of aggression and depression/anxiety, and archival (academic achievement) data. The self-report and peer-nominated assessments were administered individually for first graders and in the child's regular classroom for second and fourth graders. Individual administration was conducted by one investigator, and classroom administration was conducted by one investigator and two monitors. All investigators and monitors were trained extensively in the assessment of children in urban settings. In both individual and group administrations, the investigator read each question aloud. For children who spoke only Spanish, all measures were translated and back-translated, and were administered by investigators who were native Spanish speakers. No difficulties in understanding the self-report or peer-nomination measures were noted. One year later (Time 2), in the spring of 1992, teacher ratings of aggression and archival (academic achievement) data were again collected.

Community data on indicators of chronic environmental stress were gathered from available school, census, and demographic records. There was initial concern that ethnicity and environmental stress would be confounded, with African-American children overrepresented in the highly disadvantaged communities (Wilson, 1987). However, because all schools were drawn from urban neighborhoods with a high concentration of lower-class and lower-middle-class minority families, the correlation between ethnicity and ND level was only moderate. Therefore, ethnicity was retained as a separate variable, although it is clear that ethnicity and community are not independent.

ND. Because almost all students in all schools lived in the adjacent neighborhoods, environmental stress was initially assessed from school data. A school was considered located in a *high-ND* setting if approximately two thirds of the children in the school received free lunch, and a school was considered located in a *moderate-ND* setting if fewer than one third of the students received free lunch. This procedure resulted in three schools being classified as high ND and three schools being classified as moderate ND.

ND level was confirmed with data on median family income, percentage of residents receiving public aid,

Table 1. *Demographic Distribution of Sample*

Race and Grade	Girls	Boys
African American		
First Grade	35	32
Second Grade	31	35
Fourth Grade	39	48
Hispanic		
First Grade	28	19
Second Grade	30	32
Fourth Grade	33	22

type of housing (public housing vs. rentals and other private dwellings), number of abandoned buildings, and violent crime rates. According to these data, the three schools rated as high ND were located in neighborhoods with median family incomes ranging from $8,900 to $15,000 (Donnelly Marketing Information Services [DMIS], 1991). An average of 41% of the residents of these communities received some form of public aid (Illinois Department of Public Aid, 1992). Housing in these neighborhoods included high-rise and low-rise public housing developments and/or between 100 and 200 abandoned buildings (Chandler & Herrmann, 1992). These schools were also located in police districts where violent crime rates were at least 50% higher than citywide figures (Chicago Police Index [CPI], 1991).

The three schools considered to be moderate ND were located in neighborhoods with median family incomes at or above $25,000 (DMIS, 1991), with approximately 6% of residents receiving public aid. Housing in these neighborhoods typically consisted of rental apartments, condominiums, and two- and three-story single-family dwellings. There were fewer than 100 abandoned buildings in these neighborhoods (Chandler & Herrmann, 1992). These three schools were also located in police districts where the violent crime rate was at least 50% lower than the citywide average (CPI, 1991).

Stressful life events. The occurrence of such events was measured by the Stress Index, a 16-item self-report scale consisting of three subscales: Circumscribed Events (4 items), Life Transitions (6 items), and Exposure to Violence (6 items). Items for the circumscribed events and life transitions subscales were taken from the corresponding scales of the Social Stress Measure developed by Tolan et al. (1988). Items were selected from the two original scales of the Social Stress Measure if they had been rated by at least 85% of children as having a "negative" impact, did not describe an event which could possibly be confounded with child maladjustment (e.g., suspended from school), and were considered appropriate for urban, minority, elementary-school children. Exposure to Violence items were developed for the present study and included types of violent events most likely to be witnessed or experienced by school-age children. To reassess the classification of items into these three subscales, two independent raters categorized all items according to specified operational definitions, and 100% agreement was obtained. Children completed the index by indicating whether or not they had experienced each of the stressful events during the past year. The 16-item scale is presented in Table 2.

Peer-nominations of aggression. The Peer-Nominated Aggression Scale (Eron, Walder, & Lefkowitz,

Table 2. *Stress Index Items (and Subscale)*

During the last year:
1. Did your family move to a new home or apartment? (T)
2. Did your family's property get wrecked or damaged due to fire, burglary, or other disaster? (C)
3. Has anyone in your family gotten married? (T)
4. Has your family had a new baby come into the family? (T)
5. Has anyone moved out of your home? (T)
6. Did a family member die? (C)
7. Did another close relative or friend die? (C)
8. Has a family member become seriously ill, injured badly, and/or had to stay at the hospital? (C)
9. Has a family member been robbed or attacked? (V)
10. Has someone else you know, other than a member of your family, gotten beaten, attacked, or really hurt by others? (V)
11. Have you seen anyone beaten, shot, or really hurt by someone? (V)
12. Did you change where you went to school? (T)
13. Have you seen or been around people shooting guns? (V)
14. Did you have to go live in a foster home? (T)
15. Have you been afraid to go outside and play, or have your parents made you stay inside because of gangs or drugs in your neighborhood? (V)
16. Have you had to hide someplace because of shootings in your neighborhood? (V)

Note: T = Life Transitions; C = Circumscribed Events; V = Exposure to Violence.

1972) was used as a measure of children's aggression. This 10-item scale has been used for over 30 years with demonstrated reliability and validity for children of different socioeconomic and ethnic groups (Eron et al., 1972; Huesmann & Eron, 1986). In this procedure, each child is presented with a series of printed pages, each listing of all children in his or her classroom, with the names grouped by sex. The child is asked to circle every name that fits the question at the top of the page (e.g., "Who pushes and shoves other children?"). The investigator reads each question aloud and paces the child (children) so that exactly the same amount of time is spent on each question. A child's score is derived by taking the number of times the child is nominated by other children and dividing by the total number of times the child could have been nominated. Scores thus range from 0 to 1.

Teacher ratings of depression/anxiety and aggression. During the first wave of data collection (Time 1), teachers rated all permission children on the complete Child Behavior Checklist–Teacher Report Form (CBCL–TRF; Achenbach & Edelbrock, 1986). This reliable and well-validated measure contains a list of 118 behavior-problem items that the teacher rates on a 3-point scale ranging from *not true* (0) to *very true* (2). For the purposes of the current study, only the 17-item Depression scale, the 25-item Anxiety scale, and the 23-item Aggression scale were of interest. Because of the high intercorrelation between the Depression and Anxiety scales ($r = .87$), these two scales were averaged to form a Depression/Anxiety scale. Because peer nominations of aggression were also available at Time 1, they were used for analyses of Time 1 data in lieu of the teacher ratings in order to maximize the independence of ratings on the variables of interest. During the second wave of data collection, teacher ratings were obtained on the Aggression scale only. Due to unavailability of peer ratings of aggression at Time 2, both Time 1 and Time 2 teacher ratings were used in the prospective analyses.

Academic achievement. The Reading and Math scales of the Iowa Test of Basic Skills were used to measure academic achievement. Children's percentile scores on these two scales were averaged to yield a total achievement score.

Results

The results of this study are presented in three major sections. First, mean levels of stressors are reported by ND, sex, ethnicity, and grade. Next, cross-sectional relations among stressors and both peer-rated aggression and teacher-rated depression/anxiety are reported. Finally, the longitudinal relations between stressors and subsequent teacher-rated aggression and academic achievement are reported.

Exposure to Stressors

Means and standard deviations for total stress (all 16 items) and for the three subscales of the Stress Index are reported in Table 3. For each of the four dependent stress measures, a 2 (ND) $\times$ 2 (Sex) $\times$ 2 (Ethnicity) $\times$ 3 (Grade) analysis of variance was performed. Subse-quent to a significant main effect or interaction, post hoc comparisons were performed using a Bonferroni comparison test.

For total stress, significant main effects were revealed for ND, $F(1, 369) = 23.98$, $p < .001$, and grade, $F(2, 369) = 7.39$, $p < .001$. Children from schools in high-ND areas reported more stressors than children from schools in moderate-ND neighborhoods. Post hoc comparisons indicated that first graders reported significantly more total stress than did second graders ($p < .05$) and fourth graders ($p < .001$), and that second and fourth graders did not differ from each other. A significant Sex $\times$ Ethnicity interaction also was revealed, $F(1, 369) = 4.05$, $p < .05$. Post hoc comparisons indicated that African-American girls reported significantly more stressors ($M = 7.0$) than did any other group ($p < .05$), and the other groups did not differ significantly.

For the Life Transitions subscale, a significant ND $\times$ Grade interaction was revealed, $F(2, 369) = 3.11$, $p < .05$. Post hoc comparisons showed that among children attending schools in high-ND settings, first graders reported significantly more transitions than fourth graders ($p < .01$), and first and second graders did not differ in their exposure to transitions. Among children at schools in moderate-ND settings, there were no grade differences in the number of transitions experienced.

For the Circumscribed Events subscale, a main effect was revealed for ND, $F(1, 369) = 10.18$, $p < .01$. Children from schools in high-ND settings reported more circumscribed events than did children from schools in moderate-ND areas. No significant interactions were revealed.

For the Exposure to Violence subscale, a significant Sex $\times$ Grade interaction, $F(2, 369) = 3.18$, $p < .05$, and a Sex $\times$ ND interaction, $F(1, 369) = 3.90$, $p < .05$, were revealed. Post hoc comparisons for the Sex $\times$ Grade interaction indicated that first- and second-grade girls

Table 3. *Means and Standard Deviations for Children's Stress Exposure*

Group	Total Stress		Life Transitions		Circumscribed Events		Exposure to Violence	
	M	*SD*	*M*	*SD*	*M*	*SD*	*M*	*SD*
All Children	5.6	3.2	2.0	1.4	1.4	1.1	2.2	1.6
Neighborhood Disadvantage								
High ND	6.6	3.2	2.3	1.4	1.7	1.1	2.6	1.6
Moderate ND	4.3	2.6	1.7	1.2	1.1	1.0	1.6	1.4
Sex								
Girls	5.9	3.1	2.1	1.3	1.5	1.1	2.3	1.6
Boys	5.3	3.2	2.0	1.4	1.3	1.1	2.0	1.6
Ethnicity								
African Americans	6.5	3.2	2.2	1.4	1.7	1.1	2.6	1.6
Hispanics	4.5	2.7	1.8	1.3	1.1	1.0	1.6	1.4
Grade								
First	6.7	3.0	2.5	1.3	1.7	1.1	2.5	1.6
Second	5.4	3.4	2.0	1.4	1.3	1.1	2.1	1.6
Fourth	5.1	2.9	1.8	1.3	1.4	1.1	1.9	1.5

Note: Scores ranged from 0 to 16 for total stress, 0 to 6 for Life Transitions, 0 to 4 for Circumscribed Events, and 0 to 6 for Exposure to Violence.

reported significantly more exposure to violence than did fourth-grade boys ($p < .05$), with no other significant differences. Post hoc comparisons for the Sex × ND interaction indicated that boys in schools located in moderate-ND settings reported less exposure to violence than did girls in moderate-ND schools ($p < .05$) and children in high-ND areas ($p < .001$), whereas the other groups did not differ.

Cross-Sectional Relations Among Stressors and Adjustment

Prior to analyzing the relations between stressful life events and behavioral outcomes, the dependent variables were tested for normality. As expected for measures of behavior problems, the distribution of outcome variables was skewed. Thus, square-root transformations were applied to the dependent measures to provide a more normal distribution.

Intercorrelations were calculated among aggression, depression/anxiety, total stress, and the three stress subscales. Results are presented in Table 4. As expected, the Circumscribed Events, Transitions, and Exposure to Violence subscales of the Stress Index showed significant positive intercorrelations. In addition, total stress, Life Transitions, and Exposure to Violence were significantly positively correlated with aggression. None of the stress indices correlated with depression/anxiety, although depression/anxiety correlated significantly with aggression.

Next, multivariate linear models were used to determine the relations between stressful life events and both aggression and depression/anxiety. Four separate multivariate models were used, for total stress, Life Transitions, Circumscribed Events, and Exposure to Violence. For each analysis, the main effects of the stressor variable, sex, grade, ethnicity, and ND, and the separate interactions of stress with sex, grade, ethnicity, and ND were entered into the equation, with aggression and depression/anxiety as criterion variables. As the main effects for the stress scales and the interactions between stress and the demographic variables were the

primary interest of this study, only these results are reported.

The multivariate analyses were significant for: total stress, $F(2, 348) = 6.42$, $p < .01$; Life Transitions, $F(2, 348) = 7.40$, $p < .01$; and Exposure to Violence, $F(2, 348) = 7.09$, $p < .001$. Multivariate analyses also revealed significant interactions between total stress and ethnicity, $F(2, 348) = 3.49$, $p < .05$, and between total stress and ND, $F(2, 348) = 4.63$, $p < .01$. Similarly, there were significant interactions between Life Transitions and ethnicity, $F(2, 348) = 3.75$, $p < .05$, and between Life Transitions and ND, $F(2, 348) = 3.39$, $p < .05$. Finally, a significant interaction was revealed between Exposure to Violence and ND, $F(2, 348) = 4.32$, $p < .01$.

F values for univariate analyses are reported in Table 5. For aggression, significant main effects were revealed for total stress, Life Transitions, and Exposure to Violence. The regression weights showed that stress and aggression were positively related. There were also significant interactions between ND and both total stress and Exposure to Violence. Interactions were interpreted by performing separate Pearson product–moment correlations between the stress subscales and aggression for each group, followed by Bonferroni corrections to demonstrate significance. Results revealed that the relation between total stress and aggression was significant only for children living in high-ND communities ($r = .35$, $p < .001$). Similarly, for Exposure to Violence, Bonferroni-adjusted correlations indicated that this relation was significant only for children living in high-ND areas ($r = .32$, $p < .001$).

For depression/anxiety, no significant main effects were revealed, although there were significant interactions between ND and both total stress and Life Transitions, and between ethnicity and total stress and Life Transitions. However, interpretation of these interactions by Bonferroni-adjusted Pearson correlations revealed that the relations between total stress, Life Transitions, and depression/anxiety did not reach significance for children from either moderate- or high-ND communities or for African-American or Hispanic children.

Table 4. *Intercorrelations Among Stress and Adjustment Variables at Time 1*

	2	3	4	5	6
Stress					
1. Total Stress	.76**	.74**	.83**	.24**	.04
2. Life Transitions		.38**	.39**	.18*	.03
3. Circumscribed Events			.46**	.15	.00
4. Exposure to Violence				.22**	.05
Adjustment					
5. Peer-Rated Aggression					.23**
6. Teacher-Rated Depression/Anxiety					

*$p < .01$. **$p < .001$.

Table 5. *F Values of Univariate Analyses Examining the Relations Between Stress and Adjustment at Time 1*

Main Effects and Interaction Terms	Peer-Rated Aggression	Teacher-Rated Depression/ Anxiety
Total Stress	12.32***	2.07
Total Stress × Sex	0.05	3.83
Total Stress × Grade	1.32	2.65
Total Stress × Ethnicity	1.60	6.41*
Total Stress × ND[a]	6.16*	4.97*
Life Transitions	7.40**	0.64
Transitions × Sex	0.94	2.51
Transitions × Grade	2.33	0.47
Transitions × Ethnicity	0.06	7.37**
Transitions × ND	1.19	6.46**
Circumscribed Events	3.73	0.10
Events × Sex	1.08	1.24
Events × Grade	2.05	2.35
Events × Ethnicity	0.05	1.01
Events × ND	2.12	1.86
Exposure to Violence	12.87***	3.45
Violence × Sex	0.86	2.73
Violence × Grade	0.69	1.58
Violence × Ethnicity	3.74	3.54
Violence × ND	8.19**	1.53

[a]ND = Neighborhood Disadvantage.
*$p < .05.$ **$p < .01.$ ***$p < .001.$

Table 6. *Hierarchical Multiple-Regression Analyses to Predict Subsequent (Time 2) Aggression*

Step	Independent Variable Entered	Beta	Increase in R^2
1	Time 1 Aggression	.39***	
2	Total Stress Controlling for Time 1 Aggression	.13*	.013
3	Transitions Controlling for Time 1 Aggression	−.01	.000
4	Circumscribed Events Controlling for Time 1 Aggression	.28**	.037
5	Exposure to Violence Controlling for Time 1 Aggression	.14*	.014

*$p < .05.$ **$p < .01.$ ***$p < .001.$

Prospective Relations Between Stress and Subsequent Aggression and Academic Achievement

Next, the relations of stress and teacher-rated aggression and academic achievement measured 1 year later were examined.

First, a set of separate hierarchical regression analyses were performed for total stress and each of the stress subscales in the prediction of Time 2 aggression. For each analysis, initial (Time 1) teacher-rated aggression,

Time 1 stress, and the interaction term were entered in order to determine the effect of stress on subsequent aggression while controlling for initial levels of the behavior.

As presented in Table 6, total stress, Circumscribed Events, and Exposure to Violence predicted subsequent aggression. After controlling for the effects of Time 1 aggression, total stress accounted for an additional 1.3% of the variance, Circumscribed Events accounted for an additional 3.7%, and Exposure to Violence accounted for an additional 1.4% of the variance in Time 2 aggression ratings.

An identical set of analyses were conducted to predict Time 2 academic achievement. As shown in Table 7, regression analyses predicting Time 2 academic achievement from Time 1 stress did not reach significance for total stress or for any of the three stress subscales.

Discussion

Stress Exposure in Urban Minority Children

This study examined the occurrence of stressful life events in African-American and Hispanic elementary school children living in areas of high and moderate ND. Children living in high-ND communities reported experiencing significantly more stressors during the preceding year than did children living in more moderate-ND communities, but even children in the moderate group reported experiencing a relatively high number of stressful events when compared to what had been documented in previous studies.

For example, in a study of predominantly Caucasian, middle-class, elementary-school children, Dubow et al. (1991) found that over a 1-year period, children experienced, on average, slightly more than 2 stressors (of

Table 7. *Hierarchical Multiple-Regression Analyses to Predict Subsequent (Time 2) Academic Achievement*

Step	Independent Variable Entered	Beta	Increase in R^2
1	Time 1 Achievement	.78*	
2	Total Stress Controlling for Time 1 Achievement	−.05	.000
3	Transitions Controlling for Time 1 Achievement	−.06	.000
4	Circumscribed Events Controlling for Time 1 Achievement	−.03	.000
5	Exposure to Violence Controlling for Time 1 Achievement	−.02	.000

*$p < .001.$

32 possible events listed). Yet, in our study, children in moderate ND communities reported experiencing more than 4 stressful life events of 16 possible choices, and children in high ND communities had experienced close to 7 of these stressors during the previous year. This finding is striking given the fact that prior studies, using measures with similar items, have found that children experience comparable numbers of stressors over their entire lifetimes (Work, Cowen, Parker, & Wyman, 1990).

Compared to these studies, these findings demonstrate that urban minority children are acutely exposed to a multitude of stressful life events, and that these stressors also increase with corresponding increases in chronic stressors such as ND. Each of the three types of stressful life events were more frequent in the high-ND communities, although in some cases only for younger children (life transitions). Of course, with respect to exposure to violence, it is not surprising that children in high-ND communities reported observing more violence, because ND is, in part, defined by higher communitywide crime rates. Still, this finding confirms that children are observing such violent behavior firsthand in their neighborhoods. With regard to life transitions and circumscribed events, it may be the case that limited community resources, weakened social supports, and high crime rates in the most distressed neighborhoods may additionally destabilize families, particularly families with young children. Thus, the fragile quality of life under highly stressful community conditions seems to portend more negative life events.

Stress and Adjustment

The relations between stressful life events and three indices of adjustment (aggression, depression/anxiety, and academic achievement) were measured both concurrently and prospectively. The differential effects on adjustment of three types of stressful life events—life transitions, circumscribed events, and observation of violence were also explored. Furthermore, we sought to determine whether the hypothesized relations obtained under varying ND levels. Drawing on research indicating that the effects of stressors are multiplicative, it was expected that children in high-ND communities would be more adversely affected by stressful events and would evidence corresponding decreases in adjustment.

Findings indicate that stressful life events in urban settings contribute significantly to children's aggressive behavior. Stressful life events were concurrently related to children's peer-nominated aggression and predicted increases in teacher-rated aggression 1 year later. Looking at the differential effects of different types of stressful life events, exposure to violence predicted both concurrent and prospective aggressive behavior. Interestingly, life transitions were related to concurrent but not future aggression, with circumscribed events seeming to exert their effects only over time. It may be that life transitions such as a move, a marriage, or a new baby, require short-term readjustments which only temporarily change behavior, whereas in contrast, circumscribed events, such as the death of a relative, are more traumatic and may portend more serious long-term consequences. It is also possible that results were affected by the relative ambiguity of valence of items in the Life Transitions subscale, whereas the Circumscribed Events items were more clearly negative. In any case, the total number of stressors did predict both concurrent and future aggression, providing support for the notion that the accumulation of stressors is particularly critical in determining maladjustment (Seifer & Sameroff, 1987).

In addition, these relations did not vary by sex, ethnicity, or grade. The lack of sex differences contrasts with findings from previous studies (e.g., Masten et al., 1988) that the relations between stress and various adjustment criteria differed between boys and girls. It may be that environmental variables are most critical in the link between stress exposure and aggression in urban communities. Perhaps, in the face of such persistent and extreme conditions, family relationships become strained, children become fearful of victimization, and opportunities for success through conventional channels are limited. Parental feelings of powerlessness and fears about child victimization may lead them to use more power-assertive and authoritarian parenting practices, which, in turn, may contribute to an increase in their children's aggressive behavior (McLoyd, 1990). Children may learn that being tough and aggressive both minimizes the emotional impact of persistent stressors and maximizes their ability to survive under difficult and extreme environmental conditions.

Consistent with this notion, in general, children living under high-ND conditions were most adversely affected by stressful events. In fact, the concurrent relation between stress and aggression, for both total number of stressors and Exposure to Violence scores, was significant only for children from high-ND communities. It appears that for children from high-ND areas, experiencing stressors and being exposed to violence contributes to aggressive behavior. Repeated observations of violence may serve both to promote internal standards of behavior accepting of violence (Huesmann, Guerra, Miller, & Zelli, 1992), and to direct one's efforts toward avoiding victimization. In fact, this interpretation is consistent with our findings that stress did not relate significantly to depression/anxiety. In an environment where resources are scarce and violence is pervasive, children might be discouraged from depressive or anxious reactions to stressful events, because children who cry or frighten easily would be less likely to achieve instrumental goals and could be easy targets for victimization by others.

Of course, the lack of a relation between stress and depression/anxiety is inconsistent with past research and should be interpreted cautiously. In this study, we used only concurrent teacher ratings, as opposed to child self-report of depression and anxiety. Considering the low rates of concordance between child and teacher reports (Achenbach & Edelbrock, 1989), particularly with regard to internalizing symptoms (Offord & Fleming, 1991), this finding may be related to the inherent limitations of others' reports of such symptoms. However, it is also possible that the relations obtained in past studies relying exclusively on self-report data of both stress and depression were inflated because of common-method variance.

The finding that stress was not related to symptoms of depression and anxiety might also be a consequence of the age range sampled, because past research linking stress and internalizing symptoms has been conducted with older children and adolescents (Compas et al., 1989; Larson & Ham, 1993; Mullins, Siegel, & Hodges, 1985). Because few studies have examined symptoms of depression and/or anxiety as related to stress in elementary-age children, future studies should address the influence of developmental level in moderating this relation.

It is clear that these results should be interpreted with caution. First, significant correlations between predictors and adjustment variables were low to modest, although in some cases (i.e., academic achievement), the stability of the criterion variable was exceedingly high ($r = .78$) and could have limited our ability to observe significant effects for stressors. This demonstrates the complex nature of these relations and that these variables tap into a small component of the etiology of child adjustment. In addition, as the Stress Index consisted of 16 items, this measure clearly did not assess the full range of potentially stressful events. Several events judged to be too sensitive were omitted from the scale, such as family drug use, arrest or imprisonment, parental job status, financial problems, and physical or sexual abuse. Had these and other events been included, stronger relations between stress and maladjustment may have been found.

Second, the cross-sectional analyses conducted here do not enable us to infer causal relations between stress and adjustment, nor do they indicate directionality. Still, because the stressful events examined in this study are largely independent of the child's functioning and represent recollections of events occurring during the previous 12 months, it is more appropriate to suggest that the experience of stressful life events contributes to aggressive behavior, rather than the opposite. This notion was supported by the prospective analyses,

which indicated that exposure to stressors predicted subsequent teacher-rated aggression. However, because the Time 2 analyses were based on a more highly stressed and depressed/anxious sample, results of the prospective analyses may have been biased in some fashion. Future studies should implement prospective longitudinal methods, which would be particularly valuable in advancing our knowledge of the developmental pathways and causal relations between stress and adjustment.

References

Achenbach, T. M., & Edelbrock, C. (1986). *Manual for the Teacher's Report Form and Teacher Version of the Child Behavior Profile.* Burlington: University of Vermont, Department of Psychiatry.

Achenbach, T. M., & Edelbrock, C. (1989). Diagnostic, taxonomic, and assessment issues. In T. H. Ollendick & M. Hersen (Eds.), *Handbook of child psychopathology* (2nd ed., pp. 53–69). New York: Plenum.

Chandler, S., & Herrmann, A. (1992, November 22). Battling neighborhood blight: Empty homes hurt stability, neighbors say. *Chicago Sun-Times*, p. 3.

Chicago Police Department. (1991). Crime index. Chicago: Author.

Compas, B. E. (1987). Coping with stress during childhood and adolescence. *Psychological Bulletin, 101,* 393–403.

Compas, B. E., Howell, D. C., Phares, V., Williams, R. A., & Giunta, C. T. (1989). Risk factors for emotional/behavioral problems in young adolescents: A prospective analysis of adolescent and parental stress and symptoms. *Journal of Consulting and Clinical Psychology, 57,* 732–740.

Donnelley Marketing Information Services. (1991). *Market profile analysis: Consumer and business demographic reports.* Chicago: Author.

Dubois, D. L., Felner, R. D., Brand, R. D., Adan, A. M., & Evans, E. G. (1992). A prospective study of life stress, social support, and adaptation in early adolescence. *Child Development, 53,* 542–557.

Dubow, E. F., Tisak, J., Causey, D., Hryshko, A., & Reid, G. (1991). A two-year longitudinal study of stressful life events, social support, and social problem-solving skills: Contributions to children's behavioral and academic adjustment. *Child Development, 62,* 583–599.

Eron, L. D., Walder, L. O., & Lefkowitz, M. M. (1972). *The learning of aggression in children.* Boston: Little, Brown.

Federal Bureau of Investigation. (1990). *Uniform crime reports.* Washington, DC: Author.

Felner, R. D., Farber, S. S., & Primavera, J. (1983). Transitions and stressful life events: A model for primary prevention. In R. D. Felner, L. A. Jason, J. N. Moritsugu, & S. S. Farber (Eds.), *Preventive psychology: Theory, research and practice* (pp. 199–215). New York: Pergamon.

Forehand, R., Middleton, L., & Long, N. (1987). Adolescent functioning as a consequence of recent parental divorce and the parent–adolescent relationship. *Journal of Applied Developmental Psychology, 8,* 305–315.

Garbarino, J., Kostelny, K., & Dubrow, N. (1991). What children can tell us about living in danger. *American Psychologist, 46,* 376–382.

Garmezy, N. (1987). Stress, competence, and development: Continuities in the study of schizophrenic adults, children vulnerable to psychopathology, and the search for stress-resistant children. *American Journal of Orthopsychiatry, 57,* 159–174.

Hetherington, E. M. (1989). Coping with family transitions: Winners, losers, and survivors. *Child Development, 60,* 1–14.

Huesmann, L. R., & Eron, L. D. (Eds.). (1986). *Television and the aggressive child: A cross-national comparison.* Hillsdale, NJ: Lawrence Erlbaum Associates, Inc.

Huesmann, L. R., Guerra, N. G., Miller, L., & Zelli, A. (1992). The role of social norms in the development of aggressive behavior. In A. Fraczek & H. Zumkley (Eds.), *Socialization and aggression* (pp. 139–152). New York: Springer-Verlag.

Illinois Department of Public Aid. (1992). [Data on public aid recipients]. Unpublished raw data.

Johnson, J. H. (1986). *Life events as stressors in childhood and adolescence.* Newbury Park, CA: Sage.

Larson, R., & Ham, M. (1993). Stress and "Storm and Stress" in early adolescence: The relationship of negative events with dysphoric affect. *Developmental Psychology, 29,* 130–140.

Masten, A. S., Garmezy, N., Tellegen, A., Pellegrini, D. S., Larkin, K., & Larsen, A. (1988). Competence and stress in school children: The moderating effects of individual and family qualities. *Journal of Child Psychology and Psychiatry, 29,* 745–764.

McLoyd, V. C. (1990). The impact of economic hardship on Black families and children: Psychological distress, parenting, and socioemotional development. *Child Development, 61,* 311–346.

Mullins, L. L., Siegel, L. J., & Hodges, K. (1985). Cognitive problem-solving and life event correlates of depressive symptoms in children. *Journal of Abnormal Child Psychology, 13,* 305–314.

Offord, D. R., & Fleming, J. E. (1991). Epidemiology. In M. Lewis (Ed.), *Child and adolescent psychiatry: A comprehensive textbook* (pp. 1156–1168). Baltimore: Williams & Wilkins.

Pryor-Brown, L., & Cowen, E. L. (1989). Stressful life events, support, and children's school adjustment. *Journal of Clinical Child Psychology, 18,* 214–220.

Rowlison, R., & Felner, R. D. (1988). Major life events, hassles, and adaptation in adolescence: Confounding in the conceptualization and measurement of life stress and adjustment revisited. *Journal of Personality and Social Psychology, 55,* 432–444.

Rutter, M. (1983). Stress, coping, and development: Some issues and some questions. In N. Garmezy & M. Rutter (Eds.), *Stress, coping, and development in children* (pp. 1–42). New York: McGraw-Hill.

Rutter, M. (1989). Psychiatric disorder in parents as a risk factor for children. In D. Schaffer, I. Philips, & N. B. Enzer (Eds.), *Prevention of mental disorders, alcohol and other drug use in children and adolescents* (OSAP Prevention Monograph No. 2, DHHS Publication No. ADM 89–1646). Washington, DC: U.S. Government Printing Office.

Seifer, R., & Sameroff, A. J. (1987). Multiple determinants of risk and vulnerability. In E. J. Anthony & B. J. Cohler (Eds.), *The invulnerable child* (pp. 51–69). New York: Guilford.

Tolan, P. H. (1988). Socioeconomic, family, and social stress correlates of adolescent antisocial and delinquent behavior. *Journal of Abnormal Child Psychology, 16,* 317–331.

Tolan, P. H., Miller, L., & Thomas, P. J. (1988). Perceptions and experience of types of social stress and self-image among adolescents. *Journal of Youth and Adolescence, 17,* 147–163.

Vaux, A., & Ruggerio, M. (1983). Stressful life change and delinquent behavior. *American Journal of Community Psychology, 11,* 169–183.

Wagner, B. M., Compas, B. E., & Howell, D. C. (1988). Daily and major life events: A test of an integrative model of psychosocial stress. *American Journal of Community Psychology, 16,* 189–205.

Wilson, W. J. (1987). *The truly disadvantaged: The inner city, the underclass, and public policy.* Chicago: University of Chicago Press.

Work, W. C., Cowen, E. L., Parker, G. R., & Wyman, P. A. (1990). Stress resilient children in an urban setting. *Journal of Primary Prevention, 11,* 3–18.

Wyman, P. A., Cowen, E. L., Work, W. C., & Parker, G. R. (1991). Developmental and family milieu correlates of resilience in urban children who have experienced major life stress. *American Journal of Community Psychology, 19,* 405–426.

Received August 17, 1993
Final revision received February 25, 1994

Journal of Clinical Child Psychology
1994, Vol. 23, 401–412

Effects of Poverty and Quality of the Home Environment on Changes in the Academic and Behavioral Adjustment of Elementary School-Age Children

Eric F. Dubow and Maria F. Ippolito
Bowling Green State University

Examined the effects of poverty and the quality of the home environment on changes in the academic and behavioral adjustment of elementary school-age children. Analyses are based on a subset of children (n = 473) from a national data set. The children completed an academic achievement measure in 1986 (when they were 5 to 8 years old) and again in 1990. Mothers provided ratings of their children's behavior at the same time points. Results showed that prior poverty status (number of years in poverty from 1982 to 1985) predicted decreases in math and reading scores and increases in antisocial behavior (from 1986 to 1990). However, number of years in poverty between the 1986 assessment and the 1990 assessment failed to predict changes in adjustment over and above prior poverty status. Quality of the home environment between the two assessments predicted positive changes in adjustment after accounting for poverty status. These effects were independent of child characteristics (i.e., sex, age, and race) and relevant family background/demographic risk factors that are associated with poverty (i.e., number of children at home, presence of a father figure, mother's age at child's birth, and mother's education).

The rate of child poverty is higher in the United States than in any other industrialized country (Jones-Wilson, 1991). By 1989, 39.5% of America's poor were children (Jones-Wilson, 1991), with the poverty rate among American children increasing from 20.6% in 1990 to 21.8% in 1991. Thus, 900,000 children joined the ranks of the poor in 1991, bringing the total number of American children living in poverty to 14.3 million (Strawn, 1992). Furthermore, it has been projected that, by the year 2000, the proportion of American children living in poverty will increase to one in three (Jones-Wilson, 1991). Given the growing number of impoverished children and the reduced "safety net" of government support services (Strawn, 1992), research designed to pinpoint the optimal timing of intervention and identify factors that moderate the devastating effects of child poverty is of critical importance.

The focus of this study is the relation between parental poverty status and children's academic achievement and behavior problems. In particular, we examined whether the following variables contribute to predicting changes in children's academic and behav-

ioral adjustment during the elementary-school years: (a) poverty status during the 4 years prior to the initial assessment of academic and behavioral functioning (i.e., poverty status primarily during the toddler and preschool years), (b) poverty status during the 4 years between the two assessments of academic and behavioral functioning (i.e., poverty status primarily during the elementary school years), and (c) the quality of the home environment. In addition, we assessed the contributions of a number of variables generally associated with poverty. Specifically, we included the following: (a) maternal age at the time of the child's birth, because teenage pregnancy has been found to be associated with impoverishment (Dubow & Luster, 1990; Jens & Gordon, 1991); (b) the presence of a spouse or partner in the home, because single parenthood has frequently been found to be a significant correlate of poverty (Blum, Boyle, & Offord, 1988; Coulton & Pandey, 1992; Entwisle & Alexander, 1992; Garbarino, 1992; Jens & Gordon, 1991; Ledingham & Crombie, 1988; Rycraft, 1990); (c) the number of other children under 18 years old living in the home, because number of siblings has been found to be associated with poverty status (Jens & Gordon, 1991); (d) level of maternal education, because lower educational attainment by parents has been variously associated with low socioeconomic status (SES; Garbardino, 1992; Wilson & Matheny, 1983); and (e) deficits in children's academic

We gratefully acknowledge the suggestions of three anonymous reviewers who commented on an earlier version of this article.

Requests for reprints should be sent to Eric F. Dubow, Department of Psychology, Bowling Green State University, Bowling Green, OH 43403–0228.

achievement (Coulton & Pandey, 1992; Ninio, 1990) and mental development (Wilson & Matheny, 1983). Thus, because poverty is clearly more complex than family income level, we attempted to examine simultaneously the effects of poverty and these additional family variables that often occur in the context of poverty.

Economic Status, Academic Achievement, and Behavioral Problems

The relation between parental SES and children's academic achievement is well documented. As the result of a meta-analysis of 200 studies of SES as a correlate of individual academic achievement, White (1982) concluded that the median correlation between SES and academic achievement was relatively weak (r = .22). However, White (1982) qualified this conclusion, calling attention to the varying definitions of SES (e.g., parental income, education, and occupation) used across studies. He found income to be the "highest single correlate of academic achievement . . . [and] that measures of SES that combine two or more indicators are more highly correlated with academic achievement than any single indicator" (p. 470). Of note is the fact that we utilized the dichotomous variable of poverty status as the index of SES deprivation. However, the dichotomous variable of poverty status, as utilized here, is summed over several years and is based on a number of indicators, such as total net family income (including the value of noncash assistance, e.g., food stamps), family size, and state of residence (Center for Human Resource Research [CHHR], 1992).

Of particular interest with regard to the relation between SES and achievement is Wilson and Matheny's (1983) longitudinal study of twins. In this study, SES (based on head-of-household occupation) did not contribute significantly to variation in mental ability (as measured by the Bayley Scales of Infant Development; Bayley, 1969) at 6 months. However, by 24 months and at 3 and 6 years of age, SES significantly predicted mental ability (as measured by the Bayley Scales of Infant Development, McCarthy Scales of Children's Abilities, and the Wechsler Preschool and Primary Scales of Intelligence, respectively; McCarthy, 1972; Wechsler, 1967). Seifer and Sameroff (1987), Laosa (1984), and Church and Katigbak (1991) also reported significant relations between SES and mental ability for urban preschoolers, Hispanic toddlers, and Philippine preschoolers, respectively.

With regard to school-age children, SES and grade point average (Masten, Garmezy, Tellegen, Pellegrini, Larkin, & Larsen, 1988), SES and reading and math achievement (Hare, 1980), SES and mathematics achievement test scores (Entwisle & Alexander, 1992), and SES and academic achievement (Cherian, 1991) were found to be significantly related. And, in a 2-year study of all California high schools, Fetler (1989) found a significant negative correlation between receipt of Aid to Families with Dependent Children funds and academic achievement.

A number of researchers acknowledged the potential role of inherited mental ability in determining scholastic achievement and controlled for the effects of parental IQ and education (Bergeman & Plomin, 1988; Bradley et al., 1989; Church & Katigbak, 1991; Entwisle & Alexander, 1992; Laosa, 1984; Norman & Breznitz, 1992; Wilson & Matheny, 1983). In addition, Bell, Aftansas, and Abrahamson (1976) matched their low- and middle-SES subjects on IQ and sex. Nevertheless, low-SES children scored significantly below middle-SES children on a measure of school readiness administered prior to first-grade entry. These low-SES children later scored significantly lower on reading and mathematics achievement tests administered at the end of the first school year, even when the school readiness differences were removed via covariation. Norman and Breznitz (1992) also matched their first-grade subjects on IQ and assessed achievement using standardized reading and arithmetic tests. They found that low-SES students' performance was significantly inferior to the performance of high-SES students with regard to both measures of achievement.

There is a dearth of empirical studies of the interrelation between SES and child behavior problems. However, SES and behavior problems (measured by the Revised Behavior Problem Checklist; Quay & Peterson, 1983) were found to be significantly correlated in kindergarten children (Morrison, Mantzicopoulos, & Carte, 1989). In addition, after a review of studies of academic underachievement and behavior problems conducted from 1975 to 1991, Hinshaw (1992) concluded that "aggressive and conduct-disordered behavior is associated with SES" (p. 147) in preadolescents. Also pertinent is Achenbach, Howell, Quay, and Conners's (1991) study of problems and competencies, which sampled 5,200 children between 4 and 16 years old across geographic regions, ethnicity, and SES. SES significantly predicted behavior problems (although the authors pointed out that SES accounted for only a small amount of the variation in behavior scores). Furthermore, when behavior rating scores were trichotomized, the proportion of children with clinically high levels of behavior problems was significantly greater in families receiving various forms of public assistance (e.g., Aid to Families with Dependent Children; Aid for Women, Infants, and Children; and food stamps).

Contribution of Quality of Home Environment

According to Greaney (1986), "Conventional measures of home background, such as SES, underestimate the effects of home on the child's mental and scholastic development. These measures tend to focus on what parents *are* and not on what they *do*" (p. 814).

As the result of a meta-analysis, White (1982) concluded that "measures of home atmosphere . . . account for from 4 to 11 times as much of the variation in academic achievement as do traditional measures of SES" (p. 470).

The preponderance of research assessing the impact of children's home environment targets preschool children and focuses primarily on the relation between adequacy of home environment and mental development (Bergeman & Plomin, 1988; Bradley & Caldwell, 1984; Bradley, Caldwell, & Elardo, 1977; Bradley, Caldwell, Rock, & Harris, 1986; Bradley et al., 1989; Church & Katigbak, 1991; Luster & Dubow, 1992; Portes, 1991; Richter & Grieve, 1991). Share, Jorm, Maclean, Matthews, and Waterman (1983) found that the reading achievement and oral language abilities of children at the time of school entry were associated with home educational processes (e.g., as parents reading to children, parents reading for recreation, library usage, number of books owned by the child, and amount of television viewing). Wilson and Matheny (1983) found that the contribution of adequacy of home environment (based on maternal interviews and direct observation) steadily increased starting at the first time of measurement (6 months) such that, by 6 years of age, adequacy of home environment contributed significantly to mental development (assessed by the Wechsler Preschool and Primary Scales of Intelligence; Wechsler, 1967), even when maternal cognitive ability, temperament, social-affect ratings, and parents' education were also considered. In Ninio's (1990) longitudinal study, second-grade reading comprehension and arithmetic scores were significantly predicted by environmental opportunities (e.g., availability of books, toys, and freedom of exploration in the home) after SES and number of children in the home had been statistically controlled. Parenting quality (assessed via maternal interviews) also significantly predicted grade point average in elementary school children with SES partialled out (Masten et al., 1988). Dubow and Luster (1990) found that the Emotional Support and Cognitive Stimulation scales of the Home Observation for Measurement of the Environment (HOME; Caldwell & Bradley, 1984), a combined interview/observational assessment of the quality of the home environment including the quality of parenting, significantly predicted behavior problems in general and antisocial behavior in particular, as well as reading and math achievement. Dubow and Luster reported that, although the contribution of HOME scores was minimal when a number of risk factors (e.g., poverty, number of children in the home, maternal education, and self-esteem) and other protective factors (e.g., child's self-esteem and IQ) were also included, high HOME scores were significantly associated with higher levels of academic achievement and lower levels of behavior problems in at-risk children who were classified on the basis of exposure to environmental risk factors (e.g., poverty and low maternal education). Given the preceding research results, we expected that the quality of the home environment may contribute to predicting children's academic achievement and behavior problems over and above the effects of poverty.

Implications for Long-Term Effects of Poverty on Children's Adjustment

Longitudinal studies are necessary to assess the long-term impact of poverty on children's adjustment. Although a number of studies just cited were longitudinal in nature, they were generally of relatively short duration (1 to 2 years) and assessed parental SES on only one occasion (e.g., Bell et al., 1976; Bradley et al., 1989; Entwisle & Alexander, 1992). Also, these studies did not assess poverty status per se; rather, they included families of lower SES. Thus, the extent of long-term effects of being in poverty during the early years (toddlerhood and preschool age) on children's academic and behavioral adjustment during the elementary school years is unclear. In addition, what are the effects of continued poverty status during the elementary school years on changes in adjustment? Can a positive home environment during these years influence more positive outcomes even in the face of economic deprivation?

The National Longitudinal Survey of Youth (NLSY; CHHR, 1992)—with its oversampling of poor respondents across geographic regions, ethnicity, and age— provides a unique opportunity for an analysis of the prospective impact of poverty on children. In particular, the focus of our study is a preliminary examination of the impact of early chronic poverty and recent poverty on changes in children's academic and behavioral adjustment. We hope that answers to questions about the impact of poverty on children across time will highlight the importance of the timing of intervention to achieve the maximum impact. We feel that it is also important to examine factors that may contribute to positive adjustment, even in the context of poverty, to further inform intervention efforts. The NLSY project collected longitudinal data on the quality of the home environment, affording us the opportunity to examine the contributions of poverty and the home environment to predicting changes in elementary school children's adjustment.

Method

Subjects

This study is based on analyses of the merged mother–child data set of the NLSY (CHHR, 1992). The

NLSY included a national probability sample of 6,283 women between the ages of 14 to 21 who were initially interviewed in 1979; some degree of oversampling was shown to increase the size of poor and minority groups. Attempts were made to reinterview the women each year between 1979 and 1990. In addition, in 1986, 1988, and 1990, extensive data were collected about the psychological and academic functioning of the children of these women. By 1990, 4,180 (67%) of the women had given birth to 8,513 children (2.04 children per mother). In 1990, 88% of the mothers were interviewed, some data were available for 90% of the children, and 65% of the children were actually interviewed.

The focus of this article is on the effects of chronic poverty on the academic and behavioral adjustment of elementary school-age children. In 1986, the time of the first child assessment, 5-year-olds were administered an individual achievement test. Parents also completed a behavior rating scale for these children. These same academic and behavioral adjustment measures were also collected in 1990. Because we were interested in the effects of poverty on changes during these 4 years in elementary school-age children's adjustment, we included in our analyses children who were 5 to 8 years old in 1986. Most of these children would have been in elementary school between 1986 and 1990. The total sample of 5- to 8-year-olds in 1986 was 1,632. However, to be included in our analyses, it was necessary to collect poverty data from the mother every single year from 1983 to 1990. Thus, our analyses examine a subset of 473 children who met these criteria.

The two groups of subjects—the 473 children for whom there was complete poverty data and the 1,159 children who were omitted—were compared to determine if they differed substantially. With regard to race, 21% of the omitted group ($n = 1,159$) were Hispanic, 33% were African American, and 46% were members of other races; the comparative values for the included group ($n = 473$) were 13%, 38%, and 49%, respectively, suggesting that Hispanics were somewhat more likely to drop out of the longitudinal analyses. The percentages of boys and girls were identical in the included and omitted groups: 53% boys and 47% girls. Table 1 compares the two groups with respect to additional variables of interest.

Although many of the t tests assessing group differences in the variables listed in Table 1 were significant, an examination of the means reveals that these differences were quite modest. For example, Peabody Individual Achievement Tests (PIATs; Dunn & Markwardt, 1970) Math scores for the included group were approximately 2 points higher than those of the omitted group, and PIAT Reading Recognition scores for the included group were approximately 3 points higher than those of the omitted group, suggesting that the significant differences between the omitted and in-

cluded subjects were, for the most part, modest and attributable to the large sample sizes.

The distributions of the demographic characteristics of the sample included in our analyses reflect the oversampling of minority and poor respondents. As just noted, 51% of the sample were minorities (13% Hispanic and 38% African American), and approximately one third were living below the poverty line each year from 1982 to 1989. As to the mothers' characteristics, 25% did not complete high school by 1990, and 21% were under 18 when their children were born. For current (1990) living situation, 33% of the mothers had no spouse or partner living in the home, and 19% had four or more children.

The mean age of the 473 children in 1990 was 133.10 months ($SD = 13.36$, range = 111 to 162), and 53% of the children were boys. Compared to their peers in the general population, the children in this sample were in the normal range for math and reading achievement scores on the PIAT and slightly above the general population mean in terms of total behavior problems as assessed by the Behavior Problems Index (BPI; Peterson & Zill, 1986; see Table 1).

Measures

Poverty. For this study, poverty status is based on total net family income, including the value of noncash assistance such as food stamps, corrected for family size and state of residence (CHHR, 1992). For each year of the NLSY data collection, a poverty variable was created that indicates whether a family's poverty status during the past calendar year was above or below either official poverty income guidelines set by the U.S. Department of Health and Human Services or projected poverty income levels as computed by the CHHR (1992). We created two poverty scores for the purposes of this study. *Prior poverty* reflects the total number of years that the family was living below the poverty line from 1982 to 1985, the 4 years prior to the first child assessment in 1986. *Recent poverty* reflects the total number of years that the family was living below the poverty line from 1986 to 1989, the 4 years between the two child assessments. Scores for prior poverty and recent poverty each ranged from 0 to 4.

HOME. The HOME (Caldwell & Bradley, 1984) was used as an index of the quality of cognitive stimulation and emotional support provided in the home. Items tap aspects of the home environment such as maternal warmth and acceptance toward the child, organization of the environment, and provision of opportunities for learning and cultural experiences. This observation/interview instrument is reliable over time and predicts children's subsequent cognitive development (Bradley, 1982). Abbreviated versions of the

Table 1. *Comparative Means and Standard Deviations of Included and Omitted Subjects*

| | Subjects | | | | |
| | Included[a] | | Omitted[b] | | |
Variables	M	SD	M	SD	t
Demographic/Background Variables					
Mother's Age at Child's Birth	19.27	1.98	18.92	1.98	−3.24**
Mother's Age in 1990	30.40	1.91	30.11	1.95	−2.77**
Mother's Education as of 1990	11.86	1.77	11.16	2.14	−6.28**
Child's Age in 1990 (in Months)	133.10	13.36	134.00	13.66	1.20
Birth Order of Child	1.42	.69	1.49	.76	1.81
Years Spouse/Partner in Home[c]	2.66	1.70	2.33	1.67	−3.63**
Average Family Income[c]	25,900.41	29,760.91	22,775.92	38,459.95	−1.58
Children in Home[d]	2.57	1.09	2.64	1.34	.94
Child Variables					
1986 BPI[e] Antisocial	108.01	13.79	108.81	13.98	1.02
1990 BPI[e] Antisocial	109.00	13.23	110.15	14.61	1.34
1986 HOME[f] (Standardized)	.00	1.00	−.21	1.08	−3.53**
1990 HOME[f] (Standardized)	.00	1.00	−.28	1.06	−4.48**
1986 PIAT[g] Math	99.36	12.27	97.48	12.76	−2.62**
1990 PIAT[g] Math	97.27	13.03	95.55	13.60	−2.06*
1986 PIAT[g] Reading	106.02	11.65	103.65	12.92	−3.32**
1990 PIAT[g] Reading	101.97	14.55	98.50	15.45	−3.67**

[a] n = 473. [b] ns range from 578 to 1,159. [c] For the years 1987 to 1990. [d] Average number of other children under 18 living in the home for the years 1987 to 1990. [e] Behavior Problem Index (Peterson & Zill, 1986). [f] Home Observation for Measurement of the Environment (Caldwell & Bradley, 1984). [g] Peabody Individual Achievement Tests (Dunn & Markwardt, 1970).
*p < .05. **p < .01.

HOME (for children of different ages) were designed for the NLSY study in consultation with the original developers of the measure. Baker and Mott (1989) reported that the items from the HOME included in the shortened versions were selected based on reliability coefficients, discrimination indices, validity coefficients, and factor loadings from prior published and unpublished research. Three versions of the HOME were used in this study: the preschool version (for 5-year-olds), the younger elementary-aged version (for 6- to 9-year-olds), and the older children version (for 10- to 12-year-olds). There are 26 items on the preschool version and 27 items on the two other versions. Each item is scored as 0 (*indicating the absence of quality stimulation*) or 1 (*indicating the presence of quality stimulation*). Coefficient alphas (Baker, 1993) are as follows: .73 for the preschool version, .73 for the elementary school-age version, and .68 for the older children version. Note that these internal consistency estimates for the shortened versions of the HOME are somewhat lower than those of the original versions, which were in the .90s (e.g., Caldwell & Bradley, 1984), this may be due in part to the smaller number of items on the shortened versions.

Some similarities and differences among the three versions of the HOME should be noted. Like the original HOME inventories, the shortened versions include both observation and interview items. Identical or highly similar items across all versions deal with the organization of the physical environment (e.g., reason-ably clean, free from clutter, and not dark or perceptually monotonous), the emotional climate of the home (e.g., mother conveys positive feelings and use of physical punishment), and cognitively stimulating activities (e.g., access to books, trips to museums, and parent reads to child). Differences among the measures, however, reflect differences in developmental tasks. For example, the preschool version includes items dealing with teaching the child specific information (e.g., letter, colors, and numbers), whereas the two other versions include items dealing with the child's activities outside of the home (e.g., organizational memberships) and responsibilities in the home (e.g., self-care routines and cleaning his or her room). Scores for all versions are standardized with a mean of 100 and a standard deviation of 15. For the purposes of this study, we computed a composite HOME score to reflect the quality of the environment between 1986 and 1990 by standardizing the scores for each of these 2 years and summing these scores.

Academic achievement. We examined children's scores on the Math and Reading Recognition sections of the PIAT (Dunn & Markwardt, 1970). (The Reading Comprehension section was not examined due to the lower response rates for this measure.) Dunn and Markwardt presented adequate reliability and validity data for the PIAT on a national standardization sample. PIAT scores reported in this article are standard scores with a mean of 100 and a standard deviation of 15.

Behavioral adjustment. Mothers completed the 28-item BPI (Peterson & Zill, 1986). This 3-point scale was derived from Achenbach and Edelbrock's (1981) Child Behavior Checklist. Items represent problem behaviors such as antisocial behavior, hyperactivity, anxiety, and peer conflict. Mothers respond to each item using the following statements: *often true,* (1) *sometimes true* (2), or *not true* (3). Baker (1993) reported a coefficient alpha of .88 for the total score and alphas ranging from .57 to .71 across the subscales. In our study, we focus on the total score and the Antisocial Behavior Problems subscale ($\alpha = .67$). Total and subscale scores were standardized with a mean of 100 and a standard deviation of 15.

Results

Preliminary Analyses: Poverty and Its Correlates

First, we examined the distributions of the two poverty measures. Prior poverty reflects the number of years in which the family lived below the poverty line during the 4 years prior to the first child assessment in 1986: Results show that 47% were never below the poverty line; 13% were below the poverty line for only 1 year; 9% were below the poverty line for 2 years; 11% were below the poverty line for 3 years; and 20% were below the poverty line for all 4 years. Recent poverty reflects the number of years the family lived below the poverty line from 1986 to 1989, between the two child assessments: Results show that 52% were never below the poverty line; 12% were below the poverty line for only 1 year; 8% were below the poverty line for 2 years; 11% were below the poverty line for 3 years; and 17% were below the poverty line for all 4 years. The correlation between the number of years in poverty prior to and between the two assessments was $r = .79$, $p < .01$.

Next, we examined the zero-order correlations among the poverty scores, the quality of the home environment, and children's adjustment scores. Table 2 shows that the more years the family was below the poverty line either prior to or between assessments, the poorer the quality of cognitive stimulation and emotional support provided to the child ($rs = -.51$). In addition, the greater the number of years in poverty prior to the first child assessment in 1986, the lower the child's 1986 math and reading achievement scores, and the higher was the child's 1986 antisocial behavior score (absolute rs ranged from .20 to .23). Similarly, the greater the number of years between the 1986 and 1990 assessments that the family was living below the poverty line, the lower the child's 1990 math and reading achievement scores and the higher the child's 1990 antisocial behavior score (absolute rs ranged from .26 to .31). (Correlations of the poverty scores with BPI Total

Behavior Problems and all subscales of the BPI other than Antisocial Behavior Problems were generally below $r = .20$. Thus, for simplicity, these results are not included in Table 2. In addition, only the Total Behavior Problems score and the antisocial behavior score were retained for the subsequent regression analyses.)

Hierarchical Regressions Predicting Children's Adjustment From Poverty Scores and the Quality of the Home Environment

The major focus of this study was to examine the contributions of poverty and the quality of the home environment to predicting changes in children's academic and behavioral adjustment during the elementary school years. We examined math and reading academic achievement scores separately because they were only moderately related ($rs = .48$ in 1986 and .59 in 1990). We only examined Total Behavior Problems, and Antisocial Behavior Problems more specifically, because the other BPI subscales were weakly related to poverty. Thus, we computed four hierarchical regression equations, one predicting each 1990 adjustment measure.

In Step 1 of each regression equation, we entered the child's 1986 level of adjustment and the prior poverty score. Significant effects for prior poverty would demonstrate prospective effects of poverty on later changes in adjustment. In Step 2, we entered recent poverty scores (i.e., number of years in poverty between the 1986 and 1990 assessment) and the composite score for the quality of the home environment between 1986 and 1990. Significant effects for recent poverty scores would demonstrate the effects of continued poverty during the time between the two assessments on changes in adjustment during the same 4 years. Significant effects for the home environment measure would demonstrate the degree to which the quality of the home environment between assessments is associated with changes in adjustment during these 4 years. Finally, in Step 3, we entered the Recent Poverty × Home Environment interaction to examine whether the quality of the home environment may buffer the potential negative effects of recent poverty on changes in children's adjustment.

Table 3 shows the results for PIAT reading, math, and BPI antisocial behavior. In Step 1, initial adjustment scores and prior poverty accounted for 23% to 36% of the variance in later adjustment scores. The highly significant effects for initial adjustment reflect the relatively strong stability of academic and behavioral adjustment over 4 years. However, despite this stability, the number of years in poverty from 1982 to 1985 was significantly related to changes in adjustment between 1986 and 1990, likely illustrating the long-term debilitating effects of early poverty on the development of academic skills and positive social behavior. In Step 2, recent poverty and the quality of the home environment contributed modest (1% to 4%) but significant additional variance to predicting 1990 adjustment above and beyond initial adjustment and prior poverty. Recent poverty failed to add incremental variance in predicting changes in adjustment above and beyond the contribution of prior poverty. (The significant positive standardized beta weight for recent poverty in predicting PIAT Math achievement is due to a suppressor effect [see Cohen & Cohen, 1975]; as Table 2 shows, the zero-order correlation between recent poverty and 1990 PIAT Math is −.28.) However, the results show that a positive home environment between 1986 and 1990 is related to improvement in both math and reading achievement and decreases in antisocial behavior above and beyond the effects of initial adjustment and poverty.

In Step 3, the Recent Poverty × Home Environment interaction failed to account for more than 1% of the variance, so these results are not included in Table 3. Thus, there was no evidence that a positive home environment would help buffer the potentially negative effects of recent poverty on changes in adjustment. Rather, the significant main effects for home environment suggest that a cognitively stimulating and emotionally supportive home environment is associated with positive changes in adjustment irrespective of level of recent poverty. (Results of the hierarchical regression predicting total BPI scores are not presented in Table 3. The only significant effect was for initial Total Behavior Problems predicting later Total Behavior Problems. Neither the poverty scores nor the quality of the home environment contributed significant incremental variance to predicting changes in total behavior problems between 1986 and 1990.)

Table 2. *Correlations Among Poverty, Home Environment, and Adjustment Measures*

Variables	Variables							
	1	2	3	4	5	6	7	8
1. Prior Poverty[a]								
2. Recent Poverty[b]	.79*							
3. Home Environment[c]	−.51*	−.51*						
4. 1986 PIAT Math	−.23*	−.24*	.31*					
5. 1990 PIAT Math	−.34*	−.28*	.40*	.56*				
6. 1986 PIAT Reading	−.23*	−.21*	.24*	.48*	.48*			
7. 1990 PIAT Reading	−.31*	−.31*	.38*	.44*	.59*	.50*		
8. 1986 BPI Antisocial	.20*	.25*	−.30*	−.25*	−.26*	−.22*	−.24*	
9. 1990 BPI Antisocial	.19*	.26*	−.29*	−.17*	−.19*	−.13*	−.27*	.49*

[a]Number of years in poverty status from 1982 to 1985. [b]Number of years in poverty status from 1986 to 1989. [c]These scores are the sum of the standardized home environment scores based on the 1986 and 1990 assessments.
*p < .05.

Table 3. *Hierarchical Regressions Predicting Current Academic and Behavioral Adjustment From Prior Poverty, Recent Poverty, and Recent Quality of the Home Environment*

	Current Adjustment[a]					
	PIAT Math[b]		PIAT Reading[c]		BPI Antisocial[d]	
Predictors	Δ R²	β	Δ R²	β	Δ R²	β
Step 1						
Prior Scores	.36		.29		.23	
Adjustment[e]		.50***		.45***		.47***
Poverty[f]		−.23***		−.21***		.12***
F		122.67***		88.39***		73.17***
Step 2						
Recent Scores	.04		.04		.01	
Poverty[g]		.13**		.06		.00
Home Environment[h]		24***		.22***		−.11*
F		9.44***		8.75***		2.68*

Note: Beta weights are standardized. [a]The current adjustment measures were administered in 1990. [b]$n = 437$. [c]$n = 434$. [d]$n = 437$. [e]The prior adjustment measures were administered in 1986. [f]Number of years in poverty status from 1982 to 1985. [g]Number of years in poverty status from 1986 to 1989. [h]These scores are the sum of the standardized home environment scores from the 1986 and 1990 assessments.
*p < .10. **p < .05. ***p < .01.

Contribution of Demographic Variables

It was of interest to examine whether the contribution of poverty to predicting changes in children's adjustment was independent of the effects of basic child demographic variables (i.e., sex, age, and race) on adjustment. We computed analyses of covariance (ANCOVAs) in which sex, age, and race were the independent variables, initial adjustment and prior poverty were the covariates, and later adjustment served as the dependent measure. These ANCOVAs essentially replicate Step 1 of the hierarchical regressions reported in the previous section, except for the addition of the child demographic variables. The results show that the initial adjustment and prior poverty variables remained significant predictors of 1990 adjustment, but none of the child demographic variables was a significant predictor. Thus, the effects of prior poverty on changes in children's academic and behavioral adjustment were independent of the child's sex, age, and race.

Next, we examined whether the role of poverty in predicting children's adjustment was due to poverty's association with several family background/demographic risk factors previously shown to be associated with children's maladjustment. Children appear to be at increased risk for developing problems if they come from homes in which there are many children (e.g., Barocas, Seifer, & Sameroff, 1985; Furstenberg, Brooks-Gunn, & Morgan, 1987) or homes in which the father is absent (Furstenberg et al., 1987; Werner, 1985). Other factors related to poverty that place a child at risk for maladjustment include being born to teenage mothers and low levels of maternal education (e.g., Brooks-Gunn & Furstenberg, 1986; Dubow & Luster, 1990). All of these variables were available in the NLSY data set.

We recomputed the hierarchical regressions as follows. In Step 1, along with initial adjustment and prior poverty, we entered the number of children in the home (averaged over the years from 1982 to 1985), number of years in which there was a father or father figure in the home (from 1982 to 1985), and mother's age at child's birth. In Step 2, along with recent poverty and the quality of the home environment, we entered the number of children in the home (averaged over the years from 1986 to 1989), number of years in which there was a father or father figure in the home (from 1986 to 1989), and mother's highest level of education. The results for the poverty and home environment measures were nearly identical to those from the regressions just reported when these family background/demographic variable were not entered. And, more important, these family background/demographic variables were rarely significant predictors of 1990 adjustment scores (i.e., their standardized beta weights never reached .15). Thus, the effects of poverty and the home environment on changes in academic and behavioral adjustment, as reported in the previous section, are significant irrespective of number of children in the home, number of years in which a father or father figure was present, mother's age at the child's birth, or mother's education.

Discussion

Brooks-Gunn, Phelps, and Elder (1991) have referred to "long-term carefully preserved longitudinal studies . . . [as] the backbone of developmental psychology (p. 907). Data sets that include multiple variables and have been accumulated over a number of years provide invaluable opportunities to augment core findings of developmental psychology. In our study, the NLSY data set permitted a prospective examination of a large sample of economically and ethnically diverse children across a time span of several years. In contrast, the preponderance of extant developmental research continues to focus on small, homogeneous samples of Caucasian, middle-class children (Chase-Lansdale, Mott, Brooks-Gunn, & Philips, 1991). Many of these studies are also cross-sectional in design and "cross-sectional information only provides a brief, static snapshot of a slice of an individual's or family's life" (Brooks-Gunn et al., 1991, p. 900). Although the contribution of such small sample, short-term studies is important to the understanding of development, there is considerable potential for gaining additional knowledge about human development by capitalizing on the availability of longitudinal national data sets. The use of this latter methodology permitted us to juxtapose multiple "snapshots," accumulated across time, of a group of demographically diverse children. Chase-Lansdale et al. (1991) characterized national data sets as a resource that permits building the scaffolds that then guide the fruitful analysis of behavior at the micro level (using smaller sample, short-term studies). Such microlevel studies can then, in turn, suggest questions to be addressed using available archival data sets.

Impact of Poverty on Academic and Behavioral Adjustment

Approximately 500,000 American children drop out of school each year; during the 1980s, "families headed by high school dropouts experienced a 17.3% decline in income" (Garbarino, 1992, p. 223), whereas the incomes of families headed by college graduates increased significantly during that same time period.

In addition, level of academic achievement tends to be stable over time (Slaughter & Epps, 1987). In a 2-year study of all California high schools, Fetler (1989) found low academic achievement to be significantly associated with high dropout rates even when background variables such as receiving Aid to Families with Dependent Children funds, enrollment in academic courses, and total school enrollment were controlled. In addition, Cassidy and Lynn (1991) found educational status at age 16 to be a direct predictor of SES at age 23. According to Birch and Gussow (1970), "Poverty produces educational failure, and since lack of education reduces opportunities for employment, it in turn contributes to the perpetuation of poverty" (p. 24; see also Garmezy, 1991; Ramey & Ramey, 1990; Rycraft, 1990). Given the connections between academic achievement, future academic attainment, and SES, the findings of this study—that poverty during the toddler/preschool years is a significant predictor of declines in academic achievement during elementary school—take on added importance.

In part, our study was a preliminary effort to segment the impact of poverty (early vs. recent) on children's level of academic adjustment during the elementary school years. We found that early poverty status primarily during the toddler and preschool years explained a significant proportion of the variance in changes in academic adjustment during the elementary school years. However, recent poverty (primarily during the elementary school years) did not significantly predict changes in elementary school academic achievement after accounting for early poverty.

First, it is immediately apparent that our findings with regard to recent poverty must be interpreted with caution. As Pedhazur (1982) pointed out, one appropriate use of hierarchical regression analysis is as follows:

> The study of the effect of an independent variable(s) on a dependent variable after having controlled for another variable(s). . . . The important thing to bear in mind is that such an analysis is not intended to provide information about the relative importance of variables, but rather about the effect of a variable(s) after having controlled for another variable(s). (p. 178)

Our intent was not to assess the relative importance of prior versus recent poverty but to examine the effect of recent poverty once poverty during the preschool years had been statistically controlled. That is, although the impact of recent poverty, when examined after having controlled for early poverty, appeared to be nonsignificant, it is well known that for many children—including those in our sample—poverty is highly stable across time (Rycraft, 1990). In addition, despite the failure of recent poverty to explain significant additional variation in the adjustment measures, recent poverty may act to sustain the established developmental course.

Second, we have added to previous findings about the negative impact of poverty on children and children's adjustment (e.g., Entwisle & Alexander, 1992; Garbarino, 1992; Garmezy, 1991; Ramey & Ramey, 1990; Rycraft, 1990). Our analyses demonstrated that poverty during the early years had a significant impact years later on declines in children's levels of academic achievement and increases in antisocial behavior independent of the contribution of other risk factors that we considered (the presence of a father figure, the number of children in the home during the toddler/preschool and elementary school years, mother's age at the time of the child's birth, and maternal education). Although it is undeniable that these additional risk factors can have a negative impact on the children who experience them, it was chronic prior poverty that emerged as the strongest single indicator of later failure to achieve in school and antisocial behavior.

Impoverishment no doubt results in parental focus on economic concerns. Perhaps this emphasis on economic matters interferes with the parents' ability to provide adequate emotional and environmental support for their children's academic and social development (e.g., parental warmth and encouragement, access to cultural experiences such as museums and books, and a clean and orderly home). A number of authors have confirmed the relation between a lack of parental support and academic underachievement (Cassidy & Lynn, 1991; Garmezy, 1991; Portes, 1991). Furthermore, it is likely that when parents do not support children's early academic efforts, the result may be a longstanding failure of children to place value on academic achievement.

In addition, our finding that early poverty predicts increased antisocial behavior during the elementary school years is compatible with Ramey and Ramey's (1990) conclusion that chronic poverty is associated not only with lags in development and educational achievement but also with deficits in social development. These authors suggested that intergenerational poverty is sometimes associated with "increased hostility toward the mainstream society" (p. 3), as reflected in increases in antisocial behavior. Disruptions in family supportiveness and cohesion often associated with chronic poverty may impair the development of positive social values and increase the likelihood of antisocial behavior (see Haddad, Barocas, & Hollenbeck, 1991).

Quality of Home Environment

Whereas a number of researchers have suggested educational intervention as the ideal means of reversing the academic deficits of economically disadvantaged children (Ramey & Ramey, 1990; Schweinhart & Weikart, 1988), Gallagher (1991) was adamant that educational interventions with children constitute "'weak treatment' unless supplemented by many other interventions at many social levels" (p. 437).

It may be that intervention programs that define specific ways in which parents can improve the home environment could augment the small-to-moderate gains brought about by direct educational intervention with disadvantaged children (Gallagher, 1991; Ramey & Ramey, 1990; see also Hanson & Lynch's, 1992, discussion of family-focused as opposed to child-focused interventions). We found that a cognitively stimulating and emotionally supportive home environment predicted increases in academic achievement and decreases in antisocial behavior scores during the elementary school years, independent of the effects of poverty status and the other risk factors previously enumerated. Garmezy (1991) similarly identified environmental inadequacy as a factor that contributes to the risk of school failure and future unemployment or underemployment in the children of poverty in his model of transgenerational poverty.

Note that the home environment variable utilized in our analyses was a composite score based on the quality of the recent home environment (i.e., during the elementary school years). It may be that if prior home environment scores—like prior poverty—had been partialled from recent measures, the quality of the recent home environment would not have significantly predicted academic achievement or antisocial behavior. This does not minimize the fact that the quality of the home environment either during the toddler/preschool years (a relation we were unable to explore given the limitations of the NLSY data set) or the quality of the recent home environment (as demonstrated here) can have a significant impact on children's adjustment. Intervention programs that seek to alleviate the detrimental effects of poverty must extend their scope beyond the education of at-risk children to include the education of those who are responsible for creating the home environments of these children.

Limitations and Implications for Future Research

A few limitations of this study should be highlighted. First, a word of caution is in order regarding the drawbacks of using the NLSY data set. Of primary interest is attrition due to failure to obtain consistently all of the targeted measures for each interview year. Attrition in such long-term studies can be due to systematic factors. Thus, there is some concern that the children dropped from our study may be, for example, the most academically deficient or the most impoverished. However, the analyses suggested that the sample that was omitted differed little from those included in the analyses on most demographic and child measures.

In addition to incomplete data for a large number of potential subjects, Chase-Lansdale (1991) pointed out that many of the subscales utilized in the NLSY data

set are shortened forms of the original instruments; interobserver reliabilities were not assessed, "a problem in particular for the short form of the HOME, which includes both maternal report and interviewer observation of family life" (p. 923). Also, the measures of behavioral adjustment included in this data set are based solely on maternal reports.

Future research should segment the impact of the quality of the home environment (i.e., during the toddler/preschool years vs. the elementary school years) to determine the optimal timing of the suggested parental education programs. In addition, to achieve unambiguous test results of the relative effects of prior and recent poverty, future research should attempt to assess the effects of moving out of poverty status on changes in adjustment; the group moving out of poverty could then be compared to children who remain in poverty over long periods of time. Unfortunately, given the stability of poverty status over time, such a study would require extensive tracking of a large sample of individuals in poverty who are likely to move out of poverty status (e.g., a sample of parents in poor families who take part in job-training intervention programs).

References

Achenbach, T. M., & Edelbrock, C. (1981). Behavioral problems and competence reported by parents of normal and disturbed children aged four through sixteen. *Monographs of the Society for Research in Child Development, 46*(1, Serial No. 188).

Achenbach, T. M., Howell, C. T., Quay, H. C., & Conners, C. K. (1991). National survey of problems and competencies among four- to-sixteen-year-olds. *Monographs of the Society for Research in Child Development, 58*(3, Serial No. 225).

Baker, P. C. (1993). [Reliability of the 1990 child assessment scores]. Unpublished raw data.

Baker, P. C., & Mott, F. L. (1989). *NLSY child handbook 1989: A guide and resource for the National Longitudinal Survey of Youth 1986 child data.* Columbus: Center for Human Resource Research.

Bayley, N. (1969). *Bayley Scales of infant development.* New York: Psychological Corporation.

Barocas, R., Seifer, R., & Sameroff, A. (1985). Defining environmental risk: Multiple dimensions of psychological vulnerability. *American Journal of Community Psychology, 13,* 433–447.

Bell, A. E., Aftanas, M. S., & Abrahamson, D. S. (1976). Scholastic progress of children from different socio-economic groups, matched for IQ. *Developmental Medicine and Child Neurology, 18,* 717–727.

Bergeman, C. S., & Plomin, R. (1988). Parental mediators of the genetic relationship between home environment and infant mental development. *British Journal of Developmental Psychology, 6,* 11–19.

Birch, H. G., & Gussow, J. D. (1970). *Disadvantaged children.* New York: Harcourt, Brace and World.

Blum, H. M., Boyle, M. H., & Offord, D. R. (1988). Single-parent families: Child psychiatric disorder and school performance. *Journal of the American Academy of Child and Adolescent Psychiatry, 27,* 214–218.

Bradley, R. H. (1982). The HOME inventory: A review of the first fifteen years. In N. J. Anastasiow, W. Frankenburg, & A. Fandall (Eds.), *Identifying the developmentally delayed child* (pp. 87–100). Baltimore: University Park Press.

Bradley, R. H., & Caldwell, B. M. (1984). The relation of infants' home environments to achievement test performance in first grade: A follow-up study. *Child Development, 55*, 803–809.

Bradley, R. H., Caldwell, B. M., & Elardo, R. (1977). Home environment, social status, and mental test performance. *Journal of Educational Psychology, 69*, 697–701.

Bradley, R. H., Caldwell, B. M., Rock, S. L., & Harris, P. T. (1986). Early home environment and the development of competence: Findings from the Little Rock longitudinal study. *Children's Environments Quarterly, 3*, 10–22.

Bradley, R. H., Caldwell, B. M., Rock, S. L., Ramey, C. T., Barnard, K. E., Gray, C., Hammond, M. A., Mitchell, S., Gottfried, A. W., Siegel, L., & Johnson, D. L. (1989). Home environment and cognitive development in the first 3 years of life: A collaborative study involving six sites and three ethnic groups in North America. *Developmental Psychology, 25*, 217–235.

Brooks-Gunn, J., & Furstenberg, F. (1986). The children of adolescent mothers: Physical, academic, and psychological outcomes. *Developmental Review, 6*, 224–251.

Brooks-Gunn, J., Phelps, E., & Elder, G. H., Jr. (1991). Studying lives through time: Secondary data analysis in developmental psychology. *Developmental Psychology, 27*, 800–910.

Caldwell, B., & Bradley, R. (1984). *Home observation for measurement of the environment.* Little Rock: University of Arkansas at Little Rock.

Cassidy, T., & Lynn, R. (1991). Achievement motivation, educational attainment, cycles of disadvantage and social competence: Some longitudinal data. *Journal of Educational Psychology, 61*, 1–12.

Center for Human Resource Research. (1992). *NLS users' guide 1992.* Columbus: The Ohio State University.

Chase-Lansdale, P. L., Mott, F. L., Brooks-Gunn, J., & Phillips, D. A. (1991). Children of the National Longitudinal Survey of Youth: A unique research opportunity. *Developmental Psychology, 27*, 918–931.

Cherian, V. I. (1991). The relationship between parental income and academic achievement in Xhosa children. *Journal of Social Psychology, 131*, 889–891.

Church, A. T., & Katigbak, M. S. (1991). Home environment, nutritional status, and maternal intelligence as determinants of intellectual development in rural Philippine preschool children. *Intelligence, 15*, 49–78.

Cohen, J., & Cohen, P. (1975). *Applied multiple regression/correlation analysis for the behavioral sciences.* Hillsdale, NJ: Lawrence Erlbaum Associates, Inc.

Coulton, C. J., & Pandey, S. (1992). Geographic concentration of poverty and risk to children in urban neighborhoods. *American Behavioral Scientist, 35*, 238–257.

Dubow, E. F., & Luster, T. (1990). Adjustment of children born to teenage mothers: The contribution of risk and protective factors. *Journal of Marriage and the Family, 52*, 393–404.

Dunn, L., & Markwardt, F. (1970). *Peabody Individual Achievement Tests.* Circle Pines, MN: American Guidance Service.

Entwisle, D. R., & Alexander, K. L. (1992). Summer setback: Race, poverty, school composition, and mathematics achievement in the first two years of school. *American Psychological Review, 57*, 72–84.

Fetler, M. (1989). School dropout rates, academic performance, size, and poverty: Correlates of educational reform. *Educational Evaluation and Policy Analysis, 11*, 109–116.

Furstenberg, F., Brooks-Gunn, G., & Morgan, S. P. (1987). *Adolescent mothers in later life.* Cambridge, England: Cambridge University Press.

Gallagher, J. J. (1991). Longitudinal interventions: Virtues and limitations. *American Behavioral Scientist, 34*, 431–439.

Garbarino, J. (1992). The meaning of poverty in the world of children. *American Behavioral Scientist, 35*, 220–237.

Garmezy, N. (1991). Resiliency and vulnerability to adverse developmental outcomes associated with poverty. *American Behavioral Scientist, 34*, 416–430.

Greaney, V. (1986). Parental influences on reading. *The Reading Teacher, 39*, 813–818.

Haddad, J. D., Barocas, R., & Hollenbeck, A. R. (1991). Family organization and parent attitudes of children with conduct disorder. *Journal of Clinical Child Psychology, 20*, 152–161.

Hanson, M. J., & Lynch, E. W. (1992). Family diversity: Implications for policy and practice. *Topics in Early Childhood Special Education, 12*, 283–306.

Hare, B. R. (1980). Self-perception and academic achievement: Variations in a desegregated setting. *American Journal of Psychiatry, 137*, 683–689.

Hinshaw, S. P. (1992). Externalizing behavior problems and academic underachievement in childhood and adolescence: Causal relationships and underlying mechanisms. *Psychological Bulletin, 111*, 127–155.

Jens, K. G., & Gordon, B. N. (1991). Understanding risk: Implications for tracking high-risk infants and making early service delivery decisions. *International Journal of Disability, Development and Education, 38*, 211–224.

Jones-Wilson, F. C. (1991). Alleviating the force of poverty on urban poor children. *Early Child Development and Care, 73*, 103–120.

Laosa, L. M. (1984). Ethnic, socioeconomic, and home language influences upon early performance on measures of abilities. *Journal of Educational Psychology, 76*, 1178–1198.

Ledingham, J., & Crombie, G. (1988). Promoting the mental health of children and youth: A critical review of recent literature. *Canada's Mental Health, 36*, 9–17.

Luster, T., & Dubow, E. (1992). Home environment and maternal intelligence as predictors of verbal intelligence: A comparison of preschool and school-aged children. *Merrill-Palmer Quarterly, 38*, 151–175.

Masten, A. S., Garmezy, N., Tellegen, A., Pellegrini, D. S., Larkin, K., & Larsen, A. (1988). Competence and stress in school children: The moderating effects of individual and family qualities. *Journal for Child Psychology and Psychiatry and Allied Disciplines, 29*, 745–764.

McCarthy, D. (1972). *McCarthy scales of children's abilities.* New York: Psychological Corporation.

Morrison, D., Mantzicopoulos, P., & Carte, E. (1989). Preacademic screening for learning and behavior problems. *Journal of the American Academy of Child and Adolescent Psychiatry, 28*, 101–106.

Ninio, A. (1990). Early environmental experiences and school achievement in the second grade: An Israeli study. *International Journal of Behavioral Development, 13*, 1–22.

Norman, G., & Breznitz, Z. (1992). Differences in the ability to concentrate in first-grade Israeli pupils of low and high socioeconomic status. *The Journal of Genetic Psychology, 153*, 5–17.

Pedhazur, E. J. (1982). *Multiple regression in behavioral research: Explanation and prediction.* Fort Worth, TX: Holt, Rinehart & Winston.

Peterson, J. L., & Zill, N. (1986). Marital disruption, parent–child relationships, and behavior problems in children. *Journal of Marriage and the Family, 48*, 295–307.

Portes, P. R. (1991). Assessing children's cognitive environment through parent–child interactions. *Journal of Research and Development in Education, 24*, 30–37.

Quay, H. C., & Peterson, D. R. (1983). *Revised Behavior Problem Checklist: Interim manual.* Coral Gables, FL: University of Miami.

Ramey, C. T., & Ramey, S. L. (1990). Intensive educational intervention for children of poverty. *Intelligence, 14*, 1–9.

Richter, L. M., & Grieve, K. W. (1991). Home environment and cognitive development of black infants in impoverished South African families. *Infant Mental Health Journal, 12*, 88–101.

Rycraft, J. R. (1990). Behind the walls of poverty: Economically disadvantaged gifted and talented children. *Early Child Development and Care, 63*, 139–147.

Schweinhart, L. J., & Weikart, D. P. (1988). Early childhood education for at-risk four-year-olds? Yes. *American Psychologist, 43*, 665–667.

Seifer, R., & Sameroff, A. J. (1987). Multiple determinants of risk and invulnerability. In E. J. Anthony & B. J. Cohler (Eds.), *The invulnerable child* (pp. 51–69). New York: Guilford.

Share, D. L., Jorm, A. F., Maclean, R., Matthews, R., & Waterman, B. (1983). Early reading achievement, oral language ability, and a child's home background. *Australian Psychologist, 18,* 75–87.

Slaughter, D. T., & Epps, E. G. (1987). The home environment and academic achievement of black American children and youth: An overview. *The Journal of Negro Education, 56,* 3–20.

Strawn, J. (1992). The states and the poor: Child poverty rises as the safety net shrinks. *Social Policy Report: Society for Research in Child Development, 6,* 1–19.

Wechsler, D. (1967). *Wechsler Preschool and Primary Scale of Intelligence.* New York: Psychological Corporation.

Werner, E. (1985). Stress and protective factors in children's lives. In A. R. Nichol (Ed.), *Longitudinal studies in child psychology and psychiatry* (pp. 335–355). New York: Wiley.

White, K. (1982). The relations between socioeconomic status and academic achievement. *Psychological Bulletin, 91,* 461–481.

Wilson, R. S., & Matheny, A. P., Jr. (1983). Mental development: Family environment and genetic influences. *Intelligence, 7,* 195–215.

Received August 23, 1993
Final revision received March 11, 1994

Journal of Clinical Child Psychology
1994, Vol. 23, 413–424

Poverty and the Crisis in Children's Services:
The Need for Services Integration

Robert J. Illback

R.E.A.C.H. of Louisville, Inc.

Examined the integrated services paradigm within children's services, which holds much promise as a means to create more comprehensive and coordinated systems of care for children and families living in poverty. I reviewed the development of integrated service approaches and delineated common elements of models and programs that have emerged across the nation. Implications for the practice of professional child psychology are discussed, including professional practice, training, leadership, and research considerations.

Poverty is a pervasive, complex, and refractory problem for a growing number of children and families in society, precipitating a crisis in children's services (National Commission on Children [NCC], 1991). Even a cursory review of relevant data provides clues regarding the proportions of this emerging crisis. For example, presently in the United States, approximately 14% of children and youth (numbering 14,341,000) live in conditions of poverty (Children's Defense Fund, 1992). For children younger than 6, the magnitude of the problem is even greater, with nearly 25% of children living in poverty. About 5 million youngsters live in severe poverty, with family incomes less than half the federal poverty level (NCC, 1991). Poverty cuts across racial, ethnic, and family boundaries, but it is far more prevalent for African-American (44%) and Hispanic children (36%; U.S. Department of Commerce, 1990). In 1991, the poverty rate in female-headed, single-parent families was 55%, more than five times that of married-couple families. Each year, an estimated 10,000 children die from poverty's effects, and the infant mortality rate in this country is higher than 19 other nations (NCC, 1991).

The crisis in children's services now being felt across the entire spectrum of child services (e.g., health care,

education, mental health, and social services) is, to a significant degree, associated with (and complicated by) the crushing influence of poverty. Nearly 1 million infants are born each year without prenatal care, 250,000 babies have a low birth weight, and the epidemic of substance abuse among pregnant women may affect up to 375,000 newborns per year. Less than 50% of young children in urban areas are fully immunized, resulting in a resurgence of preventable childhood diseases. As many as 35% of kindergarten children come to school unprepared for formal education (Children's Defense Fund, 1992). There are currently 2.7 million reports of child abuse and neglect each year. Between 10% and 12% of children younger than 18 suffer from a mental disorder, and nearly 50% are estimated to have serious emotional disturbances (Costello, 1986). Less than 50% get the help they need (Saxe, Cross, Silverman, Batchelor, & Dougherty, 1987). In 1991, nearly 429,000 children were in foster homes, group homes, or institutional settings, which is up from 270,000 in the early 1980s (NCC, 1991).

Moreover, it appears that disparities between the affluent and people who are economically disadvantaged are widening, further complicating service provision (NCC, 1991). The median income of young families with children dropped 32% between 1973 and 1990. Low-income working families experienced a 25% decline in the availability of health insurance from 1977 through 1987. About 40% of Caucasian babies and 90% of African-American babies of teenage mothers are born into single-parent families. (For an excellent analysis of the changing needs and circumstances of children and families, see the recent report of the NCC, 1991.)

The profound effects of poverty on the psychological development and mental health of children are well documented. Persons living in poverty are less able to

The issues discussed in this article are drawn in part from the deliberations of the Task Force on Comprehensive and Coordinated Services to Children Ages 0–10 of the American Psychological Association. The opinions expressed herein do not necessarily represent the policies or views of the association. Members and liaisons of the task force include James Paavola (Chair), Carolyn Cobb, Robert J. Illback, Herbert Joseph, Alicia Torruella, Donald Routh, Karen Carey, Sylvia Rosenfield, John Meier, Sylvia Shellenberger, and Ronda Talley.

Requests for reprints should be sent to Robert J. Illback, R.E.A.C.H. of Louisville, Inc., 101 East Kentucky Street, Louisville, KY 40203.

procure adequate housing, health care, educational services, and related social services, and they have been shown to have fewer social and community support systems (Singer & Irvin, 1989). Economic disadvantage also has been associated with health problems (Gortmaker, Walker, Weitzman, & Sobol, 1990), mental retardation (Birch, Richardson, Baird, Horobin, & Illsley, 1970), severe parental stress (Dumas & Wahler, 1983), and mental illness (Belle, 1990).

Given these immense problems, the provision of appropriate and effective services is a daunting challenge for systems of care that serve children and families living in poverty. Despite a proliferation of social, educational, mental health, and other federal, state, local, and private initiatives in the past 3 decades (e.g., Head Start, Medicare, Medicaid, maternal and child health, and nutrition programs), poverty and its sequelae continue to frustrate and impede the efforts of agencies and organizations responsible to serve these persons. Some of these difficulties are attributable to the lack of financial and programmatic resources to meet essential child and family needs (e.g., health care, food, and clothing). However, the "patchwork quilt" of health and human services available in most communities has complicated efforts to respond to needs in a thoughtful and integrative manner. The present child service system tends to be fragmented, inaccessible, duplicative, and ineffective (Saxe, Cross, & Silverman, 1988; Tuma, 1989).

The integrated services movement within children's services holds much promise as a means to create more comprehensive and coordinated systems of care for children and families living in poverty. This article reviews the development of integrated service approaches and delineates common elements of models and programs that have emerged across the nation. Implications for child psychology—to include practice, training, leadership, and research considerations—are discussed.

Evolution of the Integrated Services Concept

The growth of children's services can be traced to events beginning before the turn of the century (1880 to 1914), a time of progressive social reform in response to concern about emerging social problems related to industrialization and urbanization (Levine & Levine, 1992). Child-serving organizations have since undergone numerous transformations, most recently in the 1960s, as a function of dramatic concern for such problems as poverty, child abuse, teen pregnancy, decreases in school achievement, learning disabilities, violence, and mental illness. Consequently, social programs targeted toward children and families prolifer-

ated, as exemplified by legislation such as the Community Mental Health Centers Act (Public Law [PL] 99–660, 1970), Title I of the Elementary and Secondary Education Act (1965), the Child Abuse Prevention and Treatment Act (PL 93–247, 1974), and the Education for All Handicapped Children Act (PL 94–142, 1975).

In contrast with earlier program models, the implementation of this array of entitlement programs gave rise to highly specialized, categorical programs targeted toward narrowly defined subgroups, particularly persons who were oppressed, disabled, disadvantaged, or poverty stricken (Attkisson & Broskowski, 1978). Regulatory and funding frameworks were tied to specified eligibility criteria for each of these groups, resulting in a patchwork quilt of programs and approaches at local, regional, and state levels. Unfortunately, these large-scale social programs were often ineffective or exacerbated social problems (e.g., by creating dependency and disempowering families), and questions arose regarding the wisdom of compartmentalizing human services in this manner (Hobbs, 1975).

The emergence of systemic perspectives led to recognition that problems in living experienced by children and families were interconnected and, therefore, required an integrated response (Apter, 1982; Hobbs, 1975). Moreover, it became apparent that there was much duplication of effort across the various service systems; at times, efforts were working at cross purposes (Apter, 1982). Problems of overlapping personnel responsibilities, maldistribution of human and financial resources, ineffective practices, and evaluation findings of nonsignificance called into question the continued expansion of government-mandated entitlement programs and argued for more integrated, accountable approaches (Attkisson & Broskowski, 1978).

As early as 1968, March proposed the neighborhood-center concept, emphasizing comprehensiveness, decentralization, co-location of service components, blending resources from different programs, and the operational integration of services. The integrated services movement took root in the 1970s, when then-Secretary of Health, Education, and Welfare Elliott Richardson became interested in the concept and began to promote it within the federal bureaucracy. Early initiatives included the provision of primary health care through neighborhood health center demonstration projects (Institute of Medicine, 1982) and alternative service delivery models for special and remedial education (e.g., ungraded primaries, collaborative teaching, and curriculum-based assessment) to reduce instructional fragmentation and segregation associated with special programs (Graden, Zins, & Curtis, 1988).

Renewed interest in service integration and system restructuring continues to be fueled in part by concern for the immense cost and bureaucracy of entitlement programs (particularly in the health care arena), as well as a desire for increased accountability regarding treatment effectiveness (Kiesler, 1992). Further impetus for integrated services derives from the family support and education movement (Zigler & Black, 1989). Dunst, Trivette, Starnes, Hamby, and Gordon (1993) defined *family support* as efforts that aim to "enable and empower people by enhancing and promoting individual and family capabilities that support and strengthen family functioning" (p. 4). Central tenets of the movement, as outlined by Weissbourd and Kagan (1989), include (a) treating adults as capable and competent; (b) building on family strengths, rather than "treating" dysfunction; (c) promoting health and competency; (d) treating families as partners and active participants in program development; (e) using a broad definition of *support,* in relation to needs as perceived and experienced by families; and (f) seeking family independence and interdependence with their community.

The foci of family support programs include developing needs-based resources, facilitating self-help and social support networking, providing useful information on child development and parenting practices, intervening early, and developing community resources (Dunst et al., 1993). Many state and federal programs have adopted policies and practices that are based on family support conceptions (Roberts & Magrab, 1991), and family-centered language has become common across a range of health and human service areas, including education (e.g., preschool handicapped programs), health care (e.g., maternal and child health programs), child welfare (e.g., family preservation programs), and mental health/mental retardation (e.g., respite programs; Dunst et al., 1993).

Essential Aspects of Integrated Services

Although there may be agreement that the current service system for children and families is often fragmented, uncoordinated, and inadequate, there is not consensus regarding the features of a more comprehensive, coordinated, and effective system. Substantial literature has been generated to describe features thought to be indicative of a more responsive system, and these features reflect the values and perspectives of various individuals, families, professionals, and organizations (Edelman & Radin, 1991; Knitzer, 1982; Melaville & Blank, 1991; National Commission on Children, 1991; National Commission on Child Welfare and Family Preservation, 1990; Schorr & Schorr, 1988). The following section distills common elements of the integrated services concept.

Features of an Integrated Service System

The efficacy of services to children and families can be viewed usefully from the perspective of the families themselves. When examined in this manner (family centered vs. system centered), emphasis is placed on actual service delivery episodes and the impact these have on children and families. When children and families participate in programs that are well-integrated, services (a) are available in close proximity and are accessible without reference to physical, psychological, social, or other barriers; (b) are comprehensive and appropriate, in that they possess features that address priority needs the family has identified, at a level of service sufficient to their need; (c) are formulated and delivered at a high level of quality, such that the family perceives them as an organized whole and can participate in a consistent and effective manner; (d) promote psychological competence and selfsufficiency rather than focusing exclusively on dysfunction and pathology; (e) are oriented toward the full participation and empowerment of family members, such that they attribute change in part to their own efforts; (f) are sensitive to cultural, sex, and racial issues; (g) are driven by concern for the needs and desires of the consumers (i.e., children and families) and emphasize explicit outcomes stated in a positive manner; and, (h) stress prevention and early intervention.

In an *uncoordinated* system, individual providers and/or agencies share some aspects of their work with each other, but they essentially maintain their own sets of goals, expectations, and responsibilities in providing services to children and families. By contrast, the hallmark of an *integrated* approach involves individual providers, agencies, and families developing intervention plans, pooling resources, sharing responsibility for plan implementation, and collaborating on outcome assessment in a collaborative fashion. The greater the number of providers involved (e.g., psychologists, nurses, teachers, social workers, physicians, and day care workers), the greater the need for such collaboration. At a minimum, this may take the form of different providers (from independent agencies) communicating regularly by phone regarding a child or family. Or it may involve regular face-to-face meetings and case conferences among providers. In an ideal situation, providers and family members would work as an integrated team to design and implement needed services through approaches such as neighborhood centers, family resource centers, school-linked services, health care prevention programs, or any number of similar innovative programs and practices.

An integrated delivery system also allows for both ease of entry and flexibility of movement within and between systems of care. For example, if the point of initial contact for a family is a school setting, there would be clear connections between the school and the array of community services that the family needs, regardless of categorical restrictions or setting. This requires that individual providers and agencies see themselves as part of a larger ecology that is community wide and geared to aiding the overall climate within which children grow and develop. In this context, the specific agency through which a family seeks service becomes less important, in light of increased responsibility on the part of all agencies to consider child and family needs in a comprehensive manner.

Relatedly, the integrated service system would be organized for broad-based accountability, to benefit primarily the child and family but also the community within which the child lives, rather than only the funding entity (e.g., third-party payor). In this conception, service providers are motivated by a consumer orientation (similar to other businesses), with children and families seen as customers with whom one must collaborate (and satisfy), rather than as patients or adversaries. A well-developed, integrated service system would be more closely tied to neighborhood and community life, demonstrating concern for the quality of life in communities through community presence, resource development, advocacy, and community service and, in the process, seeking to enhance the sense of community experienced by children and families (Sarason, 1974).

For coordinated and collaborative service delivery to succeed, funding should be both flexible and shared (when possible) among agencies, such that different agencies are encouraged to develop jointly programs that serve children and families holistically (rather than to compete for funds). Funding and program decisions about how pooled or flexible funds are to be utilized are made from the bottom up by empowered frontline providers who have ongoing contact and communication with consumers (children and families).

Planning for Organizational Change

In restructuring child service organizations to achieve services integration, a number of themes and issues are likely to emerge, including the following: (a) decategorization of programs and services, (b) uniformity of eligibility standards, (c) interprofessional collaboration across levels and systems within the organization, (d) promoting innovation and flexibility, (e) focusing more on prevention and early intervention (as opposed to crisis intervention and remediation), (f) attending to the needs of consumers of services, and (g) facilitating professional development and effective working conditions (Illback & Zins, 1993). To accomplish these goals, a planned change approach is necessary.

Organizational change efforts are challenging to conceptualize and implement. Often, such efforts meet with resistance as the child service organization struggles to maintain homeostasis, leading to failure and frustration. Change initiatives have been shown to fail due to insufficient information about problems, inadequate organizational diagnosis, inattention to organizational readiness for change, simplistic intervention strategies and procedures, and lack of follow-up (Fullan, Miles, & Taylor, 1980).

Although it is not within the scope of this article to explicate the process of changing child service organizations, certain principles of organizational change are summarized: (a) Child service organizations are continually changing and evolving in response to both internal and external factors, implying the need to perceive and utilize accurately this ongoing process in the change effort; (b) change efforts that apply multiple methods and strategies (e.g., training and restructuring) are more likely to result in durable change than are approaches that are unidimensional (e.g., brief training alone); (c) successful change efforts involve balancing and controlling a large number of mediating variables involving people, procedures, and processes; (d) successful change efforts in child service organizations are dependent on timely, accurate, and continuous information about organizational functioning; (e) some child service organizations are more ready for change than others, and it may be appropriate to defer the change initiative until the organization can be made more hospitable to the intervention; (f) organizational change efforts may lead to unintended effects due to the interdependency of the organization's elements; (g) meaningful change is most likely to occur when people within the child service organization achieve a sense of "ownership" of the organizational change effort; and (h) an overriding goal of planned organizational change is the facilitation of self-evaluation and self-renewal processes that become a part of the routine of a more functional organization. (For a more thorough discussion of organizational assessment and intervention in child-serving organizations, see Illback & Zins, 1993).

Some Exemplary Programs

Considerable efforts are already underway across the country (many led by psychologists) to implement the services integration paradigm in child-serving organizations. Often, these initiatives originate within a particular service system, but they share an orientation toward family-centered, community-based, and collaborative intervention. All of the exemplary programs described next are targeted toward persons living in poverty (or serve substantial numbers of economically disadvantaged persons).

Family preservation services. Child welfare, juvenile justice, and mental health funds, in addition to private foundation monies (particularly from the Edna McConnell Clark and Annie E. Casey Foundations), are being used to support family preservation projects in numerous states and localities. Modeled after the much-replicated Homebuilders, Inc. program (Kinney, Madsen, Fleming, & Haapala, 1977), concentrated in-home and community-based services are provided by trained workers with small caseloads (as low as two) who are given programmatic flexibility and control of financial resources to meet family needs within a relatively brief time period (4 to 6 weeks). A range of cognitive, environmental, and interpersonal strategies are incorporated into these interventions, which are typically based on social-learning theory, crisis prevention and intervention strategies, and ecological perspectives on child development. The most prominent of these service integration projects have occurred in California, Iowa, Michigan, Minnesota, New Jersey, New York, Utah, and Washington. Target populations include neglected and abused children (Nelson, 1991), seriously emotionally disturbed youth (Hinckley & Ellis, 1985), and serious juvenile offenders (Haapala & Kinney, 1988; Henggeler, Melton, & Smith, 1992).

Despite problems inherent in evaluating community-based programs—including small samples, establishing viable contrast conditions, delineating demographic and program implementation variables, limitations of available instrumentation and choices of outcome measures, controlling for statistical regression effects, and inappropriate statistical analysis (Feldman, 1991; Rossi, 1992)—some important evaluative efforts have emerged. For example, in Washington, intensive family preservation services are used system wide to prevent out-of-home placement (e.g., residential treatment and foster care). A program evaluation examined 1,506 child clients (representing 1,112 families) and found that 16.9% were in out-of-home placements 12 months following intake, which was seen as favorable compared to baseline rates (Bath, Richey, & Haapala, 1992). Predictors associated with placement included child age (infants and adolescents), family income, and parental mental health. Pecora, Fraser, and Haapala (1991) reported on emerging data from a multisite evaluation (also in Washington) wherein data from a subsample of participating families were compared with those not accepted and served in a more traditional manner. Eighty-five percent of the comparison-group children were placed, whereas only 44% of the treatment-group children were out of their homes 12 months after treatment had been terminated.

In a more controlled investigation, children and families who were judged to be at imminent risk for out-of home placement in Hennepin County, Minnesota were randomly assigned to family preservation (*n* = 58) or traditional service (*n* = 58) conditions, and they were followed for 12 to 16 months (Schwartz, AuClaire, & Harris, 1991). Similar to the Washington evaluation studies, at long-term follow-up, 56% of the treatment group were placed, in contrast with 91% of the comparison group. Earlier work by these same investigators (Auclaire & Schwartz, 1986) found these two groups did not differ in the frequency of placement episodes per child during the study period, but rather they differed in the duration of placement, implying that family preservation tends not only to reduce overall placement rates but also length of time required in out-of-home placements.

These encouraging findings are tempered by Feldman's (1991) evaluation studies of five New Jersey family preservation programs. Ninety-six treatment (intensive family preservation) families were compared with 87 control (traditional community services) families. Follow-up at 9 months from termination of treatment suggested differences between treatment and control groups on out-of-home placement rates, these results dissipated by 12 months. It appears that the most significant program effects occur during and immediately following the program, but maintenance and generalization of program effects remains problematic.

Much work remains to understand relations among demographic, process, and outcome assessments in family preservation programming. Recently, Bath and Haapala (1993) studied 530 families (854 children) referred to child protective services for maltreatment. They learned that differences between neglectful and abusive families were predictive of placement, the former group having twice as high a probability of placement. Neglectful families were more prone to be poor, headed by a single parent, and have medical/mental health/substance abuse problems. The highest placement rates were seen in families referred for both abuse and neglect. Another evaluation of family preservation services with 10,191 families of status offenders in Florida (Nugent, Carpenter, & Parks, 1993) found three demographic (age, school status, and primary presenting problem), two history (involvement with dependency and delinquency systems), and three service (type of service, number of family sessions, and completion of treatment program) variables predicted positive outcomes in family preservation. (For a more in-depth review of evaluation research issues in family preservation, see Rossi, 1992; Wells & Biegel, 1991; and Yuan & Rivest, 1990.)

Systems of care in child mental health. The Child and Adolescent Service System Program initiative within the National Institute of Mental Health, begun in 1984, promotes systems change in mental health services for children with severe emotional disabilities (SEDs) by encouraging states to provide more comprehensive and coordinated services (Day & Roberts, 1991). A range of regional and statewide systems of care (service integration) initiatives are underway (many supported by the Robert Wood Johnson Foundation Mental Health Services for Youth Program), emphasizing the following: (a) the development of a full array of community-based services, (b) less restrictive child placement and prevention of out-of-home placement, (c) interagency collaboration in service planning and coordination, (d) flexible and individualized services, and (e) cost containment and efficiency (Stroul, Goldman, Lourie, Katz-Leavy, & Zeigler-Dendy, 1992). States such as California, Georgia, Kentucky, Oregon, North Carolina, Vermont, and Virginia and localities such as Cleveland, San Francisco, and Ventura County (CA) feature such efforts.

Initially funded through a Robert Wood Johnson Foundation planning grant in one region of the state (Lexington and vicinity), Kentucky's Interagency Mobilization for Progress in Adolescent and Children's Treatment (IMPACT) program represents a comprehensive, statewide restructuring of the system of care for children and adolescents with SEDs (Kentucky Cabinet for Human Resources, 1990). The program emphasizes collaboration among social service, education, mental health, and juvenile justice systems through state, regional, and local interagency councils, in addition to extensive case management, parent involvement, and flexible funding (Illback, 1993a). In Ventura County, the Children's Mental Health Initiative, funded by the California legislature, uses collaborative interagency planning to fill gaps in the prevailing service delivery array and develop some new services (Jordan & Hernandez, 1990). A longitudinal project in Fort Bragg (NC) seeks to demonstrate that coordination across the continuum of services and increased utilization of community-based alternatives can impact costs and treatment effectiveness, thereby making services available to more children and families (Heflinger et al., 1991).

Emerging evaluative information has begun to document program efficacy of these system of care initiatives. For example, the Fort Bragg demonstration project found that children in comparison sites were five times more likely to be placed in inpatient or residential settings than those served within the community-based system of care, which experienced a overall reduction from 7% to less than 1.5% of the rate of clients served in hospital or residential settings within 2 years (Bickman, 1993). Overall psychiatric hospitalization admission rates and duration of stay have been reduced in numerous localities as a function of increased community services (Behar, 1992; Georgia Division of Mental Health, Mental Retardation, & Substance Abuse, 1992; Rosenblatt & Attkisson, 1992). Vermont's New Directions program reported a 20% increase in children living at home (Vermont Department of Mental Health & Mental Retardation,

1993). Kentucky's IMPACT program demonstrated an overall decrease in the number of child placements, as compared with placement histories prior to involvement (Illback, 1993a).

In addition to positive findings regarding placement, these programs have also begun to demonstrate change in child and family functioning and family satisfaction with services. One-year follow-ups within Kentucky's IMPACT program (Illback, 1993a) and a Tennessee project (Glisson, 1992), for example, documented substantial gains in behavioral functioning on the Child Behavior Checklist (Achenbach, 1991), as compared to intake and control sites, respectively. Kentucky's IMPACT program families report that they perceive more dense and more helpful support networks, particularly in regard to the use of services such as service coordination, respite, in-home workers, and paraprofessionals (Illback, 1993a). Family satisfaction with services also has been shown to improve, as evidenced by Fort Bragg data showing program parents to be more satisfied and confident about treatment efficacy than controls (Behar, 1992). Improved youth satisfaction with services is seen in Vermont (Burchard et al., 1993), with similar findings for provider satisfaction in Virginia (Virginia Department of Mental Health, Mental Retardation, and Substance Abuse Services, 1992).

The relative cost-efficiency of these system of care interventions is dramatically shown in the Fort Bragg community mental health project, in which the total average cost per client is 51% lower for program participants ($5,380) than in comparison sites ($10,922; Behar, 1992). An analysis of estimated costs of service settings in relation to placement data reveals a substantial reduction (from $16,987 to $12,722) in the average annual cost of serving children with SEDs in Kentucky relative to the year prior to program involvement, most of which is attributable to reduced hospitalization (Illback, 1993a).

Family Support and Education Programs

Family support programs are generally aimed at increasing parental competence and ameliorating stress, presuming that healthy family systems will produce children who function higher cognitively, are less at risk for learning and behavior problems, and are more likely to become healthy and productive citizens. Thus, Iowa's Family Development and Self-Sufficiency Program aims to help high-risk Aid to Families With Dependent Children families through support and education activities that include long-term employment services, a preschool program for at-risk children, targeted Medicaid benefits, and transitional child care for those leaving the program. Hawaii sponsors a multidisciplinary Family Support Systems' Healthy Start Home

Visiting Service that provides screening, crisis intervention, parent training, respite care, male home visitors for fathers, and toy-lending libraries (National Commission on Child Welfare and Family Preservation, 1990).

There have been relatively few controlled investigations of community-based family support programs due to conceptual, practical, and methodological difficulties (Weiss & Jacobs, 1988). For instance, although the logical model for a particular program may suggest that providing social support to families will have an impact on a range of social indicators (e.g., substance abuse, dropout rates, behavior problems, and child maltreatment), establishing a direct, causal relation between the provision of such services and these presumed outcomes is almost impossible.

The inability to formulate and test a clear experimental hypothesis is especially problematic in that these programs are often "sold" to funding sources based on the expectation that they will directly impact certain high-profile indicators. In all probability, family support and education programs will not result in unidimensional change, but rather they should be viewed from a multidimensional perspective. Thus, there is a need to more closely link broad program goals with program design and evaluation, thereby broadening the outcome variables assessed. In this context, Dunst, Trivette, and Thompson (1990) suggested that systematic investigations of family support programs move from documenting the prevention of poor outcomes (absence of problems) to focusing on more positive, demonstrable, and broad-based measures (e.g., strengthening of family functioning and mobilization of resources).

Despite these inherent limitations, evaluation research advocates family support and education programs. Differences between families seeking help from family support programs and a general sample were documented in an evaluation study by Telleen (1990), who compared 79 help-seeking mothers (within a family support initiative) to 56 mothers with similar-age children. The former group reported significantly greater child behavior stresses and were more likely to attribute these to their own limitations. Notably, they did not perceive themselves as being depressed but rather as lacking in parental competence and isolated socially.

There have been some systematic investigations of community-based family support program outcomes. Halvorson (1992) reported on an evaluation of a preventive home-based program involving 12 target families. Reports of participants (i.e., teachers, parents, and children) and observational data suggest positive gains, especially in behavior problems. Utilizing a multiple-baseline design, Caro and Derevensky (1991) documented the effects of a family-focused intervention program for young children with severe disabilities.

Regular home visits and targeted behavior plans developed in conjunction with each family member were associated with positive changes in child management competencies, familial interaction patterns, parental satisfaction, and rates of progress by the children.

Telleen, Herzog, and Kilbane (1989) studied the differential impact of mothers' participation in two common family support programs: self-help discussion groups and parent education. Compared to control groups, they found that, after 3 months of program participation, mothers in both types of intervention perceived less social isolation and parenting stress. They also discovered certain intervention-specific effects, although both methods presume to improve parent–child interaction. Self-help groups appeared to serve as a surrogate informal support network, thereby reducing stress; in contrast, parent education programs appeared to alter maternal perceptions of child responsiveness in a positive direction. Following the initiation of a family support program in Michigan involving the payments of cash subsidies to families with severely handicapped children, Meyers and Marcenko (1989) found that mothers reported significantly less stress and enhanced life satisfaction, coupled with less anticipation of the need for out-of-home placement. Increases in family satisfaction with services following the implementation of a family support program have routinely been shown (Waite, 1988).

Integrated service programs for persons with mental retardation or developmental disabilities are often geared toward parent involvement, comprehensive skill training, adaptation, coping, and social and family support. Dunst, Trivette, and Deal (1988) developed an extensive theoretical framework for conceptualizing what they call "family enablement and empowerment" (p. 6) and validated numerous measures to assess their constructs within a range of human service programs. For example, Project SHaRE (Source of Help Receive and Exchanged) enables families with disabled, handicapped, and developmentally at-risk children to build and maintain social support networks. The program operates as a barter system in which individuals and groups provide assistance to one another based on reciprocal obligation. Utilizing a multitrait–multimethod evaluation design, Dunst, Trivette, Gordon, and Pletcher (1989) demonstrated that participating families can identify and meet their needs, mobilize resources, broaden social networks, and improve personal and family well-being and overall functioning.

More recently, Dunst et al. (1993) published a comprehensive and compelling analysis of the links among family support program elements, differential characteristics, and program outcomes. Based on sophisticated statistical analyses (e.g., structural equation modeling and multiple regression), they reported on data from a national study depicting relationships between family support policies and practices at state and community levels. Particularly interesting is their analysis of the association between provider helping style and family empowerment.

Despite the promise held out by these and similar findings, family support and education programs are difficult to implement in community settings, and they do not address all of the needs experienced by families. Herman and Hazel (1991) surveyed county mental health authorities in Michigan prior to and following the implementation of a policy change for programs serving individuals with disabilities. Core family support services of case management, parent training, respite, and crisis intervention were supplemented with improved parent involvement, assessment, in-home services (e.g., homemakers and home health), support groups, and counseling services across the state. They found that increases in the overall availability of services were not accompanied by improved access, as defined by the length of time families waited for services. Case management and counseling were noted as being especially difficult to make accessible. Barriers to filling service delivery gaps in family support included limited resource availability (e.g., funding and staffing), insufficient coordination among service components, and lack of commitment to the concept of paraprofessional services.

Preventive health care and health promotion. Recognition of the interrelatedness of health problems has given rise to integrated program models for preventive health care and health promotion. High rates of pregnancy, sexually transmitted disease, drug use, mental illness, and mortality among some adolescents, for example, necessitate comprehensive and integrated responses that allow for linking services across different health domains and easy access to needed services. Thus, the Michigan Department of Public Health has established Adolescent Health Delivery Demonstration programs for health education, screening, case management, and referral. These programs are located in schools and other community settings and deliver both primary and preventive care. They blend state general funds with local and in-kind contributions, while also providing a billing system to access Medicaid and other third-party payors. Multnomah County (Portland), Oregon established school-based health centers in 1986, using a combination of state, federal, and local funding. Targeted toward providing comprehensive health care for adolescents and reducing teen pregnancy, the scope of services offered includes diagnosis and treatment of minor injury and illness, management of chronic conditions, mental health services, health promotion activities, reproductive health, family planning, and AIDS education and prevention (Oomes & Owen, 1991).

In 1981, seven federal categorical maternal and child health (MCH) programs were consolidated into a single block grant, allowing states and municipalities discretion regarding MCH program development. Foci of the present program include the following: (a) reducing infant mortality, preventable diseases, and handicapping conditions; (b) increasing immunizations and health assessments; (c) promoting maternal and infant health for low income and at risk individuals; and (d) providing preventive and primary health care to children and families. A wide variety of integrated services initiatives have occurred across the country within this program model, often in collaboration with other agencies and organizations (Carlton & Poole, 1990).

School-based and school-linked services. The focus of school-based and school-linked services is to bring nonacademic services that support families and youth into school settings, the only institution with which virtually all children and families have contact. For instance, in the Memphis City Schools, a broad range of educational, mental health, and social services have been integrated within a school-based mental health center, bringing together psychologists, social workers, substance abuse counselors, and paraprofessionals within a coherent and multidisciplinary program. In addition to traditional assessment and treatment programs, the center provides teacher training, substance abuse counseling and support groups, social skills training groups, homemaker services, child abuse prevention programs, teen pregnancy programs, and a host of similar needs-driven efforts—all under the rubric of the school organization (Paavola, Hannah, & Nichol, 1989).

An effort sponsored by the Annie E. Casey Foundation is targeted toward at-risk youth in large urban areas, such as Bridgeport (CT), Little Rock, and Pittsburgh. The program involves screening, developing multidisciplinary support teams, and case management, and it seeks to improve attendance and graduation rates, increase youth employment after high school, and reduce adolescent pregnancy. In *School of the Future,* Holtzman (1992) described an ambitious project (partly funded by the Hogg Foundation for Mental Health) in four Texas cities (Austin, Dallas, Houston, and San Antonio) to foster the coordination and delivery of an extensive array of health and human services through neighborhood schools. Community renewal, family preservation, and child development are all cited as goals of this approach to serving low-income families.

Kentucky's Family Resource and Youth Service Centers were established through the Kentucky Education Reform Act of 1990 (Steffy, 1993). Each school where at least 20% of the student body is eligible for free lunch (a measure of economic disadvantage) may apply for such a center, and by the 1993–94 school year, 373 were in place. These centers provide before- and after-school child care; parent education and training; employment services; mental health counseling; and referral for medical, social, mental health, and family support services; in addition to community resource development activities.

A formative evaluation of the project (Illback, 1993b), based on 1992–93 data regarding 18,912 families and 21,270 targeted students, indicated that participants exhibited complex and interrelated difficulties, with health, behavior, emotional, and learning problems of greatest concern. Health services and referral emerged as the most frequently utilized services; parent training, child care, and counseling services also were extensively used within these centers. Preliminary outcome data suggested improvements in classroom performance variables (as rated by teachers), but more global measures of change (e.g., grades and achievement) did not register gains. Families reported receiving increased social support from both the program and informal sources in their communities (e.g., relatives, friends, and neighbors).

A related qualitative evaluation (Kalafat & Illback, 1993), based on structured interviews with key informants in 10 sites, revealed that centers helped families gain access to and integrate services, often becoming the service providers of last resort (filling service delivery gaps) in many rural communities. However, centers' ability to maintain focus on their essential mission (promoting school readiness), in light of immense family and community needs, was of concern. The most successful centers were those whose coordinator displayed personal and management characteristics that meshed with family and community needs; particularly salient characteristics were found to be community connectedness, action orientation, and persistence. Variability among coordinators was seen in dimensions such as perceptions of the mission, conceptualizations regarding family support and empowerment, and knowledge regarding best practices for program management and implementation.

Implications for Psychology

The concept of service integration has several implications for psychology as a profession. On a general level, integrated service models will increase the amount of broad-based services available to children and families living in or near poverty by increasing access to services, generating new program alternatives, and freeing up funds now tied to rigid eligibility criteria. However, it also seems likely that psychologists will remain one of a number of eligible providers to deliver such services and, therefore, continue to be in competition with other professions to demonstrate relevance and efficacy. Because decisions about service delivery are more likely to be outcome oriented, consumer driven, and cost conscious, the particular strengths of psychology (including its conceptual underpinnings, empirical base, and concern for assessing outcomes) can enable the profession to flourish in such

an environment, assuming the profession is willing to rethink and retool.

As integrated services become more prevalent in child and family service systems, a number of implications for psychological practice, training, research, and leadership are apparent.

Practice

Psychological services delivered within an integrated services framework will look and feel substantially different for practitioners who presently work in relative isolation in service systems that tend not to collaborate and are categorical in their orientation. In more integrated systems, practitioners will be able to exercise greater flexibility in the range of activities with which they engage, and they will not be as constrained in regard to funding source and program eligibility considerations. They will spend more time working as part of a team, in concert with a variety of providers, family members, caregivers, and community members. They are likely to spend more time in naturalistic home, school, and other community settings, in addition to consulting offices. They will routinely work at removing the boundaries between various social systems that impinge on children and families to coordinate activities, manage conflict, and ensure focus and quality of services. Perhaps most important, the orientation to service delivery will shift from an emphasis on ameliorating dysfunction to one of joining with families and helping them develop support systems that will enable them to attain the behavioral changes they desire (Roberts & Magrab, 1991).

It also should be acknowledged that alternative, less costly approaches to addressing child and family needs will increase within an integrated services approach. Thus, although a child problem may previously have been conceptualized exclusively within an office-based psychotherapeutic approach, using an integrated services approach, the psychologist may collaborate with caregivers, friends, relatives, and other community members to meet the needs of the individual.

Training

Service integration has important implications for training psychologists in the direction of greater breadth and flexibility. A psychologist who is serving as the only mental health professional in an elementary school or public health clinic, for example, will need to be competent in a broad number of skills and approaches, ranging from typical developmental concerns and issues to guidelines for monitoring commonly used child psychotropic medications, family interventions, and community consultation. Professionals who can operate effectively within a variety of human service settings will have greater possibilities of employment in an integrated service system than those whose background is limited to a narrow psychological practice specialty.

Three areas of psychological training appear underrepresented in current training curricula: (a) foundational knowledge about families, organizations, and communities; (b) consultation and education skill development; and (c) program management and supervision skills. Most training programs do not emphasize theoretical and empirical knowledge bases in areas such as behavioral ecology, organizational theory, prevention programming, community psychology, systems of care (e.g., health, welfare, and education), and public financing that lay the foundation for practice within an integrated service approach. Moreover, clinical coursework on family intervention may stress psychopathology from a family systems perspective but may not include family support and education approaches.

Also, consultation and educative functions have been recognized as core competencies for professional psychologists (Illback, Maher, & Kopplin, 1991). Within an integrated service system, psychologists will need more comprehensive training with family-, school-, and community-oriented consultative methods and strategies and collaborate with other professionals (Zins, Kratochwill, & Elliott, 1993). Finally, strategies associated with program management (e.g., planning, budgeting, human resource management, and information systems design) and supervision (e.g., personnel management and administrative supervision) will become more essential components of practitioners' repertoires as their responsibilities shift from direct service providers to coordinators and leaders.

Leadership

Psychologists are in an excellent position to assume leadership roles within integrated service programs, given their level of training and skills. In addition to the more traditional aspects of program administration and supervision, leadership activities can focus on establishing an integrative strategic vision for child-serving organizations, building collaborative teams, and facilitating planned organizational change. Leadership can also be expressed by being an effective team member; competent leaders are also proficient at followership and collaboration.

Research and Evaluation

Psychological research on the efficacy of integrated service delivery approaches for children and families

represents a unique contribution. Such research is distinct from traditional controlled experimentation in that the array of target problems is vast, treatment programs are diverse and multifaceted, and outcome measurement complicated. Practicing psychologists need to become proficient in a broader range of methods and procedures (e.g., quasi-experimental design, multivariate analysis, and program evaluation techniques) in order to conduct such social policy and program-related investigations. Psychologists are also in a unique position to help service systems develop and validate information systems to allow for ongoing program monitoring, management, and improvement.

Conclusion

The overall benefit of changes toward a more integrated service system is greater effectiveness in the use of psychology to advance the public interest. There are at present large numbers of children and families living in or near poverty whose needs in the area of health, mental health, education, and social welfare are not being met. In addition to the personal cost to these individuals, the prosperity of the country suffers from their resultant inability to contribute fully as citizens. By advocating for integrated services, psychology has an opportunity to exercise leadership (in collaboration with other concerned persons and professions) to secure for these children and families their right to effective, responsive, and comprehensive services.

References

Achenbach, T. M. (1991). *Manual for the Child Behavior Checklist/4–18 and 1991 Profile.* Burlington, VT: University of Vermont Department of Psychiatry.

Apter, S. J. (1982). *Troubled children, troubled systems.* New York: Pergamon.

Auclaire, P., & Schwartz, I. (1986). *An evaluation of the effectiveness of intensive home-based services as an alternative to placement for adolescents and their families.* Minneapolis: Hennepin County Services Department and the University of Minnesota, Hubert H. Humphrey Institute of Public Affairs.

Attkisson, C., & Broskowski, A. (1978). Evaluation and the emerging human services concept. In C. C. Attkisson, W. A. Hargreaves, M. J. Horowitz, & J. E. Sorensen (Eds.), *Evaluation of human services programs* (pp. 3–26). New York: Academic.

Bath, H. I., & Haapala, D. A. (1993). Intensive family preservation services with abused and neglected children: An examination of group differences. *Child Abuse and Neglect, 17,* 213–225.

Bath, H. I., Richey, C. A., & Haapala, D. A. (1992). Child age and outcome correlates in intensive family preservation services. *Children and Youth Services Review, 14,* 389–406.

Behar, L. (1992). *Fort Bragg child and adolescent mental health demonstration project.* Raleigh: North Carolina Division of Mental Health, Developmental Disabilities, and Substance Abuse Services, Child and Family Services Branch.

Belle, D. (1990). Poverty and women's mental health. *American Psychologist, 45,* 385–389.

Bickman, L. (1993). *The evaluation of the Fort Bragg demonstration project.* Nashville: Vanderbilt University, Center for Mental Health Policy.

Birch, H. G., Richardson, S. A., Baird, D., Horobin, G., & Illsley, R. (1970). *Mental subnormality in the community: A clinical and epidemiologic study.* Baltimore: Williams & Wilkins.

Burchard, J., Rosen, L., Heckman, T., Geldebien, M., Pandian, N., & Stith, A. (1993, March). *The role of youth satisfaction surveys in evaluating outcomes for children and adolescents receiving community-based, wraparound services.* Paper presented at the annual research conference of the Florida Mental Health Institue, University of South Florida, Tampa.

Carlton, T. O., & Poole, D. L. (1990). Trends in maternal and child health care: Implications for research and issues for social work practice. *Social Work in Health Care, 15,* 45–62.

Caro, P., & Derevensky, J. L. (1991). Family-focused intervention model: Implementation and research findings. *Topics in Early Childhood Special Education, 11,* 66–80.

Children's Defense Fund. (1992). *The state of America's children: 1992.* Washington, DC: Author.

Costello, E. J. (1986). Primary care pediatrics and child psychopathology: A review of diagnostic, treatment, and referral practices. *Pediatrics, 78,* 1044–1051.

Day, C., & Roberts, M. C. (1991). Activities of the child and adolescent service system program for improving mental health services for children and families. *Journal of Clinical Child Psychology, 20,* 340–350.

Dumas, J. E., & Wahler, R. G. (1983). Predictors of treatment outcome in parent training: Mother insularity and socioeconomic disadvantage. *Behavioral Assessment, 5,* 301–313.

Dunst, C. J., Trivette, C. M., & Deal, A. G. (1988). *Enabling and empowering families: Principles and guidelines for practice.* Cambridge, MA: Brookline.

Dunst, C. J., Trivette, C. M., Gordon, N. J., & Pletcher, L. L. (1989). Building and mobilizing informal support networks. In G. H. Singer & L. K. Irvin (Eds.), *Support for caregiving families: Enabling positive adaptation to disability* (pp. 121–142). Baltimore: Brookes.

Dunst, C. J., Trivette, C. M., Starnes, A. L., Hamby, D. W., & Gordon, N. J. (1993). *Building and evaluating family support initiatives: A national study of programs for persons with developmental disabilities.* Baltimore: Brookes.

Dunst, C. J., Trivette, C. M., & Thompson, R. B. (1990). Supporting and strengthening family functioning: Toward a congruence between principles and practice. *Prevention in Human Services, 9,* 19–43.

Edelman, P. B., & Radin, B. A. (1991). *Serving children and families effectively: How the past can help chart the future.* Washington, DC: Education and Human Services Consortium.

Elementary and Secondary Education Act, Title I: Compensatory Education. (1965).

Feldman, L. H. (1991). Evaluating the impact of intensive family preservation services in New Jersey. In K. Wells & D. E. Biegel (Eds.), *Family preservation services: Research and evaluation* (pp. 47–71). Newbury Park, CA: Sage.

Fullan, M., Miles, M. B., & Taylor, G. (1980). Organization development in schools: The state of the art. *Review of Educational Research, 50,* 121–183.

Georgia Division of Mental Health, Mental Retardation, & Substance Abuse. (1992). *A review of the August SED report.* Atlanta: Author.

Glisson, C. (1992). *The adjudication, placement, and psychosocial functioning of children in state custody.* Knoxville: University of Tennessee, College of Social Work.

Gortmaker, S. L., Walker, D. K., Weitzman, M., & Sobol, A. M. (1990). Chronic conditions, socioeconomic risks, and behavioral problems in children and adolescents. *Pediatrics, 85,* 267–276.

Graden, J. L., Zins, J. E., & Curtis, M. J. (1988). *Alternative educational delivery systems: Enhancing instructional options for all students.* Washington, DC: National Association of School Psychologists.

Haapala, D. A., & Kinney, J. M. (1988). Avoiding out-of-home placement of high-risk status offenders through the use of intensive home-based family preservation services. *Criminal Justice and Behavior, 15,* 334–348.

Halvorson, V. M. (1992). A home-based family intervention program. *Hospital and Community Psychiatry, 43,* 395–397.

Heflinger, C. A., Bickman, L. B., Lane, T., Keeton, W. P., Hodges, V. K., & Behar, L. B. (1991). The Fort Bragg child and adolescent demonstration: Implementing and evaluating a continuum of care. In A. Algarin & R. M. Friedman (Eds.), *A system of care for children's mental health: Expanding the research base* (pp. 83–96). Tampa: Florida Mental Health Institute.

Henggeler, S. W., Melton, G. B., & Smith, L. A. (1992). Family preservation using multisystemic therapy: An effective alternative to incarcerating serious juvenile offenders. *Journal of Consulting and Clinical Psychology, 60,* 953–961.

Herman, S. E., & Hazel, K. L. (1991). Evaluation of family support services: Changes in availability and accessibility. *Mental Retardation, 29,* 351–357.

Hinckley, E. C., & Ellis, W. F. (1985). An effective alternative to residential placement: Home-based services. *Journal of Clinical Child Psychology, 14,* 209–213.

Hobbs, N. (1975). *The futures of children.* San Francisco: Jossey-Bass.

Holtzman, W. H. (Ed.). (1992). *School of the future.* Austin, TX: American Psychological Association and Hogg Foundation for Mental Health.

Illback, R. J. (1993a). *Evaluation of the Kentucky IMPACT program for children and youth with severe emotional disabilities: Year two.* Frankfort: Kentucky Division of Mental Health, Children and Youth Services Branch.

Illback, R. J. (1993b). *Formative evaluation of the Kentucky Family Resource and Youth Service Centers: Analysis of program trends.* Frankfort: Kentucky Cabinet for Human Resources.

Illback, R. J., Maher, C. A., & Kopplin, D. (1991). Consultation and education competency. In R. Peterson, J. D. McHolland, R. J. Bent, E. Davis-Russell, G. Edwall, K. Polite, D. L. Singer, & G. Stricker (Eds.), *The core curriculum in professional psychology* (pp. 115–120). Washington, DC: American Psychological Association.

Illback, R. J., & Zins, J. E. (1993). Organizational perspectives in child consultation. In J. E. Zins, T. R. Kratochwill, & S. N. Elliott (Eds.), *Handbook of consultation services for children: Applications in educational and clinical settings* (pp. 87–109). San Francisco: Jossey-Bass.

Institute of Medicine. (1982). *Health services integration: Lessons for the 1980s.* Washington, DC: Author.

Jordan, D. D., & Hernandez, M. (1990). The Ventura planning model: A proposal for mental health reforms. *Journal of Mental Health Administration, 17,* 26–47.

Kalafat, J., & Illback, R. J. (1993). *Implementation evaluation of the Family Resource and Youth Service Centers: A qualitative analysis.* Frankfort: Kentucky Cabinet for Human Resources.

Kentucky Cabinet for Human Resources. (1990). *Kentucky's comprehensive mental health services plan on behalf of adults with severe mental illness and children and youth with severe emotional problems.* Frankfort: Author.

Kiesler, C. A. (1992). U.S. mental health policy: Doomed to fail? *American Psychologist, 47,* 1077–1082.

Kinney, J. M., Madsen, B., Fleming, T., & Haapala, D. (1977). Homebuilders: Keeping families together. *Journal of Consulting and Clinical Psychology, 45,* 667–673.

Knitzer, J. (1982). *Unclaimed children: The failure of public responsibility to children and adolescents in need of mental health services.* Washington, DC: Children's Defense Fund.

Levine, M., & Levine, A. (1992). *Helping children: A social history.* New York: Oxford University Press.

March, M. (1968). The neighborhood center concept. *Public Welfare, 26,* 97–111.

Melaville, A. I., & Blank, M. J. (1991). *What it takes: Structuring interagency partnerships to connect children and families with comprehensive services.* Washington, DC: Institute for Educational Leadership.

Meyers, J. C., & Marcenko, M. O. (1989). Impact of a cash subsidy program for families of children with severe developmental disabilities. *Mental Retardation, 27,* 383–387.

National Commission on Children. (1991). *Beyond rhetoric: A new American agenda for children and families.* Washington, DC: U.S. Government Printing Office.

National Commission on Child Welfare and Family Preservation. (1990). *A commitment to change.* Washington, DC: American Public Welfare Association.

Nelson, K. E. (1991). Populations and outcomes in five family preservation programs. In K. Wells & D. E. Biegel (Eds). *Family preservation services: Research and evaluation* (pp. 72–91). Newbury Park, CA: Sage.

Nugent, W., Carpenter, D., & Parks, J. (1993). A statewide evaluation of family preservation and family reunification services. *Research on Social Work Practice, 3,* 40–65.

Oomes, T., & Owen, T. (1991). *Promoting adolescent health and well-being through school-linked, multi-service, family-friendly programs.* Washington, DC: American Association for Marriage and Family Therapy.

Paavola, J. C., Hannah, F. P., & Nichol, G. T. (1989). The Memphis City Schools Mental Health Center: A program description. *Professional School Psychology, 4,* 61–74.

Pecora, P. J., Fraser, M. W., & Haapala, D. A. (1991). Client outcomes and issues for program design. In K. Wells & D. E. Biegel (Eds). *Family preservation services: Research and evaluation* (pp. 3–32). Newbury Park, CA: Sage.

Public Law 93–247. (1974). *Child Abuse Prevention and Treatment Act.*

Public Law 94–142. (1975). *Education for All Handicapped Children Act,* 20 U.S. §1401.

Public Law 99–660. (1970). *Community Mental Health Centers Act.*

Roberts, R. N., & Magrab, P. R. (1991). Psychologists' role in a family-centered approach to practice, training, and research with young children. *American Psychologist, 46,* 144–148.

Rosenblatt, A., & Attkisson, C. (1992). Integrating systems of care in California for youth with severe emotional disturbance: III. Answers that lead to questions about out-of-home placements and the California AB377 evalation project. *Journal of Child and Family Studies, 2,* 119–141.

Rossi, P. H. (1992). Strategies for evaluation [Special issue]. *Children and Youth Services Review, 14,* 167–191.

Sarason, S. (1974). *The psychological sense of community: Prospects for a community psychology.* San Francisco: Jossey-Bass.

Saxe, L., Cross, T., & Silverman, N. (1988). Children's mental health: The gap between what we know and what we do. *American Psychologist, 43,* 800–807.

Saxe, L., Cross, T., Silverman, N., Batchelor, W. F., & Dougherty, D. (1987). *Children's mental health: Problems and services.* Durham, NC: Duke University Press.

Schorr, L. B., & Schorr, D. (1988). Within our reach: Breaking the cycle of disadvantage. New York: Anchor.

Schwartz, I. M., AuClaire, P., & Harris, L. J. (1991). Family preservation services as an alternative to out-of-home placement of adolescents: The Hennipin County experience. In K. Wells & D. E. Biegel (Eds.), *Family preservation services: Research and evaluation* (pp. 33–46). Newbury Park, CA: Sage.

Singer, G. H., & Irvin, L. K. (1989). Family caregiving, stress, and support. In G. H. Singer & L. K. Irvin (Eds.), *Support for caregiving families: Enabling positive adaptation to disability* (pp. 3–26). Baltimore: Brookes.

Stroul, B., Goldman, S., Lourie, I., Katz-Leavy, J., & Zeigler-Dendy, C. (1992). *Profiles of local systems of care for children and adolescents with severe emotional disturbances.* Washington, DC: Georgetown University Child Development Center, CASSP Technical Assistance Center.

Telleen, S. (1990). Parental beliefs and help-seeking in mothers' use of a community-based family support program. *Journal of Community Psychology, 18,* 264–276.

Telleen, S., Herzog, A., & Kilbane, T. L. (1989). Impact of a family support program on mothers' social support and parenting stress. *American Journal of Orthopsychiatry, 59,* 410–419.

Tuma, J. (1989). Mental health services for children: The state of the art. *American Psychologist, 44,* 188–199.

U.S. Department of Commerce, Bureau of the Census. (1990). *Money income and poverty in the United States* (Serial P–60, No. 168). Washington, DC: U.S. Government Printing Office.

Vermont Department of Mental Health & Mental Retardation. (1993). *Vermont New Directions evaluation of children and adolescent services.* Waterbury, VT: Office of Research and Evaluation.

Virginia Department of Mental Health, Mental Retardation, and Substance Abuse Services. (1992). *Demonstration project interim evaluation results.* Richmond, VA: Office of Research and Evaluation.

Waite, S. (1988). Real help for families in trouble: Evaluation of a family support program. *Journal of Child Care, 3,* 47–54.

Weiss, H. B., & Jacobs, F. H. (Eds.). (1988). *Evaluating family programs.* New York: Aldine DeGruyter.

Weissbourd, B., & Kagan, S. L. (1989). Family support programs: Catalysts for change. *American Journal of Orthopsychiatry, 59,* 20–31.

Wells, K., & Biegel, D. E. (Eds.). (1991). *Family preservation services: Research and evaluation.* Newbury Park, CA: Sage.

Yuan, Y. T., & Rivest, M. (Eds.). (1990). *Preserving families: Evaluation resources for practitioners and policymakers.* Newbury Park, CA: Sage.

Zigler, E., & Black, K. B. (1989). America's family support movement: Strengths and limitations. *American Journal of Orthopsychiatry, 59,* 6–19.

Zins, J. E., Kratochwill, T. R., & Elliott, S. N. (1993). *Handbook of consultation services for children: Applications in educational and clinical settings.* San Francisco: Jossey-Bass.

Received September 9, 1993
Final revision received April 6, 1994

Journal of Clinical Child Psychology
1994, Vol. 23, 425–434

Contribution of Early Intervention and Early Caregiving Experiences to Resilience in Low-Birthweight, Premature Children Living in Poverty

Robert H. Bradley, Leanne Whiteside, and Daniel J. Mundfrom
University of Arkansas at Little Rock

Patrick H. Casey, Kelly J. Kelleher, and Sandra K. Pope
University of Arkansas for Medical Sciences

Examined the Infant Health and Development Program (IHDP) and the quality of care experienced at home by premature, low-birthweight children (LBW) living in poverty. Only 26 of 243 LBW children (11%) who received no intervention were identified as functioning in the normal range for cognitive, social/adaptive, health, and growth parameters at age 3 compared to 59 out of 153 (39%) from the intervention group. LBW children who showed early signs of resiliency differed from nonresilient children in that they were receiving more responsive, accepting, stimulating, organized care in their own homes; and they were living in safer, less crowded homes. Overall, premature, LBW children born into poverty have a very poor prognosis of functioning within normal ranges in all domains of development. However, those reared in a setting with three or more protective factors and those who participated in the IHDP intervention more often showed early signs of resiliency.

The chronic adverse conditions faced by the poor have been identified as important risk factors for a wide variety of physical, mental, and social problems (Margolis, Greenberg, & Keyes, 1992; Spurlock, Hinds, Skaggs, & Hernandez, 1987; Starfield, 1988; U.S. Department of Health and Human Services, 1991). Parker, Greer, and Zuckerman (1988) argued that children

living in poverty experience double jeopardy. First, they are exposed more frequently to such risks as medical illnesses, family stress, inadequate social support, and parental depression. Second, they experience more serious consequences from these risks than do children from higher socioeconomic status. (p. 1127)

Sameroff, Seifer, Barocas, Zax, and Greenspan (1987) showed that low socioeconomic status is often accompanied by a proliferation of social and psychological risk factors and that it is the accumulation of these detrimental circumstances that "produce morbidity in a variety of domains" (p. 349). The chronic stress and diminished material and psychological resources that often characterize poverty environments combine in synergistic fashion to the detriment of young children.

Although the relation between poverty and poor outcomes for children is well documented (Escalona, 1982; Russell, Carr-Hill, & Illsley, 1984; Werner, 1989), the precise mechanisms by which poverty exerts its negative influence on child health and development remains unclear. Most researchers hypothesize that the quality of parenting children receive and the general conditions of their physical surroundings may play the largest role (Boyce & Jemerin, 1990; Sameroff, 1983; U.S. Department of Health and Human Services, 1985). One of the pervasive effects of poverty is that it inhibits parents in their parenting role (McAdoo, 1988). Poverty often creates stresses and frustrations that constrain parents from providing the kinds of stimulating and nurturant care they desire for their children. Compared to parents who live in more affluent circumstances, poverty-stricken parents are neglectful more often because of feelings of depression and powerlessness, violent more often due to anger and substance abuse,

The Infant Health and Development Program was funded by grants from the Robert Wood Johnson Foundation to the Department of Pediatrics, Stanford University, Stanford, CA; from the Frank Porter Graham Child Development Center, University of North Carolina at Chapel Hill; and from the eight participating universities. Additional support for the National Study Office was provided to the Department of Pediatrics, Stanford University from the Pew Charitable Trusts; from the Bureau of Maternal and Child Health and Resources Development and the National Institute of Child Health and Human Development, Health Resources and Services Administration, Public Health Service (Grant MCH–06515); and from the Stanford Center for the Study of Families, Children, and Youth.

Requests for reprints should be sent to Robert H. Bradley, Center for Research on Teaching and Learning, University of Arkansas at Little Rock, 2801 South University Avenue, Little Rock, AR 72204–1099.

and disorganized more often due to feelings of alienation. In her review of the impact of economic hardship on African-American families and children, McLoyd (1990) argued that an excess of negative life events coupled with chronic undesirable conditions and the absence or disruption of marital bonds lead to psychological distress (e.g., anxiety, irritability, and depression) and to the use of physical punishment as a means of controlling children's actions. Contrarily, there is evidence that the impact of poverty on parenting is not consistent across all sociocultural groups (Garcia Coll, 1990; Laosa, 1980; McLoyd, 1990).

Despite the fact that children who grow up in conditions of poverty tend to have a higher incidence of health and developmental problems, research has shown that poverty is not uniform in its impact on children (Escalona, 1982). Boyce and Jemerin (1990) described a group of resilient children who were characterized as having environmental risk factors yet developed into well-functioning individuals, free from notable developmental problems (see also Werner, 1989). In a recent study, Bradley et al. (1994) found that, among 243 premature, low birthweight (LBW) children living in poverty, only 26 children were identified as functioning in the normal range for cognitive, social/adaptive, health, and growth parameters at age 3. These children, who showed early signs of resiliency, differed from nonresilient children in that they were receiving more responsive, accepting, stimulating, and organized care. They were also living in safer, less-crowded homes. Six protective aspects of caregiving were identified and used as part of a cumulative protection index. Children with fewer than three protective aspects of caregiving present at age 1 had only a 2% probability of being resilient; those with fewer than three protective aspects of caregiving were present at age 3 had only a 6% probability of being resilient.

Another factor that increases the probability that children born into poverty will show acceptable levels of health and developmental functioning is the availability of high-quality early intervention (Bennett, 1987; Clarke-Stewart & Fein, 1983; Ramey, Bryant, & Suarez, 1983). Reviews of studies on early intervention have shown that poor children have benefited from a variety of different programs, including those that focus directly on the child and those that provide parent education and support. Both home visitation models and models that involve center-based educational programming for children have been effective in increasing cognitive and adaptive competence in children (Farran, 1990; Olds & Kitzman, 1990). Although both biologically and environmentally at-risk children appear to benefit from high-quality intervention programs, few studies have examined the effects of intervention on children who are both biologically at risk and come from impoverished environments. The Infant Health and Development Program (IDHP, 1990)

was a multifaceted intervention designed for LBW infants and their families. This multisite, randomized, clinical trial tested the efficacy of a program consisting of high-quality pediatric follow-up for the first 3 years of life, combined with family education and support services provided in the home over those first 3 years, plus an educational day care experience beginning at age 1 and lasting until age 3. Children in the IHDP intervention group were compared to children who received only the pediatric follow-up experience. Several studies have shown the positive impact of IHDP on children's health and development through the first 3 years of life (Brooks-Gunn, Klebanov, Liaw, & Spiker, 1993; IHDP, 1990; Ramey et al., 1992).

The purpose of this study was to determine whether the percentage of premature, LBW children living in poverty who are free of major developmental problems in early childhood (i.e., they are resilient) is greater for those who received the IHDP intervention than for those who received only pediatric follow-up. Using data from the IHDP, we also examined whether an accumulation of protective caregiving experiences in the home environment increases the odds of children showing early resilience. According to Rutter (1987), identifying protective factors is not enough. It is important to move beyond identification to the delineation of protective mechanisms. Thus, we focused on specific aspects of caregiving and the caregiving context that may serve as protective mechanisms because the family environment most directly impinges on children through such aspects of caregiving.

For this study, we adopted a more holistic perspective on resilience than is typically used in studies of risk. Specifically, children living with the dual risk of prematurity and poverty are deemed to be resilient when they function well across all domains of health and development. This perspective was adopted because poverty is best viewed as "a conglomerate of conditions and events that amounts to a pervasive rather than a bounded stressor" (Huston, McLoyd, & Garcia Coll, 1994, p. 277). Likewise, prematurity is associated with a variety of conditions and events that may be reflected in a number of different vulnerabilities. For many premature children, the pervasive stress of poverty may trigger a negative cascade of psychobiological reactions, but the particular cascade of reactions will be a function of the child's specific strengths and vulnerabilities and the child's specific history of transactions with the environment. In sum, the particular developmental system affected by the combination of poverty and prematurity will vary from child to child and, for a given child, from one point in the life span to another— albeit by no means are all children negatively affected. However, if any developmental problems arise, the child's ability to function comfortably and productively across all areas of life is, to some extent, compromised.

Method

Sample

The participants in this study were consecutively-born preterm (≤ 37 weeks gestational age), LBW (≤ 2,500 g) infants enrolled from hospitals in eight cities (Little Rock, AR; Bronx, NY; Boston, MA; Miami, FL; Philadelphia, PA; Dallas, TX; Seattle, WA; New Haven, CT). This report is based on the low-income subsample from the larger IHDP. The IHDP sample, study design, enrollment criteria and measures have been described in detail elsewhere (IHDP, 1990). The IHDP was a randomized clinical trial involving 985 infants and their families. The intervention began at 40 weeks postconceptional age (after discharge from the hospital) and lasted until children were 3 years old (gestation-corrected age). All infants and their families were assessed at 40 weeks postconceptional age and at 4, 8, 12, 18, 24, 30, and 36 months gestation-corrected age. Infant and family data were collected at these visits. Cognitive assessments were performed at 12, 24, and 36 months of age, and behavioral data were collected at 24 and 36 months of age. Home visits were made at 12 and 36 months to assess the quality of the home environment. Two thirds of the infants weighed < 2,000 g at birth; the remaining one third weighed between 2,001 g and 2,500 g. Within each weight group, children were randomly assigned to intervention and follow-up groups (at a ratio of 1:2, respectively). The groups were also balanced for sex, maternal education, race, and primary language spoken in the home.

Of the 608 follow-up and 377 intervention families in the IHDP sample, children with serious chronic health problems (e.g., bronchopulmonary dysplasia, hypothyroidism, cerebral palsy, and heart problems) were excluded, leaving 896 participants. Of these 896 remaining children, 410 (243 follow-up and 167 intervention) lived in poverty, and they comprised the sample used for analyses. Poverty thresholds for 1985, as defined by the U.S. Bureau of the Census, were used at all three time points as a guide to identify families living in poverty (U.S. Department of Commerce, 1985). Poverty thresholds were based on household income and defined to be $7,500 for families of two; $10,000 for families of three; $15,000 for families of four, five, or six; $20,000 for families of seven; and $25,000 for families of eight or more. The poverty criteria for 1985 were used at each time point because the actual dollar figures used by the Bureau of the Census to determine poverty changed just slightly from 1985 to 1988 and because the information on family income in the IHDP data set was not in the form of exact dollar figures but rather in dollar ranges (e.g., $5,000 to $7,499). Because exact calculations of poverty status could not be made from these categories, we had to rely on estimates and thus opted for a more conservative operationalization of poverty status based on the 1985 guidelines. Families were considered to be living in poverty if they were below these thresholds for at least 2 years of the first 3 years of the infant's life.

In this low-income group, 15% of the mothers were Caucasian, 70% were African American, 14% were Hispanic, and 1% were from other ethnic or racial groups. At the time of birth, the average maternal age was 22.7 years ($SD = 5.4$), and 26% of the mothers were married. The target child was the first birth for 35% of the mothers, and 53% of the infants were girls. Fifty-seven percent of the mothers had not completed high school, and 29% reported receiving only their high school diploma. The mean score of mothers on the Peabody Picture Vocabulary Test (Dunn & Dunn, 1981) was 70.5 ($SD = 15.2$). By design, the maximum birthweight of the sample was 2,500 g, and the maximum gestational age was 38 weeks. The mean birthweight was 1,789 g ($SD = 466$ g), and the mean gestational age was 33.17 weeks ($SD = 2.69$). Twenty-one percent of the infants were small for gestational age based on birthweight. Bivariate analyses revealed no differences between intervention and follow-up groups on any of these demographic indices. Of the 410 families living in poverty, 57 (35 follow-up, 22 intervention) were missing data. The specific cases excluded from particular analyses varied from one analysis to another. For most analyses, there were fewer than 25 cases with missing data. There was a small difference in the percentage of missing data from African-American families as compared to families from the other racial and ethnic groups.

Intervention

Infants in both intervention and follow-up groups received basic pediatric services (including periodic medical, developmental, and familial assessments) from 40 weeks corrected age (corrected for prematurity) to 36 months corrected age. The IHDP, lasting from the time of hospital discharge to age 3, consisted of weekly home visits through age 1 and biweekly visits thereafter. Children in the intervention group also attended a child development center (at least 4 hr per day, 5 days per week) beginning at age 1 and terminating at age 3. The home visit component included using a problem-solving curriculum (Wasik, 1984). A coordinated educational curriculum of learning games and activities was used for both the home visit component and the child development center component (Sparling & Lewis, 1985). Although efforts were made to individualize curricula for both parents and children at all sites, every effort was made (including extensive training and monitoring) to ensure that the assessments and the program were implemented in the same way at all sites.

Measures

Because the IHDP was structured as a multisite clinical trial, it was essential that study measures be given consistently across all sites. For this reason, substantial training was provided to all data collectors to ensure proper administration of the measures. In addition, periodic reliability checks were made on all data collectors to determine whether each was properly administering the measures. All measures were given in English. (Note that one of the criteria for participation was competence in spoken English.) Most of the data collectors were Caucasian women; only a few women were minorities. Data collectors were randomly assigned to each assessment performed both in the home and in the clinic; thus, there were many instances in which data were not collected by a person of the same ethnic background as the participant.

Conditions and acts of caregiving. With respect to the conditions and acts of caregiving experienced directly by the child during the first 3 years of life, Bradley et al. (1994) found that six conditions consistently afforded a measure of protection from the generally deleterious consequences of prematurity compounded by poverty. These conditions were (a) low density in the home, (b) a safe area in which to play, (c) responsivity of the parent, (d) acceptance of the child, (e) variety of experiences for the child, and (f) the availability of enriching learning materials. These conditions were selected because they appeared likely to foster capacities or motivational sets in the child that the child could use to engage more successfully in the pervasive risks present in a poverty environment (for a discussion of protective mechanisms, see Rutter, 1987). Low density in the home and a safe area in which to play were included even though these conditions may result in a reduction of risk and in the facilitation of children's capacities to engage in risk situations successfully.

The information on Conditions (b) to (f) was obtained from the Home Observation for Measurement of the Environment inventory (HOME; Caldwell & Bradley, 1984). Specifically, the Infant–Toddler (IT–HOME) and Early Childhood (EC–HOME) versions of HOME were administered to 1-year-old and 3-year-old children, respectively, of the participating families. The HOME inventories are designed to measure the quality and quantity of stimulation and support available to a child in the home environment. The HOME utilizes both observation and interview done in the home that lasts about 1 hr. The home visitor allows natural interactions between caregiver and child. Substantial validity and reliability data are presented in the HOME technical manual (Caldwell & Bradley, 1984). The HOME inventory has been used for a wide variety of sociocultural groups (Bradley & Caldwell, 1988).

There is a reasonable amount of evidence in support of the validity of the measure as used with Caucasian and African-American families; however, there is less evidence regarding its use with Hispanics (Bradley et al., 1989). Cronbach alphas were calculated on the IT–HOME total score for Caucasian (.79), African-American (.81), and Hispanic (.74) families from the IHDP sample. Alphas were also calculated on the EC–HOME total score for Caucasian (.87), African-American (.86), and Hispanic (.84) families.

Scores from the HOME administered at 12 months were adjusted with an algorithm that used the mean and standard deviation from the standardization sample and the 36-month HOME scores from each site from the current sample. This action was taken due to evidence of inflation in scores on the 12-month IT–HOME intervention at several sites. The site variations occurred despite careful training on IT–HOME and monitoring during the periods of data collection. The degree of inflation was small; thus, it was difficult to detect during the actual process of data collection at 1 year. The site variations were reduced by additional training prior to the 36-month EC–HOME data collections.

Child outcomes. We used four child outcome measures collected when children were age 3. The Stanford–Binet Intelligence Test (3rd ed.; Terman & Merrill, 1973) was administered by trained IHDP staff. Mothers completed the Child Behavior Checklist (CBCL; Achenbach, Edelbrock, & Howell, 1987), a widely used measure of maladaptive behavior in children. The CBCL consists of 100 items reflecting social withdrawal, depression, sleep problems, somatic problems, and aggressive or destructive behavior. Cronbach alphas were calculated for the Total Problems subscale score on the CBCL. The estimates for Hispanic, Caucasian, and African-American children were .93, .93, and .94, respectively. Health status was assessed by the mothers' response to the question: "At this time, your child's health is excellent, is that true or false?" Possible answers ranged from *definitely false* to *definitely true*. This one-item measure of health status was used because it was determined to be the best of the health status measures available from the IHDP data set. Growth status was evaluated using the ratio of the child's weight to height at age 3, and this ratio was then compared to standard growth curves for 3-year-old children.

Procedure

Identification of resilient children. To classify children as *resilient,* we began with the assumption that resilient children should be functioning essentially within acceptable ranges with respect to health and development (see Bradley et al., 1994). They should not be children whose health or developmental limitations make them candidates for any special medical, educational, or other psychosocial interventions—other than some minor temporary assistance. Limitations in four areas of development were considered for purposes of analysis: cognitive competence, behavioral competence, health status, and growth status. Children were considered resilient if they were functioning in acceptable ranges for all four health/developmental areas at age 3.

Minimum performance on the Stanford–Binet Intelligence Test necessary to be considered resilient was an IQ score of 85. Scores on the CBCL range from 0 to 200, with higher scores indicating more maladaptive behavior. Raw scores of 65 or higher on the Total Problems subscale generally are considered clinically significant. Thus, to be regarded resilient, children had to attain scores less than 65. For a child to be considered resilient with respect to health status, the mother had to answer either "true" or "definitely true" when asked if the child's health was excellent. Children whose weight:height ratios were between the 10th and the 90th percentile, compared to norms for 3-year-old children, were considered resilient.

The approach used to define resilience differs from that used in most other studies of resilience in that it characterizes resilience as a multidimensional outcome. Most previous investigations have looked at the concept of resilience in terms of a particular adverse outcome (e.g., poor school performance, teenage pregnancy, mental illness, and drug use). The concern here was not with any particular adverse outcome. Rather, it was whether children who had already experienced one adverse outcome (prematurity) were likely to experience subsequent adverse outcomes as well. Sameroff (1983), Escalona (1982), and others showed that prematurity alone (i.e., independent of poor-quality caregiving) is unlikely to lead to poor cognitive performance or to any other one particular adverse developmental outcome. However, research has shown an increased incidence of a number of developmental problems when prematurity is accompanied by a poor social environment (Bradley & Casey, 1992). In effect, although there may not be a high probability of diminished functioning in any one particular developmental domain as a consequence of the joint occurrence of prematurity and poverty, the likelihood of diminished functioning in some domain seemed considerable, with different vulnerabilities and different specific patterns of care leading to different developmental problems. That premature children living in poverty would escape all forms of developmental problems seemed unlikely.

Preliminary analyses. Data analyses for this study are based on analyses completed as part of the earlier study of children in the IHDP follow-up group (Bradley et al., 1994). For the follow-up group, we examined the extent to which each individual environmental variable

may serve as a "protective" one. Once variables were identified as being protective, a criterion value was selected for each variable to maximize the discrimination between resilient and nonresilient children, using receiver-operating curves (ROCs; Herman, Irwig, & Groeneveld, 1988; Last, 1983). There is a degree of artificiality in establishing criterion values in this fashion. It required that children be treated as resilient based on data collected at a single age point (3 years) even though there is plasticity in development (Lerner, 1985). It also means that the points of maximum discriminability identified using ROCs were based on the same sample as was used in the analyses that followed, thus limiting generalizability. Despite these limitations, epidemiologists have recommended ROCs as a useful technique for such applications (Erdreich & Lee, 1981). Furthermore, there was no basis in theory or previous research to suggest that any other procedure for establishing cutoff points would be generally applicable to the six caregiving conditions as measured.

The next phase of the preliminary analysis consisted of estimating the level of protection afforded children by each of the aspects of the home environment identified as being protective in the first phase. The impact of the protective experiences was interpreted using the epidemiological concept of relative risk. Relative risk is expressed mathematically as the ratio of the percentage of persons in an exposed group who have bad outcomes:the percentage of persons in a nonexposed group who have bad outcomes. Because we were concerned with resilience (i.e., a good outcome), not with bad outcomes, we reversed the notion and called it *relative protection*. It indicates the odds of children being resilient when protective conditions are present compared to circumstances when the protective conditions are not present (Herman et al., 1988).

The final phase of analysis focused on determining whether the likelihood of being resilient at age 3 was increased when children had multiple protective experiences in the home environment. To investigate the effect of multiple-protective factors, a cumulative protection index was computed as the number of protective factors present at 12 months. The same procedure was applied to protective factors at 36 months. ROCs were also used in this phase of the analysis to determine the number of protective factors that maximized discrimination between resilient and nonresilient groups.

Results

Primary Analyses: Effects of Intervention

In the follow-up group, only 12% (26 of 223) of preterm LBW infants in poverty were classified as resilient. This percentage is significantly lower than the

39% incidence of resilience (59 of 153) in the intervention group, $\chi^2(1, N = 376) = 37.5$, $p < .001$. Fifty-seven percent of the intervention group (91 of 160) scored above the threshold score of 85 on the Stanford–Binet Intelligence Test compared to only 26% (62 of 235) of the follow-up group, $\chi^2(1, N = 395) = 37.3$, $p < .001$. Eighty-five percent of the intervention group (132 of 156) scored less than 65 on the Total Problems subscale of the CBCL (i.e., outside the maladaptive range) compared to 73% (168 of 229) of the follow-up group, $\chi^2(1, N = 395) = 6.8$, $p < .001$. Ninety percent of the children from both groups were considered in good health by their mothers, and about 71% were between the 10th and the 90th percentile weight for their height, indicating proportionate growth.

Secondary Analyses: Protective Qualities of Caregiving

In the previous study (Bradley et al., 1994), IT–HOME and EC–HOME subscale scores were dichotomized using ROCs. The same criterion values were used in these analyses. At 12 months, the criterion value used for the Variety subscale was approximately 1 SD below the normative mean; for the Responsivity subscale, it was approximately ½ SD above the mean for the norm group (Caldwell & Bradley, 1984). At 36 months, the criterion values for both the Responsivity and the Acceptance subscales were approximately 1 SD above the mean for the norm group. Thresholds for all remaining subscales were set at approximately the mean of the normative sample.

To evaluate the effect of multiple-protective agents, a cumulative protection index consisting of the number of protective agents was calculated. The six variables found to be significant in the previous study (Bradley et al., 1994) were included in the cumulative protection index (see Table 1). These variables were the Learning Materials, Variety, Acceptance, and Responsivity subscales from HOME; a safe play area; and home density

less than 1. The cumulative index is incremented by 1 for each protective agent present. Thus, the index ranges from 0 to 6. For the intervention group at 12 months, there was no difference between resilient and nonresilient children in terms of the number of protective agents present in the home environment. However, resilient intervention children had significantly more, $t(151) = 2.96$, $p < .05$, home environment protective agents ($n = 59$, $M = 3.2$) at 36 months than did nonresilient children ($n = 94$, $M = 2.3$).

In the previous study of only follow-up children, the ROC analysis of the sensitivity and specificity for the cumulative protection index at both 12 and 36 months indicated that maximum discrimination between resilient and nonresilient groups occurred at three or more protective agents. In this study we examined the positive and negative predictive values of having three or more protective agents. The positive predictive value is the probability that a child is actually resilient given that three or more protective agents are present. The negative predictive value is the probability that a child is nonresilient given that two or fewer protective agents are present (Hennekens, 1987, cited in Mayrent, 1987). The moderate positive predictive value at 12 months (.42) indicates that 42 of 100 children with three or more protective agents are likely to be resilient. At 36 months, the positive predictive value of .45 is similar to the value at 12 months. The negative predictive value of .73 at 12 months indicates that 73 of 100 children are likely to be nonresilient if two or fewer protective agents are present. The negative predictive value of .68 at 36 months is nearly as high.

Table 1 summarizes the analyses of multiple-protective agents at both 12 and 36 months. As shown, intervention children with three or more protective agents were only a little more likely to be resilient than nonresilient.

Figure 1 includes information from both studies to give a clearer picture of the combined effects of protective home factors and intervention. For example, only 2% (1 of 57) of follow-up children with fewer than three

Table 1. *Comparison of Resilient and Nonresilient Children From the IHDP Intervention Group With Fewer Than Three and Three or More Protective Agents*

No. of Protective Agents	Time (Months)			
	12		36	
	Resilient	Nonresilient	Resilient	Nonresilient
0 to 2	17%	29%	42%	56%
3 or More	83%	71%	58%	44%
Relative Risk (CI)	1.56	(.89 to 2.77)	1.40	(.94 to 2.13)
Positive Predictive Value[a]		.42		.45
Negative Predictive Value[b]		.73		.68

Note: CI = confidence interval.

[a]The probability of being resilient with three or more protective agents present. [b]The probability of being nonresilient with less than three protective agents present.

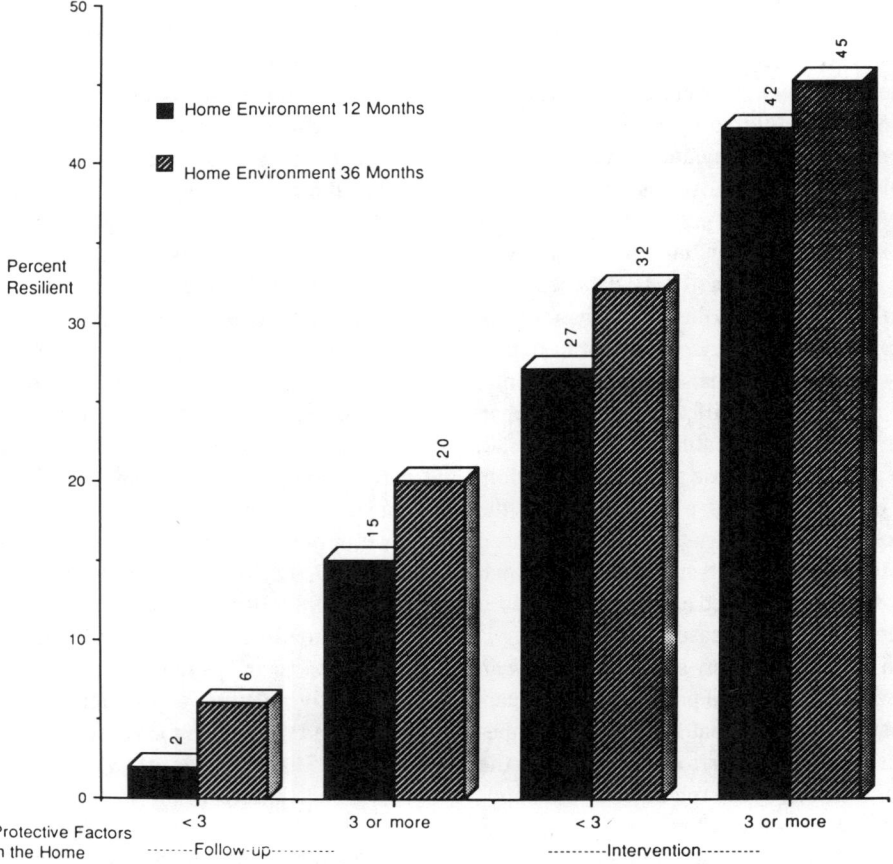

Figure 1. Percentage of resilient children by number of protective factors in the home for intervention and follow-up groups.

protective factors present in the home at 12 months were classified as resilient. By comparison, 42% (49 of 116) of the intervention children with three or more protective factors present in the home at 12 months were classified as resilient. The corresponding figures for protective factors present in the home at 36 months were 6% for follow-up children with less than three protective factors and 45% for intervention children with three or more protective factors.

Discussion

Two findings from this study are particularly striking. First, the percentage of premature, LBW children living in poverty who were regarded as resilient was substantially higher than the percentage of the follow-up group. Certainly, this figure is a function of the way in which resilience was defined; but even had criteria for defining resilience been relaxed somewhat, the difference in percentage between the two intervention and follow-up groups would still have been significant. When interpreting this finding it is important to remember that children with serious perinatal medical problems were excluded as part of the initial recruitment process for the main IHDP study, and children with serious, chronic, postnatal medical conditions such as

cerebral palsy, heart disease, and the like were excluded from the data analysis. Second, in the absence of having at least three protective caregiving experiences at 12 months, the odds that a premature, LBW child living in poverty will show early signs of resilience are low (< 28%) despite participating in an intensive, multifaceted intervention such as IHDP. Having two or fewer protective caregiving conditions at 36 months had somewhat less severe consequences (32% of those with fewer than three protective home conditions were resilient). The serious impact of "double jeopardy" accruing to the combination of prematurity and poverty was clearly evident (Parker et al., 1988). Without intervention and without protective caregiving experiences in the home, a child's chances of showing early resilience appear extraordinarily low. Even with protective home factors present, the percentage of children who manifested resiliency at age 3 was less than 20%. As striking as these findings are, it is important to acknowledge that the results could not be cross-validated on a separate sample—there were just too few children who could be classified as resilient to make it feasible.

There are three major limitations of the definition of resilience used in this study. First, resilience was defined by using criterion values for growth, health status, behavioral adjustment, and intellectual performance even though resiliency is more appropriately understood as a continuum. Resilience was treated in this way because the decision to take action on behalf of a child (preventive or interventive) is most often a dichotomous one for health providers, social service workers, and educators. Second, children were identified as resilient on the basis of developmental scores at a single age. Although this approach is not unusual, it belies the fact that adaptive functioning is subject to change over time (Lerner, 1985). Three-year functional status was used due to the limitations of the IHDP data set; thus, the results should be interpreted as indicative only of early resilience. Nonetheless, it is important to underscore that many children who manifest developmental problems early in life also manifest problems later in life. Third, our measure of health status was weak, based solely on maternal response to a single question.

It also may be something of a limitation that the percentage of children defined as nonresilient based solely on their IQ score was substantially higher than the percentage of children defined as nonresilient based on any one of the other three measures. This finding is not surprising in view of the many studies that show an association between poverty and poor intellectual performance; however, it means that intellectual competence contributes a disproportionate share to the determination of resilience. The relation between poverty and any particular poor developmental outcome is likely to vary as a function of the child's age and the ecological circumstances of the family. Had the study been done in a country where poverty is frequently associated with poor nutrition and poor health standards, growth and health status would probably have played a bigger role in determining resilience. However, because performance on intelligence tests is dependent on many factors (including good health), the percentage of nonresilient children with low IQ scores would likely be high in most conditions of poverty.

Results showing that the IHDP intervention increased the proportion of premature, LBW children living in poverty who showed early signs of resiliency extend findings from earlier studies about the IHDP (Brooks-Gunn et al., 1993; IHDP, 1990). These earlier studies, performed with the entire IHDP cohort, showed that the intervention had a positive impact on children's health and development and that it decreased the percentage of children showing developmental delays. Results of our study indicate that the intervention had a positive impact on children at particularly great risk (i.e., children living in chronic poverty). Findings also show that high-quality intervention adds to the beneficial (protective) support for development afforded to children by high-quality home experiences.

As expected, the types of caregiving variables that showed some measure of protective value in this sample were particular acts and circumstances providing stimulation, emotional support, structure, and safety to the child. These variables appear to be the types of

mechanisms through which some level of protection is afforded the child. Just as risks seem to accumulate to the detriment of children's health and development, protective mechanisms seem to accumulate to their benefit. Unfortunately, even in homes where caregiving tends to be in acceptable ranges on several dimensions, the generally pernicious joint effect of poverty and prematurity allows only a minority of infants to show early signs of resilience, albeit the percentage of children from the intervention group was substantially higher than the percentage from the follow-up group.

The kinds of caregiving experiences identified as potentially protective (availability of toys and materials, variety of stimulation, parental responsivity, acceptance of a child's behavior, and adequate space for privacy and exploration) are the kinds of experiences consistently shown to be supportive of good health and development among children in general (Bradley, Caldwell, & Rock, 1990; Kagan, 1984; Wachs & Gruen, 1982). Responsive, stimulating, organized care done in conditions of safety reduces the likelihood of both physical and psychological harm, along with their potentially negative consequences for both child behavior and subsequent caregiving acts (see, e.g., Lerner, 1985, and Sameroff, 1983, concerning the bidirectional nature of these transactions). Such care provides a basis for the development of secure emotional attachments and an emerging sense of self-efficacy (Bandura, 1977; Bretherton & Waters, 1985; Rutter, 1987). It also provides ingredients needed for early cognitive and language development (Wachs & Gruen, 1982). Unfortunately, more information on the sustenance dimension of caregiving (e.g., detailed nutrition information) was not available; thus, its potential protective value could have been more carefully examined.

Poverty and prematurity can lead to an array of morbidities in young children. Most examinations of the effects of poverty focus only on one aspect of health or development at a time (or certainly only a small number of aspects) such as poor growth. Incidence and prevalence figures for each particular aspect of health and development tend to underestimate the true impact of poverty, particularly poverty in combination with other risk factors like prematurity. The child who escapes poverty's downward impact on language development may not be so lucky when it comes to illness or growth or adaptive social functioning.

We were concerned that so many of the participants in the study were African American (about 70%) and that only 15% were Caucasian. Although poor African Americans in the sample did not differ from poor Caucasians and Hispanics on any key demographic or developmental measure, uncertainty remains with respect to the generalizability of findings. As it happened, there was a very high percentage of minority-group mothers who gave birth to premature infants at the hospitals used for recruitment in IHDP. Because African Americans have a substantially higher rate of premature deliveries than Caucasians, hospitals in areas with large African-American populations often have a disproportionate share of inborn, premature African-American infants. Nonetheless, it is important to appreciate the limitations on generalizability imposed by the high percentage of African Americans in the IHDP sample. Efforts should be made to determine particular relations among risk and protective mechanisms in different racial and ethnic groups living in poverty both in this country and elsewhere.

Finally, it is important to reiterate that a very conservative approach to identifying resilience was used in this study—one requiring that a child be within normal limits in all four areas of psychobiological functioning assessed. Clearly, however, the fact that a child does not function well in one area does not mean that the child is generally doing poorly or that the child cannot perform successfully in most areas. It is also important to reiterate that this was a study of early indications of resilience in premature, LBW children living in poverty. Whether the patterns observed would persist into later childhood cannot be determined by these data and should be investigated. Whether the patterns observed would apply to groups living in different cultural milieus (e.g., those where growth and health may more often be implicated in the determination of resilience) also cannot be determined by these data. Only when studies have been done under these other circumstances will the full impact of the intervention become clear.

References

Achenbach, T., Edelbrock, C., & Howell, C. (1987). Empirically based assessment of the behavioral/emotional problems of 2- and 3-year-old children. *Journal of Abnormal Child Psychology, 15,* 629–650.

Bandura, A. (1977). *Social learning theory.* Englewood Cliffs, NJ: Prentice-Hall.

Bennett, F. C. (1987). The effectiveness of early intervention for infants at increased biologic risk. In M. Guralnick & F. C. Bennett (Eds.), *The effectiveness of early intervention for at-risk and handicapped children* (pp. 79–112). New York: Academic.

Boyce, W. T., & Jemerin, J. M. (1990). Psychobiological differences in childhood stress response, I. Patterns of illness and susceptibility. *Developmental and Behavioral Pediatrics, 11,* 86–93.

Bradley, R. H., & Caldwell, B. M. (1988). Using the HOME Inventory to assess the family environment. *Pediatric Nursing, 14,* 97–102.

Bradley, R. H., Caldwell, B. M., & Rock, S. L. (1990). Home environment classification system: A model for assessing the home environments of developing children. *Early Education & Development, 1,* 238–265.

Bradley, R. H., Caldwell, B. M., Rock, S. L., Ramey, C. T., Barnard, K. E., Gray, C., Hammond, M. A., Mitchell, S., Gottfried, A. W., Siegel, L., & Johnson, D. L. (1989). Home environment and cognitive development in the first 3 years of life: A collaborative study involving six sites and three ethnic groups in North America. *Developmental Psychology, 25,* 217–235.

Bradley, R. H., & Casey, P. H. (1992). Family environment and

behavioral development of low-birthweight children: Annotations. *Developmental Medicine and Child Neurology, 34,* 822–826.

Bradley, R. H., Whiteside, L., Mundfrom, D. J., Casey, P. H., Kelleher, K. J., & Pope, S. K. (1994). Early indications of resilience and their relation to experiences in the home environments of low birthweight, premature children living in poverty. *Child Development, 65,* 240–260.

Bretherton, I., & Waters, E. (1985). Growing points of attachment theory and research. *Monographs of the Society for Research in Child Development, 50*(1 & 2, Serial No. 209).

Brooks-Gunn, J., Klebanov, P. K., Liaw, F., & Spiker, D. (1993). Enhancing the development of low-birthweight premature infants: Changes in cognition and behavior over the first three years. *Child Development, 64,* 736–753.

Caldwell, B. M., & Bradley, R. H. (1984). *Home Observation for Measurement of the Environment.* Little Rock: University of Arkansas at Little Rock.

Clarke-Stewart, K. A., & Fein, G. G. (1983). Early childhood programs. In E. M. Hetherington (Ed.), *Handbook of child psychology: Vol. 4. Socialization, personality, and social development* (pp. 918–999). New York: Wiley.

Dunn, L. M., & Dunn, L. M. (1981). *Peabody Picture Vocabulary Test–Revised.* Circle Pines, MN: American Guidance Service.

Erdreich, L. S., & Lee, E. T. (1981). The use of relative operating characteristic analysis in epidemiology. *American Journal of Epidemiology, 114,* 649–662.

Escalona, S. K. (1982). Babies at double hazard: Early development of infants at biologic and social risk. *Pediatrics, 70,* 670–676.

Farran, D. C. (1990). Effects of intervention with disadvantaged and disabled children: A decade review. In S. Meisels & J. Shonkoff (Eds.), *Handbook of early childhood intervention* (pp. 501–539). New York: Cambridge University Press.

Garcia Coll, C. T. (1990). Developmental outcome of minority infants: A process-oriented look into our beginnings. *Child Development, 61,* 270–289.

Herman, A. A. B., Irwig, L. M., & Groeneveld, H. T. (1988). Evaluating obstetric risk scores by receiver operating characteristic curves. *American Journal of Epidemiology, 127,* 831–842.

Huston, A. C., McLoyd, V. C., & Garcia Coll, C. (1994). Children and poverty: Issues in contemporary research. *Child Development, 65,* 275–282.

Infant Health and Development Program. (1990). Enhancing the outcomes of low-birth-weight, premature infants. *Journal of the American Medical Association, 263,* 3035–3070.

Kagan, J. (1984). *The nature of the child.* New York: Basic.

Laosa, L. M. (1980). Maternal teaching strategies in Chicano and Anglo-American families: The influence of culture and education on maternal behavior. *Child Development, 51,* 759–765.

Last, J. M. (1983). *A dictionary of epidemiology.* New York: Oxford University Press.

Lerner, R. (1985). *On the nature of human plasticity.* New York: Cambridge University Press.

Margolis, P. A., Greenberg, R. A., & Keyes, L. L. (1992). Lower respiratory illness in infants and low socioeconomic status. *American Journal of Public Health, 82,* 1119–1126.

Mayrent, S. L. (Ed.). (1987). *Epidemiology in medicine.* Boston: Little, Brown.

McAdoo, H. P. (1988). *Black families* (2nd ed.). Newbury Park, CA: Sage.

McLoyd, V.C. (1990). The impact of economic hardship on black families and children: Psychological distress, parenting, and socioemotional development. *Child Development, 61,* 311–346.

Olds, D. L., & Kitzman, H. (1990). Can home visitation improve the health of women and children at environmental risk? *Pediatrics, 86,* 108–116.

Parker, S., Greer, S., & Zuckerman, B. (1988). Double jeopardy: The impact of poverty of early child development. *The Pediatric Clinics of North America, 35,* 1127–1241.

Ramey, C. T., Bryant, D. M., & Suarez, T. M. (1983). Preschool compensatory education and the modifiability of intelligence: A critical review. In D. Detterman (Ed.), *Current topics in human intelligence* (pp. 247–296). Norwood, NJ: Ablex.

Ramey, C. T., Bryant, D. M., Wasik, B. H., Sparling, J. J., Fendt, K. H., & LaVange, L. M. (1992). The Infant Health and Development Program for low birthweight, premature infants: Program elements, family participation, and child intelligence. *Pediatrics, 90,* 454–465.

Russell, M., Carr-Hill, R., & Illsley, R. (1984). The sociological study: Differences related to the childhood environment. In R. Illsley & R. G. Mitchell (Eds.), *Low birthweight—A medical, psychological, and social study* (pp. 51–90). New York: Wiley.

Rutter, M. (1987). Psychosocial resilience and protective mechanisms. *American Journal of Orthopsychiatry, 57,* 316–331.

Sameroff, A. J. (1983). Developmental systems: Context and evolution. In W. Kessen (Ed.), *Handbook of child psychology: Vol. 1. History, theories, and methods* (pp. 238–294). New York: Wiley.

Sameroff, A. J., Seifer, R., Barocas, R., Zax, M., & Greenspan, S. (1987). Intelligence quotient scores of 4-year old children: Social–environmental risk factors. *Pediatrics, 79,* 343–350.

Sparling, J., & Lewis, I. (1985). *Partners for learning.* Winston-Salem, NC: Caplan.

Spurlock, C. W., Hinds, M. W., Skaggs, J. W., & Hernandez, C. E. (1987). Infant death rates among the poor and nonpoor in Kentucky, 1982 to 1983. *Pediatrics, 80,* 262–269.

Starfield, B. (1988). *Social factors: Poverty, class, race.* Unpublished manuscript.

Terman, L., & Merrill, M. (1973). *Stanford–Binet Intelligence Scale: Manual for the third revision, Form L–M.* Boston: Houghton Mifflin.

U.S. Department of Commerce, Bureau of the Census. (1985). *Poverty in the United States 1985* (Series P–60, No. 158). Washington, DC: U.S. Government Printing Office.

U.S. Department of Health and Human Services. (1985). *Health status of minorities and low income groups* (DHHS Publication No. [HRSA] HRS–P–DV 85–1). Washington, DC: U.S. Government Printing Office.

U.S. Department of Health and Human Services. (1991). *Healthly people 2000* (DHHS Publication No. PHS 91–50212). Washington, DC: U.S. Government Printing Office.

Wachs, T., & Gruen, G. (1982). *Early experience and human development.* New York: Plenum.

Wasik, B. (1984). *Coping with parenting through effective problem solving: A handbook for professionals.* Chapel Hill, NC: Frank Porter Graham Child Development Center.

Werner, E. (1989). High-risk children in young adulthood: A longitudinal study from birth to 32 years. *American Journal of Orthopsychiatry, 59,* 72–81.

Received September 27, 1993
Final revision received March 11, 1994

Journal of Clinical Child Psychology
1994, Vol. 23, 435–443

Role of Parental Anger in Low-Income Women: Discipline Strategy, Perceptions of Behavior Problems, and the Need for Control

Lizette Peterson, Bernard Ewigman, and Trish Vandiver

University of Missouri–Columbia

Examined anger and other variables known to be related to physical abuse by describing common child-rearing challenges to 199 low-income mothers and observing relations among their responses. Maternal anger varied extensively across the situations explored, and it was significantly related to the use of physical discipline in one third of the situations sampled. Anger was also positively related to perceived frequency of child behavior problems, and tendency to use physical discipline increased with number of perceived behavior problems. Child behaviors that underlined a challenge to the mothers' control (e.g., defiance or disobedience of a direct command) provoked the most anger. The implications of these findings for abuse prevention and positive parenting interventions for low-income families are discussed.

McLoyd (1990) offered the compelling observation that "negative parenting behavior is the primary pathway through which poverty undermines children's socioeconomic functioning" (p. 315). There are a variety of types of negative parenting behavior, ranging from an absence of concern or care for the child to severe discipline that culminates in child injury. Low-income parents are more at risk for this entire gamut of negative parenting behaviors (Elder, 1979; Galambos & Silbereisen, 1987; Lempers, Clark-Lempers, & Simons, 1989). In particular, low-income parents are more likely than middle-income parents to use authoritarian physical punishment (Daro, 1988; Trickett, Aber, Carlson, & Cicchetti, 1991). Such practices may place low-income families at higher risk for physical abuse of the child. Even when severe discipline may not constitute abuse, harsh and/or punitive parenting results in impaired parent–child relationships (Kelley, 1979; Peterson, 1989), a coercive relationship in which negative child behaviors beget negative parental responses (Patterson, 1982), and negative parental affect (Abramson, Seligman, & Teasdale, 1978).

Anger is perhaps the most prominent negative parental emotion linked to harsh discipline. Even nonabus-

ive parents recommend more negative parental responses to child misbehavior when they are angry (Dix, Reinhold, & Zambarano, 1990). Parental anger has been cited as the most common trigger for physical abuse (Averill, 1982; Whiteman, Fanshel, & Grundy, 1987), and the National Clinical Evaluation Study reported that an inability to manage anger was the variable most clearly associated with abuse (Berkeley Planning Associates, 1983).

Dix (1991) argued cogently that understanding parental emotions is essential to understanding parenting behavior and that past research on parental emotions has been inadequate in a variety of ways. Dix suggested that future research should focus on emotion as a multidimensional phenomenon, and it should consider the complex interweaving among parental affect, child elicitors of that affect, and parental goals. In this study, we sought to explore the relation among several critical correlates of parental anger in a low-income population.

The low-income population was not selected for this study because there is evidence that anger in this sample operates in a dissimilar manner than it does in middle-income families. Rather, low-income parents were selected because they are clearly at increased risk for harsh discipline and physical abuse (Garbarino, 1977; National Center for Child Abuse and Neglect, 1981; Pelton, 1978; Straus & Gelles, 1986; Straus, Gelles, & Steinmetz, 1980). If it is the case that parental anger is related to punitive discipline and abuse, then it makes sense to begin such explorations in a sample at high risk.

Anger could operate to potentiate negative parenting

This research was supported by a grant from the University of Missouri Children's Miracle Fund to Bernard Ewigman.

We thank the participating mothers and the generously helpful Women, Infants, and Children Clinic staff for their help. Gratitude is also extended to interviewers Elizabeth Kohler and Lynne Dresner; to Brenda Schick, who coded the responses; and to Darla Harmon, who assisted in data handling.

Requests for reprints should be sent to Lizette Peterson, Department of Psychology, 210 McAlester Hall, University of Missouri–Columbia, Columbia, MO 65211.

practices in a variety of ways. We hypothesized that one important link may be between anger and the selection of physical discipline, as opposed to other forms of discipline. Assuming that most parents have a variety of potential parenting techniques available to them, it may be that anger makes parents more likely to select corporal punishment rather than alternative means of discipline. Past research has linked anger to more power-assertive techniques (e.g., Dix et al., 1990); we examined the extent to which anger increased mothers' selection of physical discipline techniques following child behavior problems.

Another hypothesis was that angry parents would tend to view their children as having more negative behaviors than less angry parents. Past research suggests that angry parents tend to form more negative evaluations of their children (Brody & Forehand, 1986; Goodnow, 1988; Vasta, 1982). Our study specifically asked if angry parents perceived more behavior problems in their children. If so, the perceptions of more problems to be remediated and thus more frequent need for some form of intervention could be another vehicle for promoting increased harsh discipline.

Finally, although we did not explicitly set out to do so, we addressed one of the likely elicitors of parental anger. The parenting literature shows a strong relation between need for control and abuse (Crockenberg, 1987; Herrenkohl, Herrenkohl, & Egolf, 1983) and between a feeling of lack of control over the child and abuse (Bugental, Blue, & Cruz-cosa, 1989; Rosenberg & Reppucci, 1983). Dix (1991) argued that understanding the emotional mediators of such relations is crucial. We examined the premise that child behaviors involving the child explicitly defying parental authority would be linked to increased parental anger as well as a higher likelihood of physical discipline.

Each of the interacting factors explored here have been associated with physical discipline and abuse, and each could be the potential target for prevention and treatment efforts. Trickett et al. (1991) called for research that can evaluate the processes within low-income families that link correlates of abuse to specific abusive acts. We focused on parental anger as one of the mechanisms behind the use of physical discipline. In this study, physical discipline was regarded as a necessary (but perhaps insufficient) component of physical abuse. In addition, due to the potential negative effects of nonabusive physical discipline, physical discipline was regarded as a worthwhile focus in its own right, even though not all physical discipline is linked to abuse. Prevention and treatment efforts may benefit from an increased understanding of the relation among anger, physical discipline, behavior problems, and challenges to parental control.

Method

Subjects

Low-income mothers were recruited during weekly attendance at a women, infants, and children (WIC) clinic in a county health department. To qualify for help at a WIC clinic, at the time of the study, a woman had to fall below 185% of the federal poverty level and to be pregnant or have a child under age 5. Children of this age are most at risk for serious injury due to harsh discipline (American Humane Association, 1984) and provide many parenting challenges. To be eligible for the study, a woman must speak fluent English and be the primary caregiver of a child who was between 18 months and 5 years old. Mothers with more than one child in the age range were asked to respond to questions with respect to the child whom they felt was most difficult to manage overall. WIC clinic clients were 53% Caucasian, 40% African American, and 7% other minorities, with an average age of 23 ($SD = 4.6$).

Subjects were offered the opportunity to discuss how they managed their child in return for a small financial payment for their time ($2). Announcements of the 15-min interview opportunity were made during mandatory nutrition classes. Of the 646 women contacted, 341 did not have preschool-age children, 79 did not wish to participate in the interview, 22 agreed to participate but could not due to time constraints, and 5 did not speak sufficiently fluent English to complete the interview. The remaining 199 (66% of those eligible) completed the interviews. Of the participating subjects, 65.3% reported having a Division of Family Services worker assigned to their case, but only 3.5% acknowledged having a protective service worker (indicating documented abuse or neglect) assigned to their case.

Interviewers and Coders

Two undergraduate and two master's-level women administered the structured interview. A postgraduate-level woman unfamiliar with the child abuse literature, the interview, or the population completed the coding of disciplinary procedures into categories, and the first author served as an independent reliability coder.

Measure

The structured interview was constructed for this study. It consisted of four sections. First, eligibility criteria and contact with Division of Family Services was described. Second, general disciplinary procedures were discussed. The type of punishments typically used by the mother, the frequency of use, and the reasons for use were described.

Third, four situations that commonly occur with children of this age were described one at a time. After each was described, the mother was asked if her child ever did this behavior; if so, she was asked an open-ended question concerning what she typically did about it and to rate how angry she became on a 5-point scale ranging from *not at all angry* (1) to *ready to explode* (5). The four situations included the child becoming messy, having a tantrum, pulling items from the shelf in a grocery store, and refusing to follow directions (this item was asked of 54% of subjects and replaced a question on running out into the street). This last item was discontinued after only 46% of the subjects had responded because interviewers were concerned that, when rating their anger, subjects may have been responding to strength of other emotions, such as fear. However, data (described later) confirm a significant relation between discipline and anger ratings for this situation.

Fourth, the answers were obtained in response to each of the four common situations, a fifth situation was posed: "What is it that your child does that makes you the angriest?" Mothers described in detail the child behavior that made them the angriest. Then they described what they did about it and rated their emotion on the 5-point anger scale (just discussed). Finally, mothers were asked if they ever spank their child and, if so, how often.

Then, the mothers responded to 10 items from the Eyberg Child Behavior Inventory (ECBI), selected because they were the most frequently endorsed items in a study involving low-income women (Robinson, Eyberg, & Ross, 1980). Items 2, 4, 6, 7, 9, 10, 12, 25, 29, and 35 of the 36-item inventory were included. Mothers rated the items' intensity on a 5-point scale ranging from *never happens* (1) to *always happens* (5) and the extent to which the behavior was a problem for them according to ECBI instructions. A sample of items rather than the entire 36-item inventory was used to keep this on-site interview under 15 min.

In summary, the interview consisted of (a) background information about the mother; (b) a description of common punishments used, reasons for their use, and frequency of use; (c) the occurrence of disciplinary response to and anger provoked by vignettes about five common childrearing challenges; (d) a description of the situations that provoke the most anger, the disciplinary response to these situations, and the anger provoked; (e) an explicit question about use of spanking and frequency of spanking; and (f) a 10-item sample of the ECBI. All the data are reported just as they were asked of the subjects, except for two areas. First, the disciplinary strategies outlined in Parts 2, 3, and 4 were subjected to empirically derived coding, which revealed eight major strategies: spanking, aggressive–physical/verbal, remove from situation (including time out and response prevention), instruction, reward alter-

native, situational consequence (e.g., for "gets messy," parent would require child to clean up), allows misbehavior, and miscellaneous. Once definitions for the categories were evolved, all longhand responses were coded by both coders into these eight categories reliably ($\kappa = .74$).

Second, the parents' description of what behaviors made them the angriest were categorized. Again, eight categories were empirically derived: disobedience (doing the opposite of what is being asked), off-limits behavior (doing things the child knows are not allowed, e.g., touching the stereo), defiance (saying "no, you cannot make me," "smarting back," or "talking back"), aggression (fighting with or hurting siblings or other children, biting, and throwing objects at people), attention seeking (saying "Mommy" over and over and clinging to mother), tantrums (crying with force and/or displays, e.g., screaming and flinging extremities), unsafe behavior (touching stove and running into street), and negative affect (acting jealous, being mischievous, and sulking). Both the primary and the reliability coder again coded all interviews and demonstrated that the codes could be reliably applied ($\kappa = .75$).

Procedure

Subjects who indicated that they were eligible during a WIC in-class recruiting session were taken to a private office in the building and interviewed individually by a research assistant. During the interview, another research assistant took care of any children the mother may have brought with her. Prior to beginning the interview, women signed consent forms describing the study and the participants' rights to confidentiality, including mandatory reporting of any evidence of abuse. Following the interview, women were thanked for their assistance and paid in cash for their time.

Results

Each of the areas on the questionnaire is considered in turn, and then relations among the risk variables are discussed.

Punishments Used

After answering demographic information questions (already described), subjects outlined the punishments they most typically used. Many subjects suggested more than one type of discipline. As shown in Table 1, the most common response was to remove the child from the situation (by sending the child to a bedroom or corner or by lifting the child into a shopping cart). The second most common response (and the only other discipline type used by more than 15% of the mothers) was spanking. When a second question focused only on spanking was posed later in the interview, a similar picture emerged. As shown in Table 2, 162 of the 199 mothers (81%) acknowledged spanking sometimes, and the frequency ranged from less than 1 time per month to 10 times per day, in a relatively flat distribution.

Note that asking what kind of punishment is most typically used early in the interview and asking about spanking explicitly later in the interview resulted in a different picture of discipline. Overall, 92 of the 199 (46%) mothers spontaneously mentioned spanking early in the interview as a common disciplinary technique. Of these 92, 2 later denied spanking, 32 suggested they spanked less than three times per week, 54 spanked more than three times per week, and 4 failed to answer the latter question. In contrast, of the 107 women who did not spontaneously mention spanking,

only 29 suggested they never spank, 39 spanked less than three times per week, and 37 mothers who did not list spanking as a common disciplinary strategy later reported spanking more than three times per week, whereas 2 failed to answer the question. The bottom line is that when a parent fails to list spanking as a primary means of discipline, this does not suggest that spanking is never or only very infrequently employed.

General Reasons for Punishment

Table 3 describes the reasons mothers gave as the most frequent causes for discipline and the disciplinary strategies they employed. As shown, of the top four misbehaviors requiring punishment, three deal with direct challenges to maternal control, and these three are most likely to evoke physical discipline.

Vignettes

Table 4 shows the number of mothers ($n = 199$) who acknowledged that their child sometimes exhibited the misbehavior described in the five vignettes, including the final, "What made you angriest?" vignette. The majority of respondents mentioned a specific behavior that made them angriest and agreed that their child sometimes became messy or threw tantrums. Approximately one half the mothers agreed that their child exhibited the other misbehaviors. As shown, the type of discipline varied greatly due to the situation at hand. As shown in Figure 1, different situations evoked both differing amounts of anger and concomitantly differing amounts of physical punishment. Being messy and pulling items from shelves, for example, elicited little use of physical punishment and little anger, whereas the behavior listed as making mothers the angriest resulted in the highest anger scores and highest use of physical discipline. (Note, however, that the highest proportion of respondents listing physical discipline for any given vignette is still only 30% of the total number of subjects.) When the trend is graphed only for subjects who said they spank frequently, the pattern of the findings is almost identical (see Figure 2), although the level of physical punishment is higher. Thus, the vignettes seem to evoke anger differentially, and this occurs similarly across those subjects who do and do not use frequent physical discipline. Note also that most of these vignettes did not tap the behaviors that required the most frequent discipline (see prior section) or that made mothers the angriest (see following section).

Most Anger-Eliciting Behavior

Table 5 shows subjects' responses to the question "What makes you angriest?" Note the resemblance to

Table 1. *Number and Percentage of Parents Reporting Differing Kinds of Discipline for General Use*

Method[a]	No. Reporting	% Reporting
Removal From Situation	158	79.8
Spanking	92	46.5
Aggressive–Verbal/Physical	24	12.1
Situational Consequence	0	0.0
Instruction	23	11.6
Reward Alternative	2	1.0
Allows Misbehavior	3	1.5
Miscellaneous	6	3.0
Total Respondents	198	

[a]Based on collapsed responses to the question, "If you have to punish your child, what kind of punishment(s) do you generally use?" One subject failed to answer the question. Percentages do not sum to 100% because respondents reported more than one type of punishment.

Table 2. *How Frequently Do You Spank?*

Frequency	No. Responding	% of Those Who Spank
Never	31	N/A
< Once per Month	6	3.6
< Once Every 2 Weeks	17	10.1
< Once per Week	10	6.0
Once per Week	14	8.3
Up to Twice per Week	24	14.3
Three Times per Week	28	16.7
Four to Six Times per Week	11	6.6
Daily	12	7.1
Twice Daily	17	10.1
Up to Four Times Daily	15	9.0
Up to Ten Times Daily	8	4.8
Missing	6	3.6
Total	199	100.2[a]

[a]$n = 168$.

Table 3. *Parental Reasons to Punish*

Child Behavior	n[b]	%[c]	% Using Physical Discipline	% Using Aggressive Verbal/Physical Discipline	% Using Removal	% Using Other Discipline
			\multicolumn{4}{c}{% Reporting Each Behavior[a]}			
Disobedience	67	33.7	52.2	11.9	82.1	11.9
Off-Limits Behavior	64	32.2	48.4	12.5	71.9	20.3
Defiance	24	12.1	58.3	12.5	75.0	12.5
Aggression	64	32.2	34.4	6.3	89.1	14.1
Unsafe Behavior	19	9.5	42.1	10.5	78.9	21.1
Tantrums	9	4.5	44.4	0.0	88.9	22.2
Attention Seeking	4	2.0	25.0	25.0	100.0	0.0
Problematic Affect	4	2.0	75.0	0.0	75.0	0.0

[a]Reading across are the percentage of those saying that they did punish for this misbehavior who reported various disciplinary strategies. For example, 67 subjects reported disobedience as a common problem. Of those 67, 35 subjects (52.2%) said they used physical discipline. [b]The number of respondents (of a possible 199) who said that they punished for this child behavior. [c]Percentage of 199 respondents who said that they punished for this child behavior. Percentages do not sum to 100% because some respondents mentioned two or more kinds of child behaviors.

Table 4. *Types of Discipline Reported by Parents to Vignettes*

Discipline	Getting Messy	Throwing Tantrums	Pull Off Shelves	Run Into Street	Disobey	Angriest
	\multicolumn{6}{c}{Vignette}					
Number of Parents Acknowledging That Child Does Behavior	172	153	92	44[a]	93[b]	193
Method of Discipline[c]	\multicolumn{6}{c}{% Using}					
Spanking	3.5	14.4	15.2	27.3	23.7	30.0
Aggressive–Verbal/Physical	2.9	10.5	12.0	20.5	23.7	22.8
Situational Consequence	54.1	1.3	20.7	13.6	0.0	13.0
Removal From Situation	9.3	41.8	46.7	22.7	34.4	42.0
Instruction	17.4	15.7	33.7	45.5	55.9	24.4
Reward Alternative	3.5	9.2	9.8	2.3	1.1	3.1
Allows Misbehavior	39.5	45.1	3.3	0.0	9.7	8.8
Miscellaneous	1.2	3.3	3.3	13.6	3.2	4.1
Total %	131.4	141.3	144.7	145.5	151.7	152.9

[a]Only 46% of the parents were asked this question. [b]Only 54% of the parents were asked this question. [c]Based on collapsed responses to the "What do you do about it" portion of Questions 17, 19, 20, 21, and 22 on the current version of the survey and Question 19 on the old version of the survey. Percentages in columns can sum to greater than 100% because respondents often reported more than one type of discipline.

Table 3, which portrays the responses that parents felt most often required punishment. It is clear that the same set of behaviors are involved at very similar frequencies. Again, of the four highest frequency behaviors, three include what the mother described as the child deliberately choosing to break a parental rule and thus involve loss of control over the child. Ironically, however, the child behavior that promoted the highest proportions of mothers using physical discipline was physical aggression on the part of the child.

ECBI

Only 10 of the 36 ECBI items were administered. The possible scores ranged from 10 to 50, and actual scores ranged from 12 to 46. The mean was 29.67.

Unfortunately, because we employed high base-rate questions out of the context of the standardized questionnaire and used a 5-point scale rather than the standard 7-point scale, it is not possible to compare these values to published norms.

Relations Between Measures

As implied earlier, although the vignettes varied both in how much verbally aggressive or physical discipline and how much anger they evoked, for most vignettes, anger and type of discipline (nonaggressive vs. physically or verbally aggressive) were unrelated (point biserial $r = .10$ for getting messy, $r = .07$ for throwing tantrums, $r = .07$ for disobedience, and $r = .19$ for what makes mother angriest). In contrast, moderately signif-

439

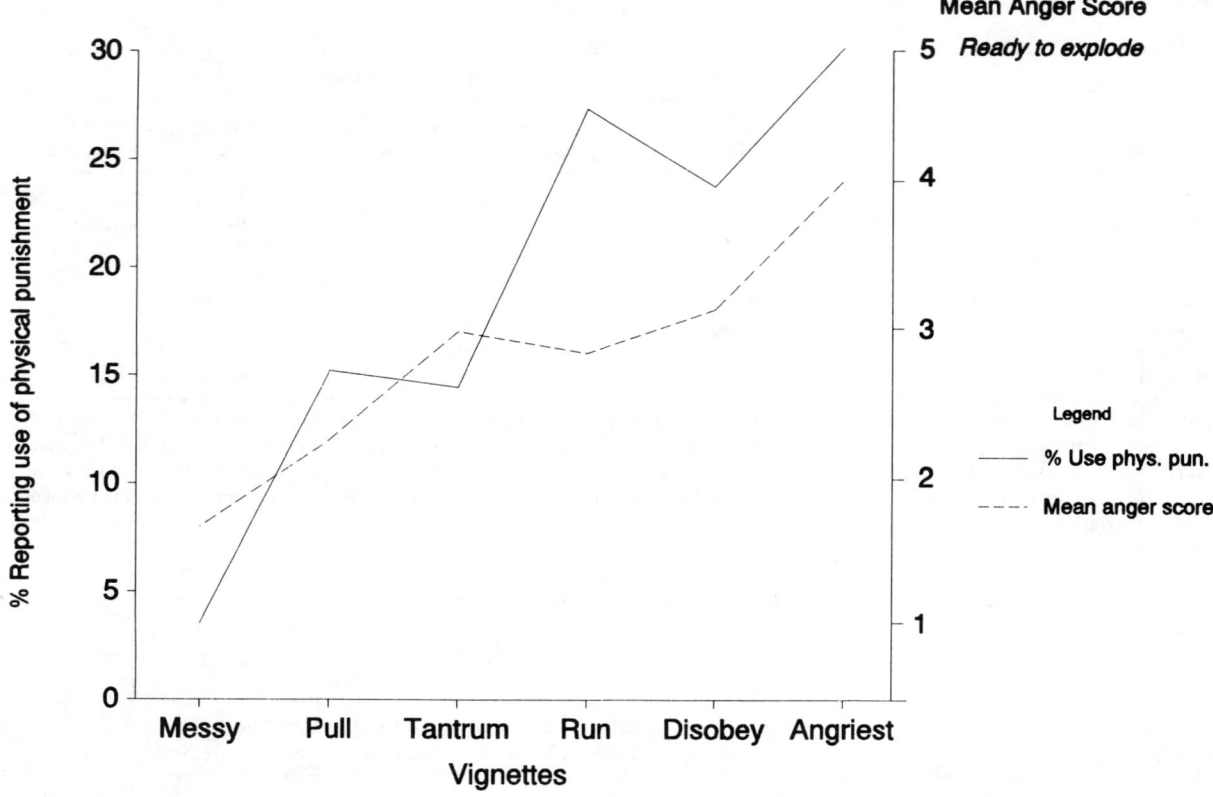

Figure 1. Percentage of mothers advocating punishment and mean anger score for each vignette for all mothers.

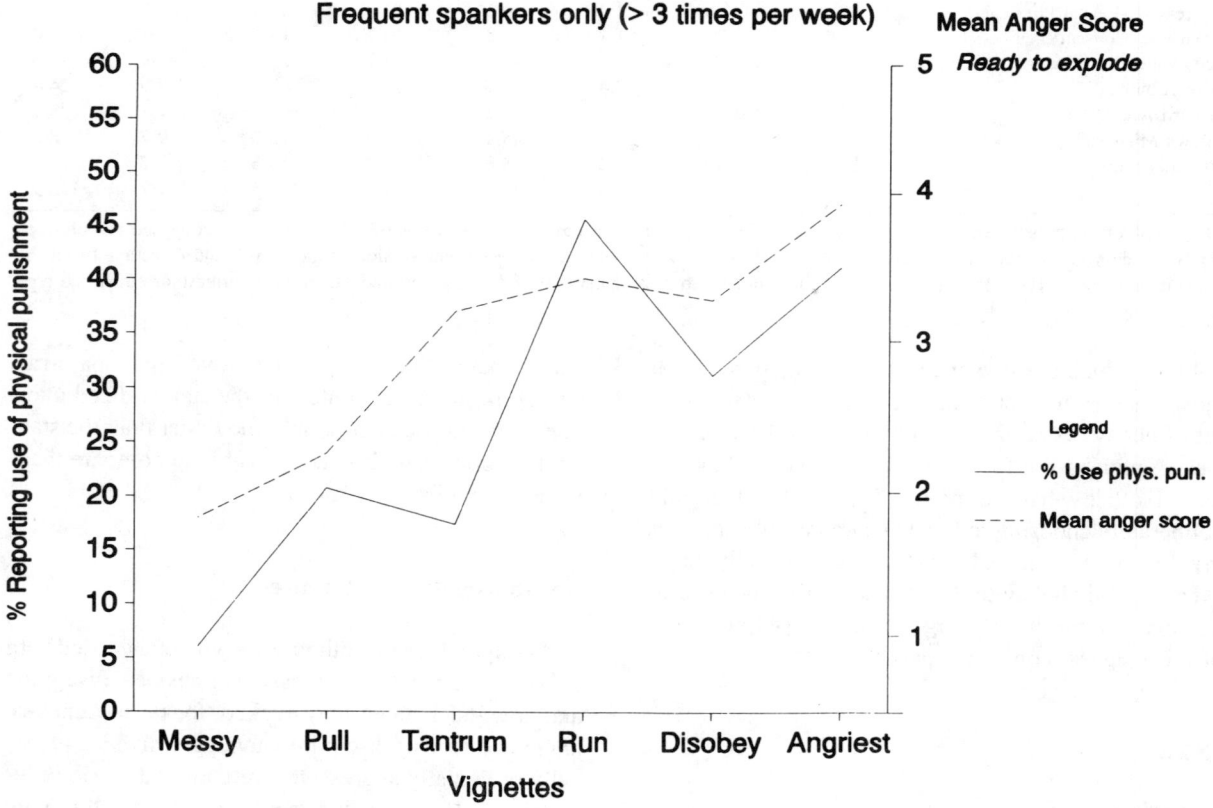

Figure 2. Percentage of mothers advocating punishment and mean anger score for each vignette for only those mothers advocating spanking more than three times per week.

Table 5. *Parental Response to "What Makes You Angriest?"*

| Child Behavior | n^b | $\%^c$ | % Reporting Each Behavior[a] | | | | |
			% Using Physical Discipline	% Using Aggressive Verbal/Physical Discipline	% Using Removal	% Using Other Discipline	M Anger
Disobedience	45	22.6	28.9	31.1	51.1	35.6	4.16
Off-Limits Behavior	42	21.11	31.0	14.3	47.6	61.9	3.98
Defiance	25	12.6	32.0	20.0	44.0	40.0	3.48
Aggression	51	25.6	41.2	27.5	45.1	49.0	3.71
Unsafe Behavior	6	3.0	50.0	16.7	33.3	50.0	3.83
Tantrums	33	16.6	18.2	24.2	39.4	48.5	4.06
Attention Seeking	14	7.0	7.1	14.3	2.1	78.6	3.14
Problematic Affect	6	3.0	33.3	33.3	16.7	50.0	3.67

[a]Reading across are the percentages of those saying that they did punish for this misbehavior who reported various disciplinary strategies. For example, 45 subjects reported disobedience as a common problem. Of those 45, 13 subjects (28.9%) said they used physical discipline. Percentages across Columns 3 through 6 do not sum to 100% because respondents mentioned two or more types of discipline. [b]The number of respondents (of a possible 199) who said this child behavior makes them angriest. [c]Percentage of 199 respondents who said that this child behavior makes them angriest. Percentages do not sum to 100% because some respondents mentioned two or more kinds of child behaviors. [d]Mean response to "How angry do you feel about this behavior?" regarding the child behavior listed in Column 1.

icant relations were found between anger and verbally aggressive or physical discipline for pulling things off shelves (point biserial $r = .37$), a relatively low anger provoking vignette, and running into the street (point biserial $r = .27$), the vignette that sampled the fewest subjects due to interviewers' concerns about the nature of the question. Thus, in most cases, although anger may influence extent or intensity of verbally aggressive or physical discipline (this remains for future research to determine), it did not appear to influence strongly choice of disciplinary strategy.

The extent to which mothers said they became angry when responding to the vignettes was significantly related to the view of their child as having behavior problems, as indexed by the ECBI, for half the vignettes (3 of 6 vignettes). Anger ratings for throwing tantrums ($r = .38$, $p < .001$), disobedience ($r = .36$, $p < .001$), and the behavior that made mothers the angriest ($r = .46$, $p < .001$) were related to the general rating of child behavior problems. (These ratings remained significant after Bonferroni adjustment for number of tests conducted.) Thus, the risk factors of becoming angry and perceiving the child as having behavior problems were positively related on the vignettes producing the most anger. In turn, the perception of behavior problems was moderately related to the extent to which parents spanked when frequent (three or more times per week) and infrequent (less than three times per week) spankers were considered (point biserial $r = .26$, $p < .001$.)

Discussion

In this study, we provide one of the first explorations of the relation between anger and other correlates of abusive parenting using a sample of low-income mothers. Although similar relations may occur in middle-income families, this initial study focused on low-income mothers, because they are at higher risk for many of the correlates of abuse (e.g., use of physical discipline) and physical abuse. Thus, the relation of these risk factors within this population is of interest, independent of the extent to which it may also be present in other populations (e.g., middle-income families).

Our data suggest that anger is not related to selection of physical discipline techniques, except in situations that provoke little anger in most respondents. The children's behaviors that make the mothers angriest, however, lead to physical discipline more often than do all of the other child responses described in the vignettes, but this effect is relatively small.

In contrast, maternal anger does correlate with a higher proportion of maternally perceived behavior problems, and perception of behavior problems has been linked to higher levels of abuse in low- and middle-income families. These findings were strongest for the situations that challenged the mothers' ability to control the child directly, for example, by the child deliberately disobeying a direct command or talking back. The situations rated by the mothers as making them angriest also reiterated the theme of a need to control the child, another correlate of physical abuse.

There are a number of limitations to our study that must be acknowledged. First, these data are based on verbal reports of women, some of whom are familiar with social service's response to child mistreatment and all of whom were warned, for ethical reasons, that the interviewer was mandated to report any instances of abuse revealed. Thus, although these data show substantial use of physical punishment, they probably underestimate both the intensity and frequency of physical discipline. Note, however, that the relations we did find occur despite such potential bias and thus may be particularly robust.

Second, the vignettes in the interview targeted specific behaviors suggested by the literature as being problematic for parents. Our open-ended responses revealed that the vignettes did not tap the behaviors that these mothers felt were most problematic. The most frequent consumers of many parenting strategies have been middle-class parents who may be troubled by the child getting messy or pulling items down in a grocery store. The low-income mothers, in contrast, were much more motivated to intercede with behaviors they felt undermined their authority with the child. Thus, our sample of situations failed to elicit ratings of anger and type of discipline in response to standardized descriptions of what these mothers considered to be the most problematic behavioral scenarios. Future research in this area should focus more on such problematic child behaviors in low-income families.

Finally, this is a descriptive study of low-income women only; therefore, determination of relative risk and cause–effect relations is not possible. The data do not address the differential presence of these factors in other populations (e.g., middle-income families); rather, they only explore the relations among these risk factors in this sample of low-income women. Further, these findings are limited to the specific population sampled. Although the majority of eligible subjects participated, these subjects represent only mothers in a medium-size midwestern city who are eligible to attend a WIC clinic. Because disciplinary strategies are likely to be strongly related to mothers' subculture, application of these findings should be preceded by probes to ascertain the similarity of the targeted population to the current subjects.

In summary, these data may assist us in planning preventive endeavors for these and similar low-income women. Because the parenting factors described here are clearly intertwined (as hypothesized by Dix, 1991), a successful abuse prevention program could, for example, focus on the relation of maternal anger to perception of behavior problems. Anger may increase the perception of behaviors as being problematic, or a wider range of behavior problems may escalate anger. Although the direction of causality remains to be described in future research, it may be reasonable at this time to posit a bidirectional influence and focus prevention programs accordingly. Similarly, anger does not seem to result in the choice of more physical disciplinary strategies, but it may enhance the intensity of physical discipline strategies when they are used. This is an important problem that should be addressed in future research. The majority of the women in our study reported that they relied on physical discipline. Recall that this number was higher when parents were asked directly if they "spanked" their child rather than queried in an open-ended style concerning techniques they had used. The open-ended questions may be thought to produce a more accurate picture of the discipline used.

Spank may be a middle-class term, and it may connote different things to different families. Yet, the more leading question, "How often do you spank?", promoted more reports of physical discipline than the open-ended questions. Establishing the optimum way of gathering these sensitive data is another task for future research.

In any case, given the frequent use of some form of physical discipline, the utility of preventive teaching and emphasizing the use of nonphysical discipline is clear. In addition, on a 5-point scale ranging from *not at all angry* (1) to *ready to explode* (5), mothers' responses ranged from 3.4 to 4.16. Thus, the anger-reduction interventions employed in physical abuse prevention programs (e.g., Walker, Bonner, & Kaufman, 1988; Wolfe, Sandler, & Kaufman, 1981) should be useful for this low-income sample. Finally, the situations that were rated as evoking the most anger pertained to control of the child. Trickett et al. (1991) noted that a lack of tolerance for child autonomy characterized their sample of abusive parents of 4- to 8-year-olds. Thus, instruction in developmental norms and in methods of giving up some degree of maternal control at developmentally appropriate junctures may lower maternal anger and could reduce the perceived need to punish the child, as well as yield experiential advantages to the child.

These observations can inform the development of hypotheses-testing intervention studies. It is clear that treatment of serious parenting problems such as child abuse is very difficult (e.g., Wolfe, Edwards, monion, & Koverola, 1988), and most experts believe that early preventive intervention is a preferred strategy (Daro, 1988; Walker et al., 1988; Wolfe, 1988). Our results suggest some potential targets for intervention in a low-income population to improve their parenting and to lower their elevated risk for physical child abuse.

References

Abramson, L. Y., Seligman, M., & Teasdale, J. (1978). Learned helplessness in humans: Critique and reformulation. *Journal of Abnormal Psychology, 87,* 49–74.

American Humane Association. (1984). *Highlights of official child neglect and abuse reporting—1982.* Denver: Author.

Averill, J. R. (1982). *Anger and aggression: An essay on emotion.* New York: Springer-Verlag.

Berkeley Planning Associates. (1983). *The exploration of client characteristics, services, and outcomes.* (Contract No. 105–78–1108). National Center on Child Abuse and Neglect.

Brody, G. H., & Forehand, R. (1986). Maternal perceptions of child maladjustment as a function of the combined influence of child behavior and maternal depression. *Journal of Consulting and Clinical Psychology, 54,* 237–240.

Bugental, D. B., Blue, J., & Cruzcosa, M. (1989). Perceived control over caregiving outcomes: Implications for child abuse. *Developmental Psychology, 25,* 532–539.

Crockenberg, S. (1987). Predictors and correlates of anger toward and punitive control of toddlers by adolescent mothers. *Child Development, 58,* 964–975.

Daro, D. (1988). *Confronting child abuse: Research for effective program design.* London: Free Press.

Dix, T. (1991). The affective organization of parenting: Adaptive and maladaptive processes. *Psychological Bulletin, 110,* 3–25.

Dix, T., Reinhold, D. P., & Zambarano, R. J. (1990). Mothers' judgment in moments of anger. *Merrill-Palmer Quarterly, 36,* 465–486.

Elder, G. (1979). Historical change in life patterns and personality. In P. Baltes & O. Bruin (Eds.), *Life span development and behavior* (Vol. 2, pp. 117–159). New York: Academic.

Galambos, N., & Silbereisen, R. (1987). Income change, parental life outlook, and adolescent expectations for job success. *Journal of Marriage and the Family, 49,* 141–149.

Garbarino, J. (1976). The human ecology of child maltreatment: A conceptual model for research. *Journal of Marriage and the Family, 39,* 721–735.

Goodnow, J. J. (1988). Parents' ideas, actions, and feelings: Models and methods from developmental and social psychology. *Child Development, 59,* 286–320.

Herrenkohl, R. C., Herrenkohl, E. C., & Egolf, B. P. (1983). Circumstances surrounding the occurrence of child maltreatment. *Journal of Consulting and Clinical Psychology, 51,* 424–431.

Kelley, H. H. (1979). *Personal relationships: Their structures and processes.* Hillsdale, NJ: Lawrence Erlbaum Associates, Inc.

Lempers, J., Clark-Lempers, D., & Simons, R. (1989). Economic hardship, parenting, and distress in adolescence. *Child Development, 60,* 25–49.

McLoyd, V. C. (1990). The impact of economic hardship on black families and children: Psychological distress, parenting, and socioemotional development. *Child Development, 61,* 311–346.

National Center for Child Abuse and Neglect. (1981). *Study findings: National study of the incidence and severity of child abuse and neglect* (DHHS Publication No. OHDS 81–30325). Washington, DC: U.S. Government Printing Office.

Patterson, G. R. (1982). *Coercive family process.* Eugene, OR: Castalia.

Pelton, L. H. (1978). Child abuse and neglect: The myth of classlessness. *American Journal of Orthopsychiatry, 48,* 608–617.

Peterson, D. R. (1989). Interpersonal goal conflict. In L. A. Pervin (Ed.), *Goals concepts in personality and social psychology* (pp. 327–361). Hillsdale, NJ: Lawrence Erlbaum Associates, Inc.

Robinson, E. A., Eyberg, S. M., & Ross, A. W. (1980). The standardization of an inventory of child conduct problem behaviors. *Journal of Clinical Child Psychology, 9,* 22–28.

Rosenberg, M. S., & Reppucci, N. D. (1983). Abusive mothers: Perceptions of their own and their children's behavior. *Journal of Consulting and Clinical Psychology, 51,* 674–682.

Straus, M. A., & Gelles, R. (1986). Societal change and change in family violence from 1975–1985 as revealed by two national surveys. *Journal of Marriage and the Family, 48,* 465–479.

Straus, M. A., Gelles, R. J., & Steinmetz, S. (1980). *Behind closed doors: Violence in the American family.* Garden City, NY: Doubleday/Anchor.

Trickett, P. K., Aber, J. L., Carlson, V., & Cicchetti, D. (1991). Relationship of socioeconomic status to the etiology and developmental sequelae of physical child abuse. *Developmental Psychology, 27,* 148–158.

Vasta, R. (1982). Physical child abuse: A dual-component analysis. *Developmental Review, 2,* 125–149.

Walker, C. E., Bonner, B., & Kaufman, K. (1988). *The physically and sexually abused child: Evaluation and treatment.* New York: Pergamon.

Whiteman, M., Fanshel, D., & Grundy, J. F. (1987). Cognitive–behavioral interventions aimed at anger of parents at risk of child abuse. *Social Work, 32,* 469–474.

Wolfe, D. A. (1988). Child abuse and neglect. In E. J. Mash & L. G. Terdal (Eds.), *Behavioral assessment of childhood disorders* (2nd ed., pp. 627–669). New York: Guilford.

Wolfe, D. A., Edwards, B., Monion, I., & Koverola, C. (1988). Early intervention for parents at risk of child abuse and neglect: A preliminary investigation. *Journal of Consulting and Clinical Psychology, 56,* 40–47.

Wolfe, D. A., Sandler, J., & Kaufman, K. (1981). A competency-based parent training program for child abusers. *Journal of Consulting and Clinical Psychology, 49,* 633–640.

Received October 28, 1993
Final revision received May 20, 1994

Journal of Clinical Child Psychology
1994, Vol. 23, 444–457

Economic Impact of Divorce on Children's Development: Current Findings and Policy Implications

S. Wayne Duncan
University of Washington

Examined the economic impact of divorce on families' functioning and children's mental health. U.S. Bureau of the Census (1992b, 1993) data on rates of divorce and remarriage are reviewed, as well as data on economic aspects that both predispose to and result from marital dissolution (Hernandez, 1992). Research regarding the impact of economic stress and poverty on family functioning and child mental health problems is discussed. I make five recommendations for social policy that emphasize the need for attention to economic aspects of divorce and their impact on children's and parents' adjustment and well being. Particular attention is devoted to the need for continuity in families' economic standard following divorce, enforcement of child support laws, and new treatment approaches to help children cope with their parents' divorce.

Over 1 million children and adolescents will experience their parents' divorce this year. For many children, this will initiate a series of economic changes that will significantly alter their day-to-day lives, leading to restrictions of activities, changes in residences and schools, and increasing the level of daily stress they experience. For those who are already poor, it will intensify their economic and social plight. Their difficult financial situation will be made even worse, and they will also experience the impact of divorced parents who are more stressed and less available. The impact of the economic changes concomitant with divorce has generally been little appreciated by psychologists, especially when changes are significant and, at times, place families in poverty. The central thesis of this article is that many of the problems frequently attributed to divorce per se are actually a result of divorce's economic impact; this area must be considered with other well-documented risk factors, such as high levels of marital conflict (e.g., Emery, 1982), to understand the full experience of children and parents during the course of divorce. In the following sections, I consider what we currently know about the relation of divorce rates and families' financial well-being, the impact of these economic changes on children's functioning and mental health in middle childhood, and a set of recommendations for public policy.

Poverty and Divorce in the United States: The Demographic Context

Although a national census has been taken every decade since 1790 in the United States, it was not until the 1960s that detailed data were available on the economic life of the country and, specifically, on the rates of poverty for different ethnic groups and types of families (Rivlin, 1971). In the past 25 years, improvements in survey methodology and the unprecedented development of computers have helped provide a much more accurate picture of America's families, their composition, and their economic situations. These data provide a much broader social and cultural context for understanding specific processes within families. As Furstenberg (1985) noted, it is important for psychologists to examine large, representative samples of families to appreciate the full range of families' functioning and to minimize the reliance on smaller, often less representative samples, such as those found in groups of children or families recruited for studies from mental health clinics. Such advice is especially apropos to research on divorce, in which frequent reliance on clinical samples has led to a view of divorce that is actually inaccurate for many children (Emery, 1988). In this section, I utilize some of the most recent data from the U.S. Bureau of the Census to examine trends with respect to poverty, divorce, and children in the United States.

Poverty and Children in the United States

Approximately 22% or over 14 million children and adolescents in the United States are currently living in

I thank Pam Van Dalfsen, Jane Ellis, Robert Emery, and Ross Thompson for their helpful comments on this article.

Requests for reprints should be sent to S. Wayne Duncan, Department of Psychology (NI–25), University of Washington, Seattle, WA 98195.

poverty (Bane & Ellwood, 1989; Pear, 1993b; Strawn, 1992). This rate is close to the rate of 23.1% in 1964, the year President Lyndon B. Johnson launched the Great Society programs (Schorr, 1989; U.S. Bureau of the Census, 1992a). Social historians have noted that an important impetus for the Great Society programs were the scenes of profound poverty that President John F. Kennedy had witnessed during his campaign trips through rural communities in West Virginia (de Lone, 1979; Lemann, 1988). Following Kennedy's assassination, Johnson felt the need to establish his own domestic agenda and readily supported the development of a war on poverty that was broader and more visible than the one Kennedy was considering at the time of his death (Lemann, 1988).

The programs of the Great Society contributed to a decline in the poverty rate during the 1960s. As Danziger and Danziger (1993) noted, "The poverty rate [for children] fell rapidly between 1949 and 1969, was roughly constant during the 1970s, and increased during the 1980s" (p. 60). The current rate contrasts with the significantly lower rate for children that was recorded in the 1970s and 1980s. For example, for children under 18 years old in 1970, the poverty rate was 15.1%; in 1980, it was 18.3% (Strawn, 1992). Currently, children compose the single largest group of individuals in poverty in the United States (U.S. Bureau of the Census, 1992a), and the most recent national statistics for 1992 indicate that the poverty rate is 21.9% for individuals under 18 years old (Pear, 1993b), affecting the lives of 14.6 million children and adolescents. This rate is at least twice that of any other industrialized nation (Robinson, 1993).

Determining who is in poverty hinges on the official definition of *poverty,* which was initially a controversial problem when the U.S. Department of Agriculture's "economy diet" was used as the basis for the definition (Rivlin, 1971). The debate around the definition of poverty continues today (Banerjee, 1994; Gugliotta, 1993; Ruggles, 1992). For example, in 1991, the official poverty cutoff was $13,924 for four individuals. This figure includes the cash income for the family before taxes but does not include noncash benefits such as food stamps or Medicaid. This rate resulted in the statistic that 14.2% of all Americans were below the poverty line in 1991, encompassing 35.7 million people (Gugliotta, 1993). Many economic and policy experts believe that this current federal poverty "yardstick" of $13,924 income for a family of four per year underestimates the rate of poverty because it is tied to a 1963 cost profile that is unadjusted for regional or for urban/rural differences and does not reflect the fact that today's higher housing costs consume a larger proportion of families' incomes. In addition, this definition does not reflect the fact that today's poverty income level represents a smaller proportion of the median income in the United States today than when the standard was devised (Danziger & Danziger, 1993; Gugliotta, 1993).

Note that these figures typically underestimate the true rate of families experiencing poverty. As noted by Huston (1991) and others, families whose incomes are close to the poverty range fluctuate frequently around this level, and their movement into and out of the official poverty range is generally not captured by statistics collected once per year by most panel studies or once every 10 years by the Census Bureau. Thus, it is reasonable to infer that many children experience the stress of their parents' fluctuating income but are not counted in the official poverty statistics and are ineligible for federal support programs due to their families' occasional success in rising above the required minimal level of support. Support for this argument is evident in census data that indicate substantial numbers of families with children under age 18 do not receive various forms of assistance. For example, in 1991, only 51.1% of two-parent families who met federal poverty guidelines received food stamps; this increased to 76% in mother-headed households, but still about 25% of eligible families did not receive the aid (U.S. Bureau of the Census, 1992c). Although there are a number of factors involving federal and state requirements for various programs, a detailed discussion of these factors is beyond the scope of this article (for a full discussion of these issues, see Garfinkel, 1992).

An important finding from analyses of the Census Bureau data is that poverty is not equally distributed across different ethnic groups. As shown in Figure 1, the rates for White, African-American, and Hispanic children differ dramatically. In 1991 the poverty rates for African-American, Hispanic, and White children were 45.9%, 40.4%, and 16.8%, respectively (U.S. Bureau of the Census, 1993). However, the total number of children affected varies greatly as a result of each group's size in the total U.S. population. For example, 8.8 million White children are poor, compared to 4.8 million African-American and 3.1 million Hispanic children. The fact that more nonminority children in the United States experience poverty each year than do ethnic minority children is often missed in the media, where poverty is often portrayed as primarily a problem of ethnic minorities (de Lone, 1979). As Wilson (1984) noted, this misperception can at times undermine public support for antipoverty programs because these programs are viewed as specifically benefitting a particular minority group or segment of the population.

An important, related aspect of the poverty statistics highlights the varying rates for different ethnic groups in exiting poverty. U.S. Bureau of the Census (1992c) data indicate "that about 30 percent of Whites who were poor in 1987 were able to exit poverty by 1988, compared with 17.0 percent of Blacks and 18.1 percent of persons of Hispanic origin" (p. xix). Thus, ethnic minority families are more likely to remain in poverty over

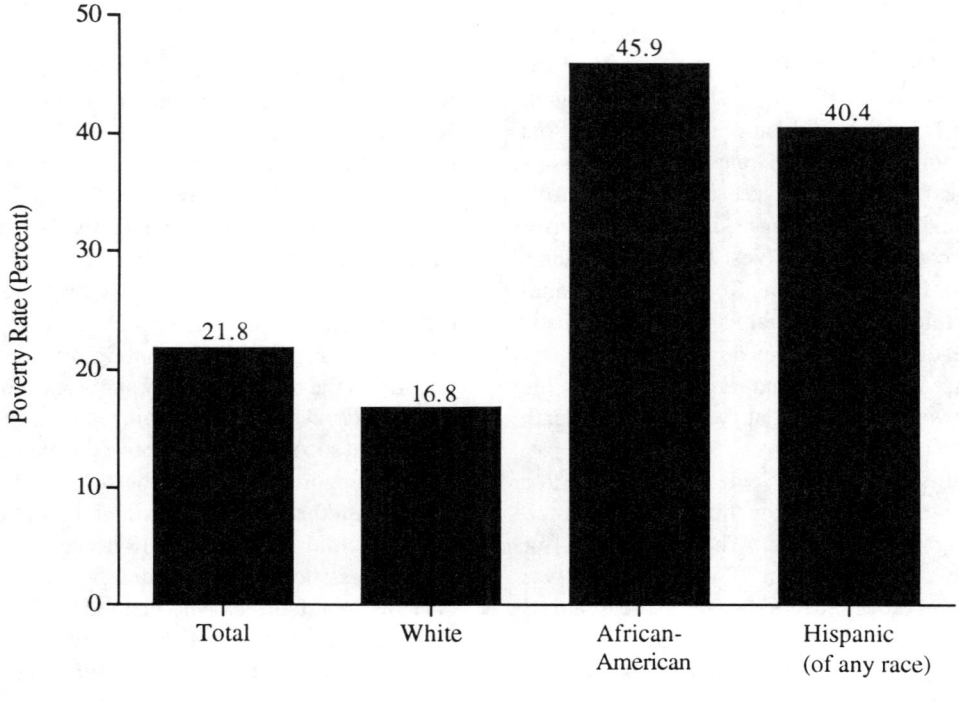

Figure 1. Childhood poverty rate by race and Hispanic origin: 1991. Adapted from *How We're Changing; Demographic State of the Nation: 1993,* by the U.S. Bureau of the Census, 1993, Washington, DC: U.S. Government Printing Office.

time, placing the children in these families at greater risk for ill effects.

The Economic Consequences of Divorce in the United States

Few changes in the family over the past 25 years have elicited the same level of discussion and, apparently, alarm as has the increasing rate of divorce among U.S. couples (Coontz, 1992; Skolnick, 1991). As federal statistics documented (U.S. Bureau of the Census, 1992b), the rate of divorce in the United States has increased dramatically since World War II. At that point, the rate was around 17 per 1,000 married women (between the ages of 14 and 44 years old) except for a postwar spurt to 24 per 1,000 from 1945 to 1947. The rate increased steadily to 40 per 1,000 in 1980, and it has leveled off at about 37 per 1,000 (U.S. Department of Commerce, 1992). Note that prior to this century divorce occurred less often, but marital desertion was significantly more common (Riley, 1991).

The current rate indicates that many children are exposed to their parents' divorce each year: In 1988, this was true for 1,044,000 children (U.S. Department of Commerce, 1992). This underestimates the rate of children's exposure to marital conflict and separations because these divorce statistics do not include either informal or legal separations. Data from the National Survey of Children (reported in

Furstenberg, 1988) suggest that divorces occur at a higher rate during the first year of marriage and continue at a relatively steady rate through the time that the children are in adolescence. Of the marriages that will end by the time their first child is age 16 (about 30%), about two thirds of these children (about 20%) will experience their parents' marital breakup prior to starting school. Thus, divorce is more likely to occur when children are in the infancy through kindergarten period. As a result, many children are adjusting to the effects of divorce during middle childhood (from age 6 to age 12) and are often experiencing their parents' subsequent remarriage.

The rates of divorce vary in different ethnic groups: African Americans and Hispanics have the highest rates, followed by Whites; Asian Americans have the lowest rate (Laosa, 1988). The divorce rate contributes to the sharp increase in single parenting over the past 2 decades, although the increase has been most heavily influenced by the dramatic rise in the number of single mothers who have never been married. Thus, 1980 census data indicated that 9.8% of African-American children under age 15 live with their divorced mother, and the same situation is true for 5.4% of Hispanic and 6.8% of White children (*Current Population Reports, Series P–23,* No. 114, 1982; cited in Laosa, 1988). Inspection of Table 1 reveals that, in 1980, divorced mothers accounted for about one half of the White single-mother households and about one fourth of Hispanic and African-American families. These data

Table 1. *Living Arrangements of Children Under 18 Years by Race and Hispanic Origin: March 1990, 1980, and 1970*

	% of Distribution		
Living Arrangement	**1990**	**1980**	**1970**
All Races Living With:			
Two Parents	72.5	76.7	85.2
One Parent	24.7	19.7	11.9
Mother Only	21.6	18.0	10.8
Father Only	3.1	1.7	1.1
Other	2.7	3.7	2.9
White Living With:			
Two Parents	79.0	82.7	89.5
One Parent	19.2	15.1	8.7
Mother Only	16.2	13.5	7.8
Father Only	3.0	1.6	0.9
Other	1.8	2.2	1.8
African American Living With:			
Two Parents	37.7	42.2	58.5
One Parent	54.8	45.8	31.8
Mother Only	51.2	43.9	29.5
Father Only	3.5	1.9	2.3
Other	7.5	12.0	9.7
Hispanic Origin[a] Living With:			
Two Parents	66.8	75.4	77.7
One Parent	30.0	21.1	NA
Mother Only	27.1	19.6	NA
Father Only	2.9	1.5	NA
Other	3.3	3.5	NA

Note: Excludes persons under 18 years old who were maintaining household or family groups. Adapted from *Marriage, Divorce, and Remarriage in the 1990's* by the U.S. Bureau of the Census, 1992b, Washington, DC: U.S. Government Printing Office.
[a]Persons of Hispanic origin may be of any race.

also help describe the pattern of children's current family lives. Also shown in Table 1, 1990 Census Bureau data indicate 79% of White children live with two parents (though both are not necessarily the biological parents), whereas this is true for 38% of African-American children and 67% of Hispanic children (U.S. Bureau of the Census, 1992b).

Women and work. It is important to consider the role of increased involvement of women in the U.S. workforce when examining divorce and poverty's influence on children's development. In 1979, Espenshade reviewed available research and noted that mothers substantially increased their work hours following divorce, presumably to increase their income to compensate for the loss of the father's income. This is consistent with more recent data (U.S. Bureau of the Census, 1991b) indicating that

> the percentage of children with a mother not working at all decreased sharply from 43 to 31 percent between the interview prior to the departure of the father from the household and the interview which covers the first

full 4-month reporting period in which he is absent from the household. (p. 11)

Unfortunately, women's salaries remain less than men's. On average, a woman makes $.70 for every $1.00 a man earns (U.S. Bureau of the Census, 1993). Thus, although a woman works equal hours, she has less to show for it than a man in an identical job. As a result of these interrelated aspects, women are at greater risk of moving into poverty than their former husbands following a divorce. Research data bear this out. Census Bureau statistics, reviewed in a National Research Council (1991) report, indicate that in 1989 70% of all women who had experienced a divorce were working outside the home in paid employment. However, this did not necessarily insulate them from severe economic effects: 17% of White, 29% of African American, and 31% of Hispanic women fell below the poverty cutoff, averaging 21% across groups. Data from the Survey of Income and Program Participation (U.S. Bureau of the Census, 1991b) indicate the percentage of families in poverty doubled during the first 4-month period of the father's absence, increasing from 18.5% to 37.6%. A ratio of the income to needs is particularly revealing because it indicates that these mother-headed households had only about 70% of the income that had been previously available when fathers were present. This occurs in spite of more mothers commencing work outside the home and more mothers increasing their paid work to full-time status. Thus, the loss of the father's income is not made up in other ways, and families' living standards drop.

Child support. Part of divorce proceedings involve the filing and judicial acceptance of a plan for financial support of the child(ren) by both parents. During most of this century, the father has typically been the noncustodial parent and has been required to pay a percentage of his income to support the child. Research indicates that the size of these awards varies as a percentage of the noncustodial father's income but is often around 20% for one child (Garfinkel, 1992). This income percentage increases with the number of children being cared for as well as when the noncustodial parent's income is small. There is some controversy regarding the regressive nature of the child-support laws due to their greater relative burden on lower income parents. For example, it is clear that this requirement also has a greater impact on ethnic minority parents, given their lower average incomes and greater average number of children (U.S. Department of Commerce, 1992).

Although child-support payments would theoretically ease the economic impact of divorce on children, often they are ineffective for many reasons. Note that child-support payments cover only a portion of the cost of rearing a child. For example, Duncan and Hoffman

(1985) reported that, in the first year following divorce (when rates of compliance are typically highest), women's child-support payments averaged only 10% of their total income. More recent data indicate that there has been an increase in child support to 17.1% of divorced women's total income, reflecting federal efforts to improve compliance (U.S. Census Bureau, 1991a). Still, in 1989 the average yearly child-support payment received by divorced mothers was only $3,322. This is consistent with the general argument that women's incomes decrease substantially during the first year following divorce. Weitzman (1985) reported that women's incomes decreased by an average of 73% in the first year following divorce, whereas Hoffman and Duncan (1988) indicated that there is a decrease of only 33% in family economic status. However, both sources agree that women's income drops substantially while their former husbands' increase.

U.S. Bureau of the Census (1991a) data indicate that 76.8% of divorced women are awarded child support at the time of their divorce. Unfortunately, the child-support payments are frequently ignored by the payer. More recent federal data indicate that about 50% of fathers pay their full child-support payment each month, about 25% pay some portion of what is ordered, and another 25% pay nothing. Thus, the typically minimal level of court-ordered support often does not even reach the mothers and children. Changes in federal and state policies with respect to the enforcement of child support have made notable progress in the amount of support collected. For example, the total amount of child support collected totalled $500 million in 1976, whereas it rose to $6 billion in 1992 (Bieniek, 1994).

In Maccoby and Mnookin's (1992) study of over 1,000 northern California families going through divorce, the authors noted that child-support awards were made in 83% of the families. Depending on the nature of the custody arrangements, the amount of support varied greatly. For example, 96% of the fathers were ordered to provide support in mother-physical/joint-legal custody cases, which was the custody arrangement in almost exactly half the families studied. Across all families in which fathers were required to pay child support, longitudinal data indicate that the level of support paid decreased over the 3 years the families were followed. For example, at 1 year following the filing of the divorce petition, 69.6% of the fathers were paying the full amount of child support ordered; 3 years later, this figure decreased to 56.5%. There was an increase (from 15.7% to 25.9%) in the fathers paying partial support, and an increase (from 14.7% to 17.6%) in fathers providing no support whatsoever during this time. These data are similar to national data for child support (Garfinkel, 1992). An interesting and important point that Maccoby and

Mnookin (1992) noted is that there was considerable variability in fathers' payment patterns:

> Nearly half of those fathers who were noncompliant at Time 2 became partially or fully compliant by Time 3. Conversely, about 35 percent of those who were fully compliant at Time 2 were only partially compliant or noncompliant by Time 3. (p. 251)

The stressfulness of this erratic support payment pattern is also important to note. Because many of the mothers were likely to be struggling to stay above the poverty line, these support payments constituted relatively small but nevertheless essential proportions of divorced families' disposable income. Maccoby and Mnookin (1992) also found that fathers who experienced unemployment were three times more likely than employed fathers not to pay child support. Although this result may not be particularly surprising, given the circumstances, it does highlight the need to view the support picture from a broader context that includes changing economic and employment patterns.

Another factor affecting the fathers' child-support compliance was their level of contact with their children. Fathers who did not regularly see their children averaged only about 52%, whereas fathers who regularly saw their mother-residence children averaged over 75% compliance with child-support payments. Many states stipulate in their laws concerning child support and visitation that parents who are failing to meet their support payments still have the right to have contact with their children. However, it is likely that many parents who are unable to make these payments (whether due to unemployment, underemployment, health care costs, etc.) may experience a sense of psychological discomfort that may begin the process of disengagement from their children. This situation may then further increase the likelihood of parents' not complying with their court-ordered financial support. Of course, it is also possible that nonresidential parents who have felt less emotionally connected with their children will be less likely to pay their court-ordered support. The link between visitation and payment of support, however, is not always consistent (see Veum, 1992, 1993).

Another aspect of this support payment noncompliance has to do with the likelihood of compliance being enforced. As Grillo (1991) noted, for many women the pursuit of a legal remedy for failure to pay child or spousal support is simply untenable. This can result from the costs often involved in litigation, threats from the ex-spouse concerning consequences of legal action, and the fact that many women are already experiencing role overload; adding the emotional, time, and financial demands of litigation to their situation becomes practically impossible.

Research Examining Poverty and Family Discontinuation

In a ground-breaking report for the U.S. Bureau of the Census, Hernandez (1992) examined the impact of poverty on families' likelihood to experience marital discontinuation, which includes separation and divorce, using the month-to-month data from the Census Bureau's ongoing Survey of Income and Program Participation (e.g., U.S. Bureau of the Census, 1991b). For the first time, it was possible to examine the interrelated factors of work, poverty, and family stability and instability using this sample of over 30,000 households. Specifically, Hernandez found that the rates of discontinuation for poor families, based on federal poverty guidelines, were about twice that of nonpoor families, as shown in Table 2. Other analyses examined family breakup by the family's ethnicity and revealed other interesting results: for poor White families, couples discontinued at a rate of 12.3% over a 2-year period in contrast to 6.9% of nonpoor married couples; for poor African-American families, couples discontinued at a rate of 21.2% in contrast to 10.5% for nonpoor couples. Interestingly, for Hispanic couples, rates of discontinuation in poor and nonpoor families were about the same—11.1% and 9.1%, respectively. These data are important. As Hernandez observed in an interview,

> Over the last decade or two, there has been a lot of emphasis on the rise of one-parent families as a cause of poverty. But this report shows that the opposite process is also important. When two-parent families fall into poverty, that significantly increases the chances that the family will break up. (Pear, 1993a, p. A6)

This study is especially noteworthy because it has provided the strongest evidence yet of what many family researchers have long suspected: Not only can divorce lead to poverty, but poverty can contribute to the likelihood of divorce.

Conclusion

The data available from the Census Bureau and from survey studies provide a useful picture of the changing context for child development. As marriages have been increasingly likely to end in divorce, the number and percentage of children spending part of their childhoods in single-parent families has notably increased. The economic consequences for many children and (typically) their mothers are generally serious and at times so severe that they lead them into poverty. Meanwhile, fathers' incomes rise, but only about half pay their full court-ordered child support. Recent data (Hernandez, 1992) have also confirmed another aspect of poverty: Families in which White or African-American parents are together but financially impoverished are about twice as likely to divorce as are more financially well-off families. Thus, poverty is a cause of marital dissolution for some families, and divorce is the pathway into poverty for other families.

Effects of Economic Factors on Mental Health Following Divorce

Economic stress has demonstrable effects on individual functioning, interpersonal relationships, and mental health. In this section, I review findings that help illuminate the impact of the economic changes on parents' and children's functioning following divorce. Although a number of different developmental periods could be considered in this review, the period of middle childhood (i.e., children between 6 and 12 years old) is emphasized. Because a large number of children in middle childhood have already experienced their parents' divorce and are coping with the consequences (Furstenberg, 1988; Heaton, 1990), it seems appropriate to assess the immediate and longer-term effects of divorce's economic impact for children in this age group. A summary of data and results from small-sample, process-oriented research (e.g., Hodges, Tierney, & Buchsbaum, 1984); national panel studies focusing on thousands of families (e.g., Peterson & Zill, 1986); and federal census data from millions of families (e.g., U.S. Bureau of the Census, 1991b) is presented in this section. The availability of both methodologically sophisticated, process-oriented family research and several large samples that are representative with respect to both ethnicity and socioeconomic status makes it possible to piece together a more complete and multifaceted picture of families' functioning following divorce.

Table 2. *Married-Couple Poverty Rate and Household Discontinuation Rate for 2-Year Period by Race and Hispanic Origin*

	Married-Couple Poverty Rate	% of Married Couples Discontinued	
		Not Poor	Poor
Families With Own Children Under 18	10.3	7.1	13.2
White	9.4	6.9	12.3
African American	16.2	10.5	21.2
Hispanic Origin[a]	22.4	9.1	11.1

Note: Adapted from *When Households Continue, Discontinue, and Form* by D. J. Hernandez, 1992, Washington, DC: U.S. Government Printing Office.
[a]Persons of Hispanic origin may be of any race.

Note that this review is selective and reflects my interpretation of the literature. Over 20 years ago, Herzog and Sudia (1973) published an influential review that described the clinical and research literature on divorce and children's development as "sprawling." At that time, they abstracted and summarized results from over 400 studies in their 90+ page review. My recent literature search for psychology articles on divorce between 1967 and 1993 produced over 3,500 citations, suggesting the complexity and difficulty in summarizing this vast literature. Consequently, I have chosen to highlight three areas that are specifically related to the economic impact of divorce on children; these include the effects on parents' mental health, changes in parenting roles and behaviors, and the specific impact on children's mental health. This section is not intended to be a comprehensive review of divorce's short- or long-term effects on children; instead, it provides a succinct summary of some of the key findings with respect to economic-linked effects. For readers who are interested in general reviews of the research literature, the volumes by Emery (1988), Hetherington and Arasteh (1988), Hodges (1991), and Pasley and Ihinger-Tallman (1987) contain helpful summaries.

The mental health of both parents is negatively affected at the time of the divorce.

Although the presence of ongoing marital conflict has been linked to a variety of mental health problems (Bond & McMahon, 1984; Jacobson, Holtzworth-Munroe, & Schmaling, 1989), the end of the marriage does not mark the beginning of optimal psychological functioning for either husbands or wives. In fact, some research has documented a significant increase in rates of mental health problems and suicide during this time (Bruce & Kim, 1992; Wasserman, 1984). Recent data from the Epidemiological Catchment Area (ECA) study indicate that separated or divorced adults are about twice as likely to meet criteria in the *Diagnostic and Statistical Manual of Mental Disorders* (3rd ed.; American Psychiatric Association, 1980) for a disorder than are married adults (Regier et al., 1993). In general, the interrelation of mental health problems and marriage is a complex one that is beyond the scope of this article; the chapter by Gotlib and McCabe (1990) contains a thorough review of this topic. Economic influences on mental health are reported by Bruce, Takeuchi, and Leaf (1991), who found that poor individuals in the ECA study had a twofold increase in the risk of having an Axis I disorder. The authors suggested that this is likely tied to increased exposure to negative life events and that future research is needed to explore whether the development of mental illness can be specifically linked to the transition into poverty. Therefore, divorce and economic stressors seem to contribute in-

dependently to the likelihood that an individual will experience mental health problems.

Economic stress often increases dramatically in women, especially custodial mothers, following a divorce. As noted earlier, mothers typically experience declines in income following divorce, whereas their ex-husbands maintain or increase their income levels. The added stress of many divorced mothers' increased work obligations and financial concerns often has an indirect impact on their mental health. The ongoing requirements of child care and maintaining a household with children often fall to the mothers, because they retain physical custody in the vast majority of cases (Emery, 1988). Household chores, home upkeep, grocery purchasing, and meal planning and preparation must all be done. Although most men have traditionally done little compared to women in caring for children and maintaining the household, what they did contribute is now absent (Hochschild, 1989; National Research Council, 1991). Thus, women frequently bear the full load of handling all aspects of family life after a divorce and suffer financial hardship.

A related issue concerns the indirect impact of economic stress and increased responsibilities on women's social support. As just noted, in attempting to survive financially, many women find it essential to increase their work hours. Besides decreasing their immediate contact with their children, increased work hours also have the effect of limiting opportunities for maintaining friendships with other adults who could provide practical assistance, as well as emotional support and encouragement. This appears especially important for women who are attempting to reorient their lives in the aftermath of a divorce (McLanahan, Wedemeyer, & Adelberg, 1981). The impact of all these changes can often lead to depression, as well as other mental health problems. As Strickland (1992) noted, "A single mother, with unpredictable or limited economic support, is at particularly high risk for depression" (p. 133).

Arendell's (1986) study illustrated many of these effects in a sample of 60 divorced mothers from the San Francisco Bay Area. Within this sample, 58 women reported drastically altered finanacial situations following their divorce and described the pain and distress this had caused for themselves and their children. Although all the women had had solid middle-class lives during marriage, it had been years since some of them had worked outside the home; most had relied heavily on their husbands' earnings for economic security. Because of out-of-date work skills, no recent employment history, and constraints due to child care and hours, many found they could compete only for low-wage positions. Even when they did get hired, the lower rates of pay for women than men in comparable jobs hindered their ability to meet their financial needs. Approximately 4 years following the divorce, only 9 of the 60 women had reversed their severe economic slide:

"Few had any savings, and most lived from paycheck to paycheck in a state of constant uncertainty" (p. 37). These financial strains produced emotional ones as well; 44 (or 73%) of the 60 recently divorced women in Arendell's study reported "frequent struggles with depression and despair" (p. 46). Twenty-six of these women admitted to having contemplated suicide. Thus, postdivorce drops in level of income for the custodial parent and children can have clear negative consequences for the mother's mental health.

Men also experience noticeable changes in their social networks despite their often unchanged employment status. The impact of the divorce is often felt on friendships that are strained by the marital problems. Husbands frequently move out of their homes and familiar neighborhoods, and as Wasserman (1984), Weiss (1975), and others noted, divorce itself significantly alters one's contact with kin and friends. Unfortunately, with respect to the economic issues affecting custodial fathers, few data are available to address these issues (Emery, 1988).

Divorced parents often exhibit decreased effectiveness in parenting during the initial years following divorce.

Changes in parenting occur following divorce at a primary level due to parents' different residences. Because 90% of children are in the physical custody of their mother, their day-to-day care is primarily her concern (Ellis, 1990). Fathers may be involved as well, especially during the first 2 years following divorce, but both parents are often emotionally preoccupied with personal issues related to their marital breakup. Consequently, several factors predispose to the likelihood of inconsistent parenting following divorce. Besides the changes in parenting that naturally occur as parenting time is split, some parents also demonstrate greater inconsistency in their parenting styles. For example, some parents become relatively more permissive and others more authoritarian then was typical for them in the past (Hetherington, M. Cox, & R. Cox, 1978).

A variety of different studies have highlighted the effects that divorce and economic changes have on divorced couples' parenting. Forgatch, Patterson, and Skinner (1988) found that 64 newly separated mothers reported significantly higher levels of recent daily hassles and major stressful life events in the previous year then did a control group. In this sample of primarily poor, White families (57% were on public assistance), mothers reported a loss of family income averaging 50% with the departure of the father. Using structural equation modeling, the researchers found that mothers' stress levels (incorporating economic stress) affected their discipline practices which, in turn, contributed to their 6- to 8-year-old sons' antisocial behavior. It was

parenting behavior that was most strongly related to children's behavior problems, but this study demonstrates the contributory role of economic and other stressors to changes in maternal discipline patterns. These changes in parenting are echoed in Hetherington's (1989) comments regarding a middle-class sample: "Divorced mothers mentioned their children less clearly than did mothers from nondivorced families. They knew less about where their children were, who they were with, and what they were doing" (pp. 5–6). Conger, Ge, Elder, Lorenz, and Simons (1994) and Hashima and Amato (1994) also suggested that parental distress stemming from economic difficulties is often clearly evident in the nature of the parent–child relationship. They noted that this distress often results in greater parental hostility and punitiveness and lessened parental support.

These changes in parenting practices and behaviors are not surprising when one considers the employment situations for many women following their divorce. During this time, women are more subject to the demands of their jobs due to their diminished income; however, they are also experiencing heightened responsibilities with respect to child care, especially when their children are ill or when they need to work in the evenings or at night. Sometimes parents in these situations are even faced with the undesirable need to leave their children alone for periods of time, which can contribute to problems with delinquency (Patterson & Stouthamer-Loeber, 1984). Given the unprecedented rates of maternal employment in general, there are fewer friends or family able to provide free or low-cost child care to poor mothers, and fathers are unlikely to make up the difference in families where the parents have divorced. A number of scholars have specifically suggested the adoption of some formal federal child care support mechanisms (e.g., McLanahan, Astone, & Marks, 1991) to ease the burden on single mothers who work outside the home.

Children's mental health is adversely affected by the economic consequences of divorce and its related events.

Life event research with adults and children has demonstrated the links between high levels of stressful life events and mental health problems (G. W. Brown & Harris, 1989). This research is particularly important due to the many changes children experience during the period of marital dissolution and, often, within a context of economic scarcity for many families. A number of studies (e.g., Hetherington et al., 1978; Wallerstein & Kelly, 1980) describe some of the life stressors children regularly experience during their parents' divorce. These typically include the marital separation, family moves, lessened contact with and supervision by parents, moving to a new school, and loss of friends. In

L. P. Brown and Cowen's (1988) study of stressful life events in fourth- through sixth-grade children, items reflecting the stressors just described were all above the midpoint of the scale, suggesting a high degree of stressfulness for these events. Of course, the ratings for the stressfulness of divorce itself are extremely high in children, consistently ranking just below the death or serious injury of a parent (e.g., Dise-Lewis, 1988).

Further support for the validity of these ratings has been demonstrated by studies that link the occurrence of various life events and children's mental health. For example, Kashani, Hodges, Simonds, and Hilderbrand (1981) found that children hospitalized for psychiatric problems reported greater frequency of parental separation or divorce, family moves, and parent–child arguments. Consistent with this line of research, Wolchik et al. (1993) found strong correlations between negative divorce events and both children's and their parents' reports of child adjustment problems (rs = .52 and .50, respectively) in their sample of inner city, poor families.

The impact of these high levels of stressful life events would likely be less if the children had adequate or high levels of social support. Unfortunately, for many children this is unlikely to be the case for several reasons. First, the children have less time with their already-stressed parents. Typically, the mother is working more and the father has moved out, beginning a steady progression of decreased contact in most families (Furstenberg, 1988). Hence, even school-age children who report that they frequently seek support from their parents (Buhrmester & Furman, 1987) find that their parents are now less available. In addition, divorce typically disrupts relationships with both extended family and friends. Therefore, the combined effect of stressful life events, decreased parent availability and effectiveness, and diminished social support all contribute to children's distress during this time.

Data from other research more directly highlight the impact of family economic stress on the children's functioning. Hodges et al. (1984) compared thirty 4-year-olds from families whose parents had been separated and divorced during the preceding 2.5 years with 60 children from families with nondivorced parents. Using teacher and parent questionnaires for assessing the children's behavior, these researchers found that the family's income level, regardless of whether parents were married or divorced, was an important predictor of children's adjustment. In addition, they noted an interaction, whereby children from divorced families whose income was perceived as inadequate by their mothers were more likely to report anxiety symptoms, be less oriented to tasks, and have higher rates of teacher-reported behavior problems. Thus, Hodges et al. (1984) observed that "income problems were more predictive of adjustment than was marital status. *Rated inadequacy of income was far more predictive of mal-*

adjustment than was absolute level [italics added]" (p. 615). These findings highlight the importance of looking both at parents' own evaluations of their family's financial situation as well as at interactions between marital status and income. These data take on added importance when viewed against the backdrop of the Census Bureau's data (reviewed in the first section), documenting the sharp drop in income for the vast majority of women who divorce. Thus, even for women who are not in the official poverty classification, the drastic decreases in family income may lead them to experience a subjective sense of impoverishment.

A sample of families used for ongoing study has been assembled as part of the National Survey of Children, a federally funded project to examine children in the United States. Currently, data are available from a sample of 2,301 children from 1,747 households in the 1976 to 1977 sample and on 1,423 children 5 years later (when the children were between 12 and 16 years old). Although a number of articles have emerged from this study (e.g., Furstenberg, Nord, Peterson & Zill, 1983; Peterson & Zill, 1986), the one of most direct relevance to this discussion is by Takeuchi, Williams, and Adair (1991). These researchers compared the functioning of 1,270 children from this sample with respect to their family's perceived financial stress or their family's receipt of welfare support. Using items adapted from the Achenbach Child Behavior Checklist (Achenbach & Edelbrock, 1983), parents were asked to rate their child's behavior on scales assessing depressive symptomatology, antisocial behavior, and impulsivity. Using welfare status as a grouping variable, these authors found that children whose families received Aid to Families With Dependent Children (AFDC) at both assessment points scored statistically higher on antisocial behavior. Note that when mothers reported more subjective financial stress, children showed significantly higher levels of impulsivity, antisocial behavior, and depressive symptoms. Analyses indicated that both perceived stress and AFDC status were making unique contributions to predicting children's behavior problems. These authors emphasized the need for more dynamic analyses of families' changing economic conditions in order to trace these effects on children's development and functioning.

Another perspective on the impact of the economics of divorce on children is Guidubaldi, Cleminshaw, Perry, and Mcloughlin (1983). They utilized 144 school psychologists in 38 states, each of whom randomly selected 2 first, third, and fifth graders from schools in their district. Consistent with Hetherington's (1989) results, Guidubaldi et al. found that children of divorced parents, especially boys, were functioning less well academically and socially than their peers from intact families. In this sample, 37.3% of single-parent households had incomes below $10,000, whereas only 3.7% of the intact families had incomes this low.

Guidubaldi et al.'s (1983) analyses, which controlled for family income, indicated that the economic status of parents was particularly important in understanding children's functioning over time. In a 2-year follow-up of 110 of these children (Guidubaldi & Perry, 1985), analyses of covariance indicated that only boys from divorced families showed greater behavior problems in 4 of 30 mental health areas examined when family income was controlled: work effort, happiness, parent–child relationships, and appropriateness of behavior. There were no adjustment or behavior differences between girls from divorced families and girls from intact homes.

These findings underscore the importance of considering changes in family income when examining factors related to children's adjustment and mental health. A notable exception to these effects of family financial status—and possibly a reason for the lack of attention to economic effects of divorce in clinical and developmental psychology—is reported in the longitudinal study by Hetherington, M. Cox, and R. Cox (1985), which is one of the most carefully conducted studies of divorce's effects on children. These investigators followed 144 middle-class White children and their parents for 6 years. Half the families had divorced 6 years earlier, on average, when the children in the research study were about 4 years old. Hetherington et al. (1985) reported that, at 6 years following the divorce, the average household income for the divorced women who had not remarried was $16,010. This is in contrast with the average income of $35,162 for remarried women and $36,900 for the nondivorced control families. In this frequently cited study, effects of financial status were not found to be significant. However, Hetherington, M. Cox, and R. Cox (1982) commented:

It may be that in our middle-class sample with an average combined maternal and paternal income of about $22,000, the range is not great enough to detect the effects of economic stress. In a lower-class sample, the greater extremes of economic duress might be associated with variations in parent–child interaction or the development of the child. (p. 245).

This interpretation seems appropriate, given that the average income for the divorced mothers was approximately three times the poverty rate for a family of four at the time (U.S. Department of Commerce, 1992). Thus, the relatively well-off nature of this group of families may have contributed to lessened attention to the economic impact of divorce on children's development.

Policy Recommendations

Psychologists are urged to consider the social policy implications of research findings (Bevan, 1980;

Culbertson, 1991; Schneider, 1990). In the area of family research, venturing into the policy arena is likely to be akin to entering a political minefield, given the highly divergent perspectives in our culture on the changing family (e.g., Coontz, 1992; Etzioni, 1993; Faludi, 1993; Whitehead, 1993). However, there is a pressing need to utilize what we currently know about divorce and its economic impact on families in order to make changes that are likely to improve the well-being of children and their parents. The recommendations made here are for policy and decision makers in government, education, and the private sector who work on issues related to children's development and mental health. Although space limitations make it impossible to develop fully all the arguments for each position, I hope that the data and examples from the two previous sections of this article will provide enough specific information that each recommendation will be seen as consistent with the earlier discussions.

Recommendation 1: Legislators, family lawyers, and judges need to consider carefully the impact of drastic changes in families' economic status on custodial parents and their children's day-to-day lives. Special attention should be given to providing sufficient economic support to the primary residential parent (who most frequently is the mother) so that the children will not suffer a sharp drop in their living standard. Legislation and, when possible, individual divorce decrees should be designed to maintain substantial continuity in living standard for the children in the family.

The provision of state-legislated levels of child support is generally inadequate for families to meet typical and desirable needs (Maccoby & Mnookin, 1992; Strawn, 1992). Although it is clear that two households cannot live as cheaply as one, it is in the best interests of the child for support awards to be at levels that provide substantial continuity with previous living standards in middle- and upper class families and that provide higher levels of support to families in the lowest income categories. The latter support for poor or poverty-level families would likely require federal government support, as argued by Ellwood (1988). Child-support levels should also be adjusted regularly to reflect the rate of inflation and the higher costs of rearing older children and adolescents.

This recommendation does not imply that financial resources should be a primary consideration in the determination of custody. Such an interpretation would be clearly contrary to a long-standing tradition of emphasizing the best interests of the child in that important determination. Instead, noncustodial parents' income should be viewed as a resource that is to be actively utilized for supporting the children's well-being; the fact that a residential parent may indirectly benefit from this support should not be reason to restrict its use. Maintaining as much continuity as reasonably possible for children in their home environments, neighborhoods, schools, friendships, and out-of-school activities should be an important consideration in determining the amount of child support essential for the residential parent. The approaches and formulae for determining the precise levels of child support vary considerably (see Bassi & Barnow, 1993), and the specific method for implementation of this recommendation in different jurisdictions with different plans for calculating child support awards is beyond the scope of this article. The objective, however, should be clear: Children need to be protected from severe economic effects stemming from their parents' decision to divorce, and child support awards would ideally provide substantial continuity in children's living standard.

Recommendation 2: Child support payments need to be consistently enforced, and vigorous efforts should be made to ensure full payments are being received by the custodial parent.

Legislation that has now been passed at the federal level (e.g., the Family Support Act; Public Law 100–485, 1988) needs to be fully funded and implemented in order to further strengthen efforts to achieve high levels of compliance with child support orders. As Garfinkel (1992) noted, current enforcement practices vary greatly. For example, in Michigan, thousands of noncustodial parents are jailed each year for nonpayment of child support, but "on a national level, only a tiny minority of nonresident parents who fail to pay child support are jailed" (p. 30). Ideally, these owers of support would be tracked through the use of income tax, Social Security, and drivers' license records so that enforcement can be rapid, consistent, and fair. This approach will require that enforcement agencies be staffed at adequate levels so that delinquencies can be traced promptly and legal action be initiated against the nonsupporting parent. It is especially important to develop approaches that are effective across different legal jurisdictions because about one third of all child-support cases involve cross-state parents (Garfinkel, 1992). Currently, estimates suggest as much as $25 billion in child support goes uncollected; this total includes that owed to divorced, separated, and never married mothers (Walsh, 1993). This large amount of uncollected support is a prominent part of current debate over federal welfare reform. The Clinton administration's plan is expected to have enhanced enforcement of child support awards as a key component, utilizing a variety of mechanisms for greater effectiveness in tracking delinquent noncustodial parents (Katz, 1994; U.S. Department of Health and Human Services, 1994).

Recommendation 3: Additional allocations of state and federal funds need to be provided to assist families when one wage earner has become unemployed and when it would be a financial hardship or an impossibility for that individual to meet the legally mandated level of support.

As documented in Maccoby and Mnookin's (1992) research, fathers' varying levels of child support is often linked to their changing employment situations (for a dissenting view, see Weitzman, 1985). Several factors have contributed to this situation, including corporations' downsizing (Fisher, 1993), increased use of temporary workers (Uchitelle, 1993), and a gradual shift to a service economy ("Jobless Rate," 1993). Furthermore, this pattern is likely to intensify in the future due to changing trade regulations (e.g., the North American Free Trade Agreement) and to continue to have a greater negative impact on ethnic minorities than other groups (Hacker, 1992; Wilson, 1987). Providing automatic support to custodial parents when the noncustodial parent is unable to pay will decrease the stress on the custodial parent and help provide for the essential needs of the children. This approach could be implemented by utilizing the mechanism already in place for automatic support withholding or by linking it with the onset of unemployment benefits for the unemployed.

Recommendation 4: Child care needs to be made more available to working parents; this could be accomplished through the use of tax credits to companies who subsidize or help underwrite the cost of developing new child care centers and by increasing the income tax credit allowed to parents for child care.

In past studies, women are more likely than men to indicate that family factors have been important influences in their career and job choices (Harris, 1981), and women continue by far (about 90%) to be the most likely parent to have physical custody of children following divorce. At the same time, women who have recently separated from their spouses increase their work hours to meet economic necessities. Affordable, quality child care is one of the most pressing problems single mothers often mention as they attempt to earn more income, juggle all of the home responsibilities, and retrain or reenter the workforce after years of absence. Special tax incentives should be offered to companies to encourage the provision of on-site daycare and after-school programs for young children and health care facilities for ill children. In addition, attention needs to be paid to the child care needs of nontraditional shift workers, such as airport and hospital workers, because nonfamily child care is virtually nonexistent for these workers, some of whom are undoubtedly divorced single parents (National Research

Council, 1991). By adding incentives to both the supply (employer) and demand (parents) sides, this approach is likely to have greater effectiveness than if only one side is affected.

Recommendation 5: New treatment approaches for assisting children and parents in dealing with the impact of divorce need to be implemented. Attention should be paid to less costly group treatment approaches for both children and for parents, as well as to nontraditional methods of supporting divorced parents.

School-based intervention programs (e.g., Alpert-Gillis, Pedro-Carroll, & Cowen, 1989) may be an effective and cost-efficient way of reaching sizable numbers of children during the critical transition periods, such as during the first year following the parents' divorce. These types of programs can be useful in screening children who may need more intensive mental health services. In addition, programs that address the issues facing parents as they divorce can be helpful in sensitizing them to issues that families commonly have during such transitions. For example, Cobb County, Georgia, has a program called Children Cope With Divorce: Seminar for Divorcing Parents (discussed in Lawson, 1992), in which divorcing parents participate in a 4-hr class on the impact of divorce on children.

Given higher rates of marital dissolution in lower income families, much can be learned from past successful programs designed for working with low-income families (e.g., Minuchin, Montalvo, Guerney, Rosman, & Schumer, 1967; Provence & Naylor, 1983). With the development of these programs, maximum accessibility can be achieved by utilizing a range of service-provision sites that permit the ready use of low-cost public transportation (e.g., schools, community centers, and churches/synagogues). In addition, culturally sensitive curricula need to be designed that reflect the diversity of family structures (Culbertson, 1993).

Finally, nontraditional methods of reaching parents need to be utilized. Cable television, educational videotapes, newsletters, and phone referral/hotline services may be useful approaches to providing divorced parents assistance that is less expensive and better suited to their employment, financial, and parenting situations.

Conclusion

Although the rate of change in families in the United States appears to be slowing (Vobejda, 1993), it is clear that one central influence on children's mental health recently has been the increased economic distress and poverty in the United States, whether as a cause or a consequence of divorce. It is likely that continuing high numbers of children and adolescents will experience the stress of their parents' marital dissolution and economic dislocation. Both at the societal level and at the individual family level, attention needs to be paid by policy experts and decision makers, legislators, family lawyers, family court judges, and mental health professionals to the effects of economic distress as a result of parental divorce on children's functioning. Changes in social policies concerning child support would be an important step in decreasing the negative effects of economic distress on children's mental health and well-being.

References

Achenbach, T. M., & Edelbrock, C. (1983). *Manual for the Child Behavior Checklist and Revised Child Behavior Profile.* Burlington, VT: Queen City Printers.

Alpert-Gillis, L. J., Pedro-Carroll, J. L., & Cowen, E. L. (1989). The Children of Divorce Intervention Program: Development, implementation, and evaluation of a program for young urban children. *Journal of Consulting and Clinical Psychology, 57,* 583–589.

American Psychiatric Association. (1980). *Diagnostic and statistical manual of mental disorders* (3rd ed.). Washington, DC: Author.

Arendell, T. (1986). *Mothers and divorce: Legal, economic, and social dilemmas.* Berkeley: University of California Press.

Bane, M. J., & Ellwood, D. T. (1989). One fifth of the nation's children: Why are they poor? *Science, 245,* 1047–1053.

Banerjee, N. (1994, May 12). Debate over measuring the poverty line will come to a head in Senate hearings. *Wall Street Journal,* p. A2.

Bassi, L. J., & Barnow, B. S. (1993). Expenditures on children and child support guidelines. *Journal of Policy Analysis and Management, 12,* 478–497.

Bevan, W. (1980). On getting in bed with a lion. *American Psychologist, 35,* 779–789.

Bieniek, M. E. (1994, January 6). The continuing crisis in child support. *The Christian Science Monitor,* p. 23.

Bond, C. R., & McMahon, R. J. (1984). Relationships between marital distress and child behavior problems, maternal personality adjustment, maternal personality, and maternal parenting behavior. *Journal of Abnormal Psychology, 93,* 348–351.

Brown, G. W., & Harris, T. O. (Eds.). (1989). *Life events and illness.* New York: Guilford.

Brown, L. P., & Cowen, E. L. (1988). Children's judgments of event upsettingness and personal experiencing of stressful events. *American Journal of Community Psychology, 16,* 123–135.

Bruce, M. L., & Kim, K. M. (1992). Differences in the effects of divorce on major depression in men and women. *American Journal of Psychiatry, 149,* 914–917.

Bruce, M. L., Takeuchi, D. T., & Leaf, P. J. (1991). Poverty and psychiatric status. *Archives of General Psychiatry, 48,* 470–474.

Buhrmester, D., & Furman, W. (1987). The development of companionship and intimacy. *Child Development, 58,* 1101–1113.

Conger, R. D., Ge, X., Elder, G. H., Jr., Lorenz, F. O., & Simons, R. L. (1994). Economic stress, coercive family process, and developmental problems of adolescents. *Child Development, 65,* 541–561.

Coontz, S. (1992). *The way we never were: American families and the nostalgia trap.* New York: Basic.

Culbertson, J. L. (1991). Child advocacy and clinical child psychology. *Journal of Clinical Child Psychology, 20,* 7–10.

Culbertson, J. L. (1993). Clinical child psychology in the 1990s: Broadening our scope. *Journal of Clinical Child Psychology, 22,* 116–122.

Danziger, S. K., & Danziger, S. (1993). Child poverty and public policy: Toward a comprehensive antipoverty agenda. *Daedalus, 122,* 57–84.

de Lone, R. H. (1979). *Small futures: Children, inequality, and the limits of liberal reform.* New York: Harcourt Brace.

Dise-Lewis, J. E. (1988). The Life Events and Coping Inventory: An assessment of stress in children. *Psychosomatic Medicine, 50,* 484–499.

Duncan, G. J., & Hoffman, S. D. (1985). A reconsideration of the economic consequences of marital dissolution. *Demography, 22,* 485–497.

Ellis, J. W. (1990). Plans, protections, and professional intervention: Innovations in divorce custody reform and the role of legal professionals. *University of Michigan Journal of Law Reform, 24,* 65–188.

Ellwood, D. T. (1988). *Poor support: Poverty in the American family.* New York: Basic.

Emery, R. E. (1982). Interparental conflict and the children of discord and divorce. *Psychological Bulletin, 92,* 310–330.

Emery, R. E. (1988). *Marriage, divorce, and children's adjustment.* Newbury Park, CA: Sage.

Espenshade, T. J. (1979). The economic consequences of divorce. *Journal of Marriage and the Family, 41,* 615–625.

Etzioni, A. (1993, September 6). How to make marriage matter. *Time,* p. 76.

Faludi, S. (1993, May/June). The kids are all right. *Utne Reader,* pp. 68–70.

Fisher, L. M. (1993, February 19). Boeing will cut one-fifth of work force in 18 months. *New York Times,* p. C1.

Forgatch, M. S., Patterson, G. R., & Skinner, M. O. (1988). A mediational model for the effect of divorce on antisocial behavior in boys. In E. M. Hetherington & J. Arasteh (Eds.), *The impact of divorce, single parenting, and stepparenting on children* (pp. 135–154). Hillsdale, NJ: Lawrence Erlbaum Associates, Inc.

Furstenberg, F. F., Jr. (1985). Sociological ventures in child development. *Child Development, 56,* 281–288.

Furstenberg, F. F., Jr. (1988). Child care after divorce and remarriage. In E. M. Hetherington & J. Arasteh (Eds.), *The impact of divorce, single parenting, and stepparenting on children* (pp. 245–261). Hillsdale, NJ: Lawrence Erlbaum Associates, Inc.

Furstenberg, F. F., Jr., Nord, C. W., Peterson, J. L., & Zill, N. (1983). The life course of children and divorce: Marital disruption and parental contact. *American Sociological Review, 48,* 656–668.

Garfinkel, I. (1992). *Assuring child support: An extension of Social Security.* New York: Russell Sage Foundation.

Gotlib, I. H., & McCabe, S. B. (1990). Marriage and psychopathology. In F. D. Fincham & T. N. Bradbury (Eds.), *The psychology of marriage: Basic issues and applications* (pp. 226–257). New York: Guilford.

Grillo, T. (1991). The mediation alternative: Process dangers for women. *Yale Law Journal, 100,* 1545–1610.

Gugliotta, G. (1993, May 24–30). Drawing the line on poverty: What must one be without to be considered poor? *Washington Post National Weekly Edition,* p. 38.

Guidubaldi, J., Cleminshaw, H. K., Perry, J. D., & Mcloughlin, C. S. (1983). The impact of parental divorce on children: Report of the nationwide NASP study. *School Psychology Review, 12,* 300–323.

Guidubaldi, J., & Perry, J. D. (1985). Divorce and mental health sequelae for children: A two-year follow-up of a nationwide sample. *Journal of the American Academy of Child Psychiatry, 24,* 531–537.

Hacker, A. (1992). *Two nations: Black and white, separate, hostile, unequal.* New York: Ballantine.

Harris, L. (1981). *The General Mills American family report 1980–81; Families at work: Strengths and strains.* Minneapolis, MN: General Mills, Inc.

Hashima, P. Y., & Amato, P. R. (1994). Poverty, social support, and parental behavior. *Child Development, 65,* 394–403.

Heaton, T. B. (1990). Marital stability throughout the child-rearing years. *Demography, 27,* 55–63.

Hernandez, D. J. (1992). *When households continue, discontinue, and form* (Current Population Reports, U.S. Bureau of the Census, Series P–23, No. 179). Washington, DC: U.S. Government Printing Office.

Herzog, E., & Sudia, C. E. (1973). Children in fatherless families. In B. M. Caldwell & H. N. Riccuiti (Eds.), *Review of child development research* (Vol. 3; pp. 141–232). Chicago: University of Chicago Press.

Hetherington, E. M. (1989). Coping with family transitions: Winners, losers, and survivors. *Child Development, 60,* 1–14.

Hetherington, E. M., & Arasteh, J. (Eds.). (1988). *The impact of divorce, single parenting, and stepparenting on children.* Hillsdale, NJ: Lawrence Erlbaum Associates, Inc.

Hetherington, E. M., Cox, M., & Cox, R. (1978). The aftermath of divorce. In J. H. Stevens, Jr. & M. Mathews (Eds.), *Mother/child, father/child relationships* (pp. 149–176). Washington, DC: National Association for the Education of Young Children.

Hetherington, E. M., Cox, M., & Cox, R. (1982). Effects of divorce on parents and children. In M. E. Lamb (Ed.), *Nontraditional families: Parenting and child development* (pp. 233–288). Hillsdale, NJ: Lawrence Erlbaum Associates, Inc.

Hetherington, E. M., Cox, M., & Cox, R. (1985). Long-term effects of divorce and remarriage on the adjustment of children. *Journal of the American Academy of Child Psychiatry, 24,* 518–530.

Hochschild, A. (1989). *The second shift.* New York: Avon.

Hodges, W. F. (1991). *Interventions for children of divorce: Custody, access, and psychotherapy* (2nd ed.). New York: Wiley.

Hodges, W. F., Tierney, C. W., & Buchsbaum, H. K. (1984). The cumulative effect of stress on preschool children of divorced and intact families. *Journal of Marriage and the Family, 46,* 611–617.

Hoffman, S. D., & Duncan, G. J. (1988). What *are* the economic consequences of divorce? *Demography, 25,* 641–645.

Huston, A. C. (Ed.). (1991). *Children in poverty: Child development and public policy.* New York: Cambridge University Press.

Jacobson, N. S., Holtzworth-Munroe, A., & Schmaling, K. B. (1989). Marital therapy and spouse involvement in the treatment of depression, agoraphobia, and alcoholism. *Journal of Consulting and Clinical Psychology, 57,* 5–10.

Jobless rate drops to 6.8%: Many temporary jobs in modest payroll rise. (1993, August 6). *Seattle Times,* p. E1.

Kashani, J. H., Hodges, K. K., Simonds, J. F., & Hilderbrand, E. (1981). Life events and hospitalization in children: A comparison with a general population. *British Journal of Psychiatry, 139,* 221–225.

Katz, J. L. (1994, January 22). Highlights of Clinton plan. *Congressional Quarterly Weekly Report,* pp. 117–122.

Laosa, L. M. (1988). Ethnicity and single parenting in the United States. In E. M. Hetherington & J. Arasteh (Eds.). *The impact of divorce, single parenting, and stepparenting on children* (pp. 23–49). Hillsdale, NJ: Lawrence Erlbaum Associates, Inc.

Lawson, C. (1992, January 23). Requiring divorce classes for the sake of the child. *New York Times,* pp. B1, B3.

Lemann, N. (1988, December). The unfinished war: The inside story of the wars behind the War on Poverty. *Atlantic Monthly, 262,* pp. 37–49, 52–56.

Maccoby, E. E., & Mnookin, R. H. (1992). *Dividing the child: Social & legal dilemmas of custody.* Cambridge, MA: Harvard University Press.

McLanahan, S. S., Astone, N. M., & Marks, N. F. (1991). The role of mother-only families in reproducing poverty. In A. C. Huston (Ed.), *Children in poverty: Child development and public policy* (pp. 51–78). New York: Cambridge University Press.

McLanahan, S. S., Wedemeyer, N. V., & Adelberg, T. (1981). Network structure, social support, and psychological well-being in the single-parent family. *Journal of Marriage and the Family,*

43, 601–612.

Minuchin, S., Montalvo, B., Guerney, B. G., Jr. , Rosman, B. L., & Schumer, F. (1967). *Families of the slums: An exploration of their structure and treatment.* New York: Basic.

National Research Council. (1991). *Work and family: Policies for a changing work force.* Washington, DC: National Academy Press.

Pasley, K., & Ihinger-Tallman, M. (1987). *Remarriage and stepparenting: Current research and theory.* New York: Guilford.

Patterson, G. R., & Stouthamer-Loeber, M. (1984). The correlation of family management practices and delinquency. *Child Development, 55*, 1299–1307.

Pear, R. (1993a, January 15). Poverty is cited as divorce factor: Poor couples are twice as likely as others to split up, U.S. report says. *New York Times*, p. A6.

Pear, R. (1993b, October 5). Poverty in U.S. grew faster than population last year. *New York Times*, p. A10.

Peterson, J. L., & Zill, N. (1986). Marital disruption, parent–child relationships, and behavior problems in children. *Journal of Marriage and the Family, 48*, 295–307.

Provence, S., & Naylor, A. (1983). *Working with disadvantaged parents and their children.* New Haven, CT: Yale University Press.

Public Law 100–485. (1988). Family Support Act of 1988, 42 U.S.C. § 667(b)(2).

Regier, D. A., Farmer, M. E., Rae, D. S., Myers, J. K., Kramer, M., Robins, L. N., George, L. K., Karno, M., & Locke, B. Z. (1993). One-month prevalence of mental disorders in the United States and sociodemographic characteristics: The Epidemiologic Catchment Area study. *Acta Psychiatrica Scandanavica, 88*, 35–47.

Riley, G. (1991). *Divorce: An American tradition.* New York: Oxford University Press.

Rivlin, A. M. (1971). *Systematic thinking for social action.* Washington, DC: Brookings Institution.

Robinson, E. (1993, September 23). U.S. lags in protecting children, UNICEF finds. *Washington Post*, p. A28.

Ruggles, P. (1992, Spring). Measuring poverty. *Focus: Newsletter of the University of Wisconsin–Madison Institute for Research on Poverty*, pp. 1–5.

Schneider, S. F. (1990). Psychology at a crossroads. *American Psychologist, 45*, 521–529.

Schorr, L. B. (1989). *Within our reach: Breaking the cycle of disadvantage.* New York: Anchor.

Skolnick, A. (1991). *Embattled paradise: The American family in an age of uncertainty.* New York: Basic.

Strawn, J. (1992). The states and the poor: Child poverty rises as the safety net shrinks. *Social Policy Report, 6*, 1–19.

Strickland, B. R. (1992). Women and depression. *Current Directions in Psychological Science, 1*, 132–135.

Takeuchi, D. T., Williams, D. R., & Adair, R. K. (1991). Economic stresss in the family and children's emotional and behavioral problems. *Journal of Marriage and the Family, 53*, 1031–1041.

Uchitelle, L. (1993, July 6). Use of temporary workers is on rise in manufacturing. *New York Times*, p. A1.

U.S. Bureau of the Census. (1991a). *Child support and alimony: 1989* (Current Population Reports, Series P–60, No. 173). Washington, DC: U.S. Government Printing Office.

U.S. Bureau of the Census. (1991b). *Family disruption and economic hardship: The short-run picture for children* (Current Population Reports, Series P–70, No. 23). Washington, DC: U.S. Government Printing Office.

U.S. Bureau of the Census. (1992a). *Income, poverty, and wealth in the United States: A chartbook* (Current Population Reports, Series P–60, No. 179). Washington, DC: U.S. Government Printing Office.

U.S. Bureau of the Census. (1992b). *Marriage, divorce, and remarriage in the 1990's* (Current Population Reports, Series P–23, No. 180). Washington, DC: U.S. Government Printing Office.

U.S. Bureau of the Census. (1992c). *Poverty in the United States: 1991* (Current Population Reports, Series P–60, No. 181). Washington, DC: U.S. Government Printing Office.

U.S. Bureau of the Census. (1993). *How we're changing; Demographic state of the nation: 1993* (Current Population Reports, Special Studies, Series P–23, No. 184). Washington, DC: U.S. Government Printing Office.

U.S. Department of Commerce. (1992). *Statistical abstract of the United States: 1992.* Lanham, MD: Bernan.

U.S. Department of Health and Human Services. (1994, March 22). *Possible elements in the welfare reform proposal.* (Available from Office of the Regional Director, Department of Health and Human Services, Region X, 2201 Sixth Avenue, Seattle, WA 98121)

Veum, J. R. (1992). Interrelation of child support, visitation, and hours of work. *Monthly Labor Review, 115*, 40–47.

Veum, J. R. (1993). The relationship between child support and visitation: Evidence from longitudinal data. *Social Science Research, 22*, 229–244.

Vobejda, B. (1993, June 28–July 4). Family circles slow their spinning: The pace of change in stabilizing. *Washington Post National Weekly Edition*, p. 37.

Wallerstein, J. S., & Kelly, J. B. (1980). *Surviving the breakup: How children and parents cope with divorce.* New York: Harper Torchbooks.

Walsh, E. (1993, January 11–17). Going after fathers who turn their backs: States are cheered by Clinton's resolve on child support. *Washington Post National Weekly Edition*, p. 32.

Wasserman, I. M. (1984). A longitudinal analysis of the linkage between suicide, unemployment, and marital dissolution. *Journal of Marriage and the Family, 46*, 853–859.

Weiss, R. S. (1975). *Marital separation.* New York: Basic.

Weitzman, L. J. (1985). *The divorce revolution: The unexpected social and economic consequences for women and children in America.* New York: Free Press.

Whitehead, B. D. (1993, April). Dan Quayle was right. *Atlantic Monthly*, pp. 47–50, 52, 55, 58, 60–62, 64–66, 70–72, 74, 77, 80, 82, 84.

Wilson, W. J. (1984). Race-specific policies and the truly disavantaged. *Yale Law & Policy Review, 2*, 272–290.

Wilson, W. J. (1987). *The truly disadvantaged: The inner city, the underclass, and public policy.* Chicago: University of Chicago Press.

Wolchik, S. A., Ramirez, R., Sandler, I. N., Fisher, J. L., Organista, P. B., & Brown, C. (1993). Inner-city, poor children of divorce: Negative divorce-related events, problematic beliefs and adjustment problems. *Journal of Divorce & Remarriage, 19*, 1–20.

Received November 5, 1993
Final revision received June 7, 1994

Acknowledgments

In addition to the regular consulting editors, the following colleagues reviewed manuscripts that were received during 1993. We greatly appreciate their contributions to the quality of the *Journal of Clinical Child Psychology*.

Arthur Anastopoulos
Brooks Applegate
Joan Asarnow

José Bauermeister
Edward Beckham
Lenore Behar
Debra Bendell-Estroff
Victor Bernstein
Elaine Blechman
Bruce Bracken
Robert Bradley
James Bray
Jeanne Brooks-Gunn
Ronald T. Brown

David Cole
Lynn Collins

Eugene D'Angelo
George DuPaul

Toni Eisenstadt
Robert Emery

Michael D. Fetter
Jack Fletcher
Paul Frick

James Garbarino
Lane Geddie
Betty Gordon
David Guevremont
Robin Gurwitch
James Gyurke

Dennis Harper
Scott Henggeler
E. Wayne Holden
Stephen R. Hooper
Honore Hughes

Nadine Kaslow
Kathy Katz
Keith Kaufman

Kathleen Lemanek
Elizabeth Lemerise
Thomas Linscheid

Lisa McElreath
Judith Meyers
Rudolf Moos
John Murray

Nga Nguyen

Eugene Pekarik

Ron Prinz

Cecil Reynolds
James Rodrigue

Karen Saywitz
Mario Scalora
Cynthia Schellenbach
Steven Shapiro
Catherine Shaw
Lisa Sheeber
Terri Shelton
Larry Siegel
Wendy Silverman
Matthew Speltz
Mary Spiers
Cyd Strauss

Kenneth Tarnowski

Eric Vernberg
Juliet Vogel

Lynn Walker
Carolyn Webster-Stratton
Bahr Weiss
John Weisz
Sandy Wurtele

INDEX

JOURNAL OF CLINICAL CHILD PSYCHOLOGY

Editor JAN L. CULBERTSON, University of Oklahoma Health Sciences Center
Associate Editors SHEILA EYBERG, University of Florida
AL J. FINCH, JR., The Citadel
Book Review Editor CYNTHIA SCHELLENBACH, Oakland University
Editorial Assistant BRENDA GENTRY

Volume 23, Numbers 1 to 4
March to December 1994

ISSN 0047-228X
Published quarterly on behalf of the Section on Clinical Child Psychology by
Lawrence Erlbaum Associates, Inc., 365 Broadway, Hillsdale, NJ 07642
Copyright © 1994 by Lawrence Erlbaum Associates, Inc.

Author Index to Volume 23

OTHER

PRESIDENTIAL ADDRESS:

Membership Application
Section on Clinical Child Psychology
Section 1, Divison 12, American Psychological Association

I wish to join Section 1, Division 12, APA. Enclosed are my dues of U.S. $31 (U.S. $24 for students). My dues include subscription to the *Journal of Clinical Child Psychology* and the Section newsletter, the right to hold office, and voting privileges (according to category).

Name _____

Address _____

_____

Membership status for which I am applying (check one):

Member (I am a member of APA and Division 12) _____

Non–Division 12 Member (I am a member of APA) _____

Associate Member (I am an Associate Member of APA or have corresponding credentials from another field). Describe _____

_____

Student Affiliate (I am a student). Describe program _____

_____

Include check for dues and mail to Debra Bendell-Estroff, Treasurer, Section 1, Niles Bldg., Kaiser Permanente, 39400 Paseo Padre Parkway, Fremont, CA 94538–2398.

Membership Application
Society of Pediatric Psychology
Section 5, Division 12, American Psychological Association

Dues for all membership except Student Associate are $40 (North American) and $40 (Foreign); Student Associate dues are $23.50. All categories receive the *Journal of Pediatric Psychology* and the Society newsletter.

Name _____

Address _____

_____

Check appropriate membership category:

Member of APA and Division 12 _____

Member only of APA _____

Associate Member of APA or possess corresponding credentials from a related field (Associate Member, no voting privileges) _____

Enrolled in a graduate or postdoctoral psychology program (Student Associate, no voting privileges) _____

Make check payable in U.S. funds to Society of Pediatric Psychology and mail to Melanie McGrath, Treasurer, Department of Psychiatry, Children's Hospital, 300 Longwood Avenue, Boston, MA 02115.

Membership Application
Division of Child, Youth, and Family Services
Division 37, American Psychological Association

I am interested in joining Division 37, APA.

Name _____

Address _____

_____

Membership status in APA (circle one):

Fellow   Member   Student   Affiliate

Note: You need not belong to the APA to qualify for membership in Division 37. Mail application to Rodney Hammond, Membership Chair, School of Professional Psychology, Wright State University, Dayton, OH 45435.

WILEY...THE PSYCHOLOGICAL EDGE

HANDBOOK OF PLAY THERAPY
VOLUME 2
Advances and Innovations

Edited by Kevin J. O'Connor and Charles E. Schaefer

A companion to the editors' successful earlier volume, Volume 2 brings the topic up to currency. It provides the reader with coverage of the application of play therapy to special populations, ranging from the aged to mentally retarded and sexually abused children, and provides a thorough overview of the advances in play therapy over the past decade.
0-471-58463-0, cloth, 500 pp. est., $55.00

HANDBOOK OF PLAY THERAPY, Volume 1
Edited by Charles E. Schaefer and
Kevin J. O'Connor
0-471-09462-5, cloth, 489 pp., $60.00

INTELLIGENT TESTING WITH THE WISC-III

Alan S. Kaufman

Revises the author's influential earlier volume on the WISC-R, superseding that previous work and bringing the subject up-to-date in line with the newer WISC-III. Setting the standard for the most revealing assessment of children's intelligence, this book covers administration, scoring, and interpretation of this widely used test.
0-471-57845-2, cloth, 458 pp., $39.95

ENCYCLOPEDIA OF PSYCHOLOGY
Second Edition, in 4 volumes

Edited by Raymond J. Corsini

The second edition of this award-winning reference work brings psychology into the 21st Century. With contributions from hundreds of experts and consultants, this updated and expanded revision provides the most current and authoritative information available.
0-471-55819-2, cloth, 2,345 pp., 4 volume set, $475.00

THE RORSCHACH:
A Comprehensive System, *Volume 3*
Assessment of Children and Adolescents,
Second Edition

John E. Exner, Jr. and Irving B. Weiner

The revised edition of the third volume in the Exner/Rorschach series, this volume is devoted to the use of the Rorschach Inkblot test with children and adolescents. This new edition updates the norms and scoring procedures based on changes that first appeared in the System in the revised Volume 2. This is the last revision planned for any volume in this series. Volumes 1 and 2 have been revised within the last 2 years and this revision of volume 3 brings the entire set up to currency.
0-471-55927-X, cloth, 480 pp. est., $70.00

The Rorschach: A Comprehensive System,
Volume 1, Basic Foundations, *Third Edition*
0-471-55902-4, cloth, 672 pp.,$65.00
The Rorschach: A Comprehensive System, Volume 2
Interpretation, *Second Edition*
0-471-85080-2, cloth, 476 pp., $65.00

CLINICIAN'S GUIDE
TO CHILD CUSTODY EVALUATIONS

Marc J. Ackerman

This practical volume, by the co-creator of the ASPECT custody evaluation instrument, provides clinicians with detailed guidelines for evaluating child custody. Covers psychological testing, clinical interviewing, handling abuse allegations, report preparation, and courtroom tesimony.
0-471-05252-3, cloth, 300 pp. est., $49.95

HANDBOOK OF CHILD BEHAVIOR THERAPY
IN THE PSYCHIATRIC SETTING

Edited by Robert T. Ammerman and Michel Hersen

Deals with applications of behavior therapy methods in medical/psychiatric settings, where there is a growing interest in such approaches to therapy but little experience or expertise.
0-471-57844-4, cloth, 560 pp. est., $75.00

UNDERSTANDING AND MANAGING
CHILDREN'S CLASSROOM BEHAVIOR

Sam Goldstein

Distills the best current findings about behavior management, and offers practical suggestions for applying new techniques in the classroom.
0-471-57946-7, cloth, 480 pp. est., $49.95

CLINICAL BEHAVIOR THERAPY
Expanded Edition

Marvin R. Goldfried and Gerald C. Davison

Written by two recognized authorities in the field, the expanded paperback edition of this classic text offers a practical introduction to cognitive-behavior therapy. Provides systematic guidelines to well-established cognitive-behavioral techniques, and covers timely therapeutic issues including formulating effective short-term interventions, establishing a therapeutic alliance, and overcoming resistance.
A volume in the Wiley Series in
Clinical Psychology and Personality
W. Edward Craighead, Series Editor
0-471-07633-3, paper, 320 pp. est., $29.95

COMING SOON FROM THE
EINSTEIN PSYCHIATRY SERIES

AVAILABLE IN MARCH 1995

TREATMENT APPROACHES
WITH SUICIDAL ADOLESCENTS

James K. Zimmerman and Gregory M. Asnis

A practical guide to identifying and treating suicidal adolescents -- using both pharmacological and psychotherapeutic treatment methods. Reviews the most current information regarding biological, psychological, and social risk factors for adolescent suicide.
0-471-10236-9, cloth, 272 pp. est., $49.95 est.

These books can be found/special ordered at a
Preferred Psychology bookstore near you or,
for more information, please write to:
L. Pearson, John Wiley & Sons, 605 Third Avenue,
New York, NY 10158,
or call 1-800-CALL-WILEY

WILEY
Publishers Since 1807
Prices subject to change without notice.